FOREIGN AFFAIRS

Special Collection

BEST OF THE YEAR—THE MAGAZINE

Introduction

Gideon Rose

2013 has been a great year for *Foreign Affairs*, and we're delighted to bring some its highlights to you in this special collection. We've pulled together ten of our top print pieces and ten Web-only ones, giving you a sample of the full range of content we offer. You'll find everything from diplomacy and national security to economics to science and technology to culture, all done with our signature combination of expertise and accessibility.

All of the pieces in this collection are great, but here are a few that are simply must-reads, if you somehow missed them:

- "Generation Kill," an interview with retired U.S. General Stanley McChrystal, in which he explains just how he revolutionized American strategy in the war on terror.
- "The Rise of Big Data," everything you need to know about the hottest trend in the technosphere (not to mention in international politics, thanks to the NSA and the Snowden revelations).
- "How Yemen Chewed Itself Dry," a look at the havoc that Yemen's qat habit is wreaking on the country's agricultural system and environment.
- "Where Have All the Workers Gone?," why people-rich China is facing labor shortages that will make governance and future development difficult.
- "Google's Original X-Man," a portrait of the smartest guy you'll ever meet, robotics genius Sebastian Thrun, who's moved from driverless cars and Google Glass to trying to disrupt the entire field of education.

GIDEON ROSE is Editor of *Foreign Affairs*.

But don't take my word for it—find your own favorites, and come back in 2014 for even more gems. We're always interested in feedback, by the way, so let us know how you think we're doing and what you'd like to see more of.

Happy Holidays,
Gideon Rose

P.S. Did I remind you that *Foreign Affairs* subscriptions make great gifts for the smart folks on your list? ☯

Can America Be Fixed?

The New Crisis of Democracy

Fareed Zakaria

In November, the American electorate, deeply unhappy with Washington and its political gridlock, voted to maintain precisely the same distribution of power—returning President Barack Obama for a second term and restoring a Democratic Senate and a Republican House of Representatives. With at least the electoral uncertainty out of the way, attention quickly turned to how the country's lawmakers would address the immediate crisis known as the fiscal cliff—the impending end-of-year tax increases and government spending cuts mandated by earlier legislation.

As the United States continues its slow but steady recovery from the depths of the financial crisis, nobody actually wants a massive austerity package to shock the economy back into recession, and so the odds have always been high that the game of budgetary chicken will stop short of disaster. Looming past the cliff, however, is a deep chasm that poses a much greater challenge—the retooling of the country's economy, society, and government necessary for the United States to perform effectively in the twenty-first century. The focus in Washington now is on taxing and cutting; it should be on reforming and investing. The United States

FAREED ZAKARIA is the host of *Fareed Zakaria GPS* on CNN, Editor-at-Large of *Time*, and the author of *The Post-American World*. Follow him on Twitter @FareedZakaria.

needs serious change in its fiscal, entitlement, infrastructure, immigration, and education policies, among others. And yet a polarized and often paralyzed Washington has pushed dealing with these problems off into the future, which will only make them more difficult and expensive to solve.

Studies show that the political divisions in Washington are at their worst since the years following the Civil War. Twice in the last three years, the world's leading power—with the largest economy, the global reserve currency, and a dominant leadership role in all international institutions—has come close to committing economic suicide. The American economy remains extremely dynamic. But one has to wonder whether the U.S. political system is capable of making the changes that will ensure continued success in a world of greater global competition and technological change. Is the current predicament, in other words, really a crisis of democracy?

That phrase might sound familiar. By the mid-1970s, growth was stagnating and inflation skyrocketing across the West. Vietnam and Watergate had undermined faith in political institutions and leaders, and newly empowered social activists were challenging establishments across the board. In a 1975 report from the Trilateral Commission entitled *The Crisis of Democracy*, distinguished scholars from the United States, Europe, and Japan argued that the democratic governments of the industrial world had simply lost their ability to function, overwhelmed by the problems they confronted. The section on the United States, written by the political scientist Samuel Huntington, was particularly gloomy.

We know how that worked out: within several years, inflation was tamed, the American economy boomed, and confidence was restored. A decade later, it was communism and the Soviet Union that collapsed, not capitalism and the West. So much for the pessimists.

And yet just over two decades further on, the advanced industrial democracies are once again filled with gloom. In Europe, economic growth has stalled, the common currency is in danger, and there is talk that the union itself might split up. Japan has had seven prime ministers in ten years, as the political system splinters, the economy stagnates, and the country slips further into decline. But the United States, given its global role, presents perhaps the most worrying case.

Is there a new crisis of democracy? Certainly, the American public seems to think so. Anger with politicians and institutions of government is much greater than it was in 1975. According to American National Election Studies polls, in 1964, 76 percent of Americans agreed with the statement "You can trust the government in Washington to do what is right just about always or most of the time." By the late 1970s, that number had dropped to the high 40s. In 2008, it was 30 percent. In January 2010, it had fallen to 19 percent.

Commentators are prone to seeing the challenges of the moment in unnecessarily apocalyptic terms. It is possible that these problems, too, will pass, that the West will muddle through somehow until it faces yet another set of challenges a generation down the road, which will again be described in an overly dramatic fashion. But it is also possible that the public is onto something. The crisis of democracy, from this perspective, never really went away; it was just papered over with temporary solutions and obscured by a series of lucky breaks. Today, the problems have mounted, and yet American democracy is more dysfunctional and commands less authority than ever—and it has fewer levers to pull in a globalized economy. This time, the pessimists might be right.

TRENDING NOW

The mid-1970s predictions of doom for Western democracy were undone by three broad economic trends: the decline of inflation, the information revolution, and globalization. In the 1970s, the world was racked by inflation, with rates stretching from low double digits in countries such as the United States and the United Kingdom to 200 percent in countries such as Brazil and Turkey. In 1979, Paul Volcker became chair of the U.S. Federal Reserve, and within a few years, his policies had broken the back of American inflation. Central banks across the world began following the Fed's example, and soon, inflation was declining everywhere.

Technological advancement has been around for centuries, but beginning in the 1980s, the widespread use of computers and then the Internet began to transform every aspect of the economy. The information revolution led to increased productivity and growth in the United States and around the world, and the revolution looks to be a permanent one.

Late in that decade, partly because the information revolution put closed economies and societies at an even greater disadvantage, the Soviet empire collapsed, and soon the Soviet Union itself followed. This allowed the Western system of interconnected free markets and societies to spread across most of the world—a process that became known as globalization. Countries with command or heavily planned economies and societies opened up and began participating in a single global market, adding vigor to both themselves and the system at large. In 1979, 75 countries were growing by at least four percent a year; in 2007, just before the financial crisis hit, the number had risen to 127.

These trends not only destroyed the East but also benefited the West. Low inflation and the information revolution enabled Western economies to grow more quickly, and globalization opened up vast new markets filled with cheap labor for Western companies to draw on and sell to. The result was a rebirth of American confidence and an expansion of the global economy with an unchallenged United States at the center. A generation on, however, the Soviet collapse is a distant memory, low inflation has become the norm, and further advances in globalization and information technology are now producing as many challenges for the West as opportunities.

The jobs and wages of American workers, for example, have come under increasing pressure. A 2011 study by the McKinsey Global Institute found that from the late 1940s until 1990, every recession and recovery in the United States followed a simple pattern. First, GDP recovered to its pre-recession level, and then, six months later (on average), the employment rate followed. But then, that pattern was broken. After the recession of the early 1990s, the employment rate returned to its pre-recession level 15 months after GDP did. In the early part of the next decade, it took 39 months. And in the current recovery, it appears that the employment rate will return to its pre-recession level a full 60 months—five years—after GDP did. The same trends that helped spur growth in the past are now driving a new normal, with jobless growth and declining wages.

MAGIC MONEY

The broad-based growth of the post-World War II era slowed during the mid-1970s and has never fully returned. The Federal Reserve Bank of Cleveland recently noted that in the United States, real GDP growth peaked in the early 1960s at more than four percent, dropped to below three percent in the late 1970s, and recovered somewhat in the 1980s only to drop further in recent years down to its current two percent. Median incomes, meanwhile, have barely risen over the last 40 years. Rather than tackle the underlying problems or accept lower standards of living, the United States responded by taking on debt. From the 1980s on, Americans have consumed more than they have produced, and they have made up the difference by borrowing.

President Ronald Reagan came to power in 1981 as a monetarist and acolyte of Milton Friedman, arguing for small government and balanced budgets. But he governed as a Keynesian, pushing through large tax cuts and a huge run-up in defense spending. (Tax cuts are just as Keynesian as government spending; both pump money into the economy and increase aggregate demand.) Reagan ended his years in office with inflation-adjusted federal spending 20 percent higher than when he started and with a skyrocketing federal deficit. For the 20 years before Reagan, the deficit was under two percent of GDP. In Reagan's two terms, it averaged over four percent of GDP. Apart from a brief period in the late 1990s, when the Clinton administration actually ran a surplus, the federal deficit has stayed above the three percent mark ever since; it is currently seven percent.

John Maynard Keynes' advice was for governments to spend during busts but save during booms. In recent decades, elected governments have found it hard to save at any time. They have run deficits during busts and during booms, as well. The U.S. Federal Reserve has kept rates low in bad times but also in good ones. It's easy to blame politicians for such one-handed Keynesianism, but the public is as much at fault. In poll after poll, Americans have voiced their preferences: they want low taxes and lots of government services. Magic is required to satisfy both demands simultaneously, and it turned out magic was available, in the form of cheap credit. The federal government borrowed heavily, and so did all other governments—state, local, and municipal—and the American people themselves. Household debt rose from $665 billion in 1974 to $13 trillion today. Over that period, consumption, fueled by cheap credit, went up and stayed up.

Other rich democracies have followed the same course. In 1980, the United States' gross government debt was 42 percent of its total GDP; it is now 107 percent. During the same period, the comparable figure for the United Kingdom moved from 46 percent to 88 percent. Most European governments (including notoriously frugal Germany) now have debt-to-GDP levels that hover around 80 percent, and some, such as Greece and Italy, have ones that are much higher. In 1980, Japan's gross government debt was 50 percent of GDP; today, it is 236 percent.

The world has turned upside down. It used to be thought that developing countries would have high debt loads, because they would borrow heavily to finance their rapid growth from low income levels. Rich countries, growing more slowly from high income levels, would have low debt loads and much greater stability. But look at the G-20 today, a group that includes the largest countries from both the developed and the developing worlds. The average debt-to-GDP ratio for the developing countries is 35 percent; for the rich countries, it is over three times as high.

REFORM AND INVEST

When Western governments and international organizations such as the International Monetary Fund offer advice to developing countries on how to spur growth, they almost always advocate structural reforms that will open up sectors of their economies to competition, allow labor to move freely between jobs, eliminate wasteful and economically distorting government subsidies, and focus government spending on pro-growth investment. When facing their own problems, however, those same Western countries have been loath to follow their own advice.

Current discussions about how to restore growth in Europe tend to focus on austerity, with economists debating the pros and cons of cutting deficits. Austerity is clearly not working, but it is just as clear that with debt burdens already at close to 90 percent of GDP, European countries cannot simply spend their way out of their current crisis. What they really need are major structural reforms designed to make themselves more competitive, coupled with some investments for future growth.

Not least because it boasts the world's reserve currency, the United States has more room to maneuver than Europe. But it, too, needs to change. It has a gargantuan tax code that, when all its rules and regulations are included, totals 73,000 pages; a burdensome litigation system; and a crazy patchwork of federal, state, and local regulations. U.S. financial institutions, for example, are often overseen by five or six different federal agencies and 50 sets of state agencies, all with overlapping authority.

If the case for reform is important, the case for investment is more urgent. In its annual study of competitiveness, the World Economic Forum consistently gives the United States poor marks for its tax and regulatory policies, ranking it 76th in 2012, for example, on the "burden of government regulations." But for all its complications, the American economy remains one of the world's most competitive, ranking seventh overall—only a modest slippage from five years ago. In contrast, the United States has dropped dramatically in its investments in human and physical capital. The

WEF ranked American infrastructure fifth in the world a decade ago but now ranks it 25th and falling. The country used to lead the world in percentage of college graduates; it is now ranked 14th. U.S. federal funding for research and development as a percentage of GDP has fallen to half the level it was in 1960—while it is rising in countries such as China, Singapore, and South Korea. The public university system in the United States—once the crown jewel of American public education—is being gutted by budget cuts.

The modern history of the United States suggests a correlation between investment and growth. In the 1950s and 1960s, the federal government spent over five percent of GDP annually on investment, and the economy boomed. Over the last 30 years, the government has been cutting back; federal spending on investment is now around three percent of GDP annually, and growth has been tepid. As the Nobel Prize-winning economist Michael Spence has noted, the United States escaped from the Great Depression not only by spending massively on World War II but also by slashing consumption and ramping up investment. Americans reduced their spending, increased their savings, and purchased war bonds. That boost in public and private investment led to a generation of postwar growth. Another generation of growth will require comparable investments.

The problems of reform and investment come together in the case of infrastructure. In 2009, the American Society of Civil Engineers gave the country's infrastructure a grade of D and calculated that repairing and renovating it would cost $2 trillion. The specific number might be an exaggeration (engineers have a vested interest in the subject), but every study shows what any traveler can plainly see: the United States is falling badly behind. This is partly a matter of crumbling bridges and highways, but it goes well beyond that. The U.S. air traffic control system is outdated and in need of a $25 billion upgrade. The U.S. energy grid is antique, and it malfunctions often enough that many households are acquiring that classic symbol of status in the developing world: a private electrical generator. The country's drinking water is carried through a network of old and leaky pipes, and its cellular and broadband systems are slow compared with those of many other advanced countries. All this translates into slower growth. And if it takes longer to fix, it will cost more, as deferred maintenance usually does.

Spending on infrastructure is hardly a panacea, however, because without careful planning and oversight, it can be inefficient and ineffective. Congress allocates money to infrastructure projects based on politics, not need or bang for the buck. The elegant solution to the problem would be to have a national infrastructure bank that is funded by a combination of government money and private capital. Such a bank would minimize waste and redundancy by having projects chosen by technocrats on merit rather than by politicians for pork. Naturally, this very idea is languishing in Congress, despite some support from prominent figures on both sides of the aisle.

The same is the case with financial reforms: the problem is not a lack of good ideas or technical feasibility but politics. The politicians who sit on the committees overseeing the current alphabet soup of ineffective agencies are happy primarily because they can raise money for their campaigns from the financial industry. The current system works better as a mechanism for campaign fundraising than it does as an instrument for financial oversight.

In 1979, the social scientist Ezra Vogel published a book titled *Japan as Number One*, predicting a rosy future for the then-rising Asian power. When *The Washington Post* asked him recently why his prediction had been so far off the mark, he pointed out that the Japanese economy was highly sophisticated and advanced, but, he confessed, he had never anticipated that its political system would seize up the way it did and allow the country to spiral downward.

Vogel was right to note that the problem was politics rather than economics. All the advanced industrial economies have weaknesses, but they also all have considerable strengths, particularly the United States. They have reached a stage of development, however, at which outmoded policies, structures, and practices have to be changed or abandoned. The problem, as the economist Mancur

Olson pointed out, is that the existing policies benefit interest groups that zealously protect the status quo. Reform requires governments to assert the national interest over such parochial interests, something that is increasingly difficult to do in a democracy.

POLITICAL DEMOGRAPHY

With only a few exceptions, the advanced industrial democracies have spent the last few decades managing or ignoring their problems rather than tackling them head-on. Soon, this option won't be available, because the crisis of democracy will be combined with a crisis of demography.

The industrial world is aging at a pace never before seen in human history. Japan is at the leading edge of this trend, predicted to go from a population of 127 million today to just 47 million by the end of the century. Europe is not far behind, with Italy and Germany approaching trajectories like Japan's. The United States is actually the outlier on this front, the only advanced industrial country not in demographic decline. In fact, because of immigration and somewhat higher fertility rates, its population is predicted to grow to 423 million by 2050, whereas, say, Germany's is predicted to shrink to 72 million. Favorable U.S. demographics, however, are offset by more expensive U.S. entitlement programs for retirees, particularly in the area of health care.

To understand this, start with a ratio of working-age citizens to those over 65. That helps determine how much revenue the government can get from workers to distribute to retirees. In the United States today, the ratio is 4.6 working people for every retiree. In 25 years, it will drop to 2.7. That shift will make a huge difference to an already worrisome situation. Current annual expenditures for the two main entitlement programs for older Americans, Social Security and Medicare, top $1 trillion. The growth of these expenditures has far outstripped inflation in the past and will likely do so for decades to come, even with the implementation of the Affordable Care Act. Throw in all other entitlement programs, the demographer Nicholas Eberstadt has calculated, and the total is $2.2 trillion—up from $24 billion a half century ago, nearly a hundredfold increase.

However worthwhile such programs may be, they are unaffordable on their current trajectories, consuming the majority of all federal spending. The economists Carmen Reinhart and Kenneth Rogoff argued in their detailed study of financial crises, *This Time Is Different*, that countries with debt-to-GDP burdens of 90 percent or more almost invariably have trouble sustaining growth and stability. Unless its current entitlement obligations are somehow reformed, with health-care costs lowered in particular, it is difficult to see how the United States can end up with a ratio much lower than that. What this means is that while the American right has to recognize that tax revenues will have to rise significantly in coming decades, the American left has to recognize that without significant reforms, entitlements may be the only thing even those increased tax revenues will cover. A recent report by Third Way, a Washington-based think tank lobbying for entitlement reform, calculates that by 2029, Social Security, Medicare, Medicaid, and interest on the debt combined will amount to 18 percent of GDP. It just so happens that 18 percent of GDP is precisely what the government has averaged in tax collections over the last 40 years.

The continued growth in entitlements is set to crowd out all other government spending, including on defense and the investments needed to help spur the next wave of economic growth. In 1960, entitlement programs amounted to well under one-third of the federal budget, with all the other functions of government taking up the remaining two-thirds. By 2010, things had flipped, with entitlement programs accounting for two-thirds of the budget and everything else crammed into one-third. On its current path, the U.S. federal government is turning into, in the journalist Ezra Klein's memorable image, an insurance company with an army. And even the army will have to shrink soon.

Rebalancing the budget to gain space for investment in the country's future is today's great American challenge. And despite what one may have gathered during the recent campaign, it is a challenge for both parties. Eberstadt points out that entitlement spending has actually grown faster under Republican presidents than under Democrats, and a *New York Times* investigation in 2012 found that two-thirds of the 100 U.S. counties most dependent on entitlement programs were heavily Republican.

Reform and investment would be difficult in the best of times, but the continuation of current global trends will make these tasks ever tougher and more urgent. Technology and globalization have made it possible to do simple manufacturing anywhere, and Americans will not be able to compete for jobs against workers in China and India who are being paid a tenth of the wages that they are. That means that the United States has no choice but to move up the value chain, relying on a highly skilled work force, superb infrastructure, massive job-training programs, and cutting-edge science and technology—all of which will not materialize without substantial investment.

The U.S. government currently spends $4 on citizens over 65 for every $1 it spends on those under 18. At some level, that is a brutal reflection of democratic power politics: seniors vote; minors do not. But it is also a statement that the country values the present more than the future.

TURNING JAPANESE

Huntington, the author of the section on the United States in the Trilateral Commission's 1975 report, used to say that it was important for a country to worry about decline, because only then would it make the changes necessary to belie the gloomy predictions. If not for fear of Sputnik, the United States would never have galvanized its scientific establishment, funded NASA, and raced to the moon. Perhaps that sort of response to today's challenges is just around the corner—perhaps Washington will be able to summon the will to pass major, far-reaching policy initiatives over the next few years, putting the United States back on a clear path to a vibrant, solvent future. But hope is not a plan, and it has to be said that at this point, such an outcome seems unlikely.

The absence of such moves will hardly spell the country's doom. Liberal democratic capitalism is clearly the only system that has the flexibility and legitimacy to endure in the modern world. If any regimes collapse in the decades ahead, they will be command systems, such as the one in China (although this is unlikely). But it is hard to see how the derailing of China's rise, were it to happen, would solve any of the problems the United States faces—and in fact, it might make them worse, if it meant that the global economy would grow at a slower pace than anticipated.

The danger for Western democracies is not death but sclerosis. The daunting challenges they face—budgetary pressures, political paralysis, demographic stress—point to slow growth rather than collapse. Muddling through the crisis will mean that these countries stay rich but slowly and steadily drift to the margins of the world. Quarrels over how to divide a smaller pie may spark some political conflict and turmoil but will produce mostly resignation to a less energetic, interesting, and productive future.

There once was an advanced industrial democracy that could not reform. It went from dominating the world economy to growing for two decades at the anemic average rate of just 0.8 percent. Many members of its aging, well-educated population continued to live pleasant lives, but they left an increasingly barren legacy for future generations. Its debt burden is now staggering, and its per capita income has dropped to 24th in the world and is falling. If the Americans and the Europeans fail to get their acts together, their future will be easy to see. All they have to do is look at Japan.

Capitalism and Inequality

What the Right and the Left Get Wrong

Jerry Z. Muller

Recent political debate in the United States and other advanced capitalist democracies has been dominated by two issues: the rise of economic inequality and the scale of government intervention to address it. As the 2012 U.S. presidential election and the battles over the "fiscal cliff" have demonstrated, the central focus of the left today is on increasing government taxing and spending, primarily to reverse the growing stratification of society, whereas the central focus of the right is on decreasing taxing and spending, primarily to ensure economic dynamism. Each side minimizes the concerns of the other, and each seems to believe that its desired policies are sufficient to ensure prosperity and social stability. Both are wrong.

Inequality is indeed increasing almost everywhere in the postindustrial capitalist world. But despite what many on the left think, this is not the result of politics, nor is politics likely to reverse it, for the problem is more deeply rooted and intractable than generally recognized. Inequality is an inevitable product of capitalist activity, and expanding equality of opportunity only increases it— because some individuals and communities are simply better able

JERRY Z. MULLER is Professor of History at the Catholic University of America and the author of *The Mind and the Market: Capitalism in Western Thought.*

than others to exploit the opportunities for development and advancement that capitalism affords. Despite what many on the right think, however, this is a problem for everybody, not just those who are doing poorly or those who are ideologically committed to egalitarianism—because if left unaddressed, rising inequality and economic insecurity can erode social order and generate a populist backlash against the capitalist system at large.

Over the last few centuries, the spread of capitalism has generated a phenomenal leap in human progress, leading to both previously unimaginable increases in material living standards and the unprecedented cultivation of all kinds of human potential. Capitalism's intrinsic dynamism, however, produces insecurity along with benefits, and so its advance has always met resistance. Much of the political and institutional history of capitalist societies, in fact, has been the record of attempts to ease or cushion that insecurity, and it was only the creation of the modern welfare state in the middle of the twentieth century that finally enabled capitalism and democracy to coexist in relative harmony.

In recent decades, developments in technology, finance, and international trade have generated new waves and forms of insecurity for leading capitalist economies, making life increasingly unequal and chancier for not only the lower and working classes but much of the middle class as well. The right has largely ignored the problem, while the left has sought to eliminate it through government action, regardless of the costs. Neither approach is viable in the long run. Contemporary capitalist polities need to accept that inequality and insecurity will continue to be the inevitable result of market operations and find ways to shield citizens from their consequences—while somehow still preserving the dynamism that produces capitalism's vast economic and cultural benefits in the first place.

COMMODIFICATION AND CULTIVATION

Capitalism is a system of economic and social relations marked by private property, the exchange of goods and services by free individuals, and the use of market mechanisms to control the production and distribution of those goods and services. Some of its elements have existed in human societies for ages, but it was only in the seventeenth and eighteenth centuries, in parts of Europe and its offshoots in North America, that they all came together in force. Throughout history, most households had consumed most of the things that they produced and produced most of what they consumed. Only at this point did a majority of the population in some countries begin to buy most of the things they consumed and do so with the proceeds gained from selling most of what they produced.

The growth of market-oriented households and what came to be called "commercial society" had profound implications for practically every aspect of human activity. Prior to capitalism, life was governed by traditional institutions that subordinated the choices and destinies of individuals to various communal, political, and religious structures. These institutions kept change to a minimum, blocking people from making much progress but also protecting them from many of life's vicissitudes. The advent of capitalism gave individuals more control over and responsibility for their own lives than ever before—which proved both liberating and terrifying, allowing for both progress and regression.

Commodification—the transformation of activities performed for private use into activities performed for sale on the open market—allowed people to use their time more efficiently, specializing in producing what they were relatively good at and buying other things from other people. New forms of commerce and manufacturing used the division of labor to produce common household items cheaply and also made a range of new goods available. The result, as the historian Jan de Vries has noted, was what contemporaries called "an awakening of the appetites of the mind"—an expansion of subjective wants and a new subjective perception of needs. This ongoing expansion of wants has been chastised by critics of capitalism from Rousseau to Marcuse as imprisoning humans in a cage of unnatural desires. But it has also been praised by defenders of the market from Voltaire onward for broadening the range of human possibility. Developing and fulfilling higher wants and needs, in this view, is the essence of civilization.

Because we tend to think of commodities as tangible physical objects, we often overlook the extent to which the creation and increasingly cheap distribution of new cultural commodities have expanded what one might call the means of self-cultivation. For the history of capitalism is also the history of the extension of communication, information, and entertainment—things to think with, and about.

Among the earliest modern commodities were printed books (in the first instance, typically the Bible), and their shrinking price and increased availability were far more historically momentous than, say, the spread of the internal combustion engine. So, too, with the spread of newsprint, which made possible the newspaper and the magazine. Those gave rise, in turn, to new markets for information and to the business of gathering and distributing news. In the eighteenth century, it took months for news from India to reach London; today, it takes moments. Books and news have made possible an expansion of not only our awareness but also our imagination, our ability to empathize with others and imagine living in new ways ourselves. Capitalism and commodification have thus facilitated both humanitarianism and new forms of self-invention.

Over the last century, the means of cultivation were expanded by the invention of recorded sound, film, and television, and with the rise of the Internet and home computing, the costs of acquiring knowledge and culture have fallen dramatically. For those so inclined, the expansion of the means of cultivation makes possible an almost unimaginable enlargement of one's range of knowledge.

FAMILY MATTERS

If capitalism has opened up ever more opportunities for the development of human potential, however, not everyone has been able to take full advantage of those opportunities or progress far once they have done so. Formal or informal barriers to equality of opportunity, for example, have historically blocked various sectors of the population—such as women, minorities, and the poor—from benefiting fully from all capitalism offers. But over time, in the advanced capitalist world, those barriers have gradually been lowered or removed, so that now opportunity is more equally available than ever before. The inequality that exists today, therefore, derives less from the unequal availability of opportunity than it does from the unequal ability to exploit opportunity. And that unequal ability, in turn, stems from differences in the inherent human potential that individuals begin with and in the ways that families and communities enable and encourage that human potential to flourish.

The role of the family in shaping individuals' ability and inclination to make use of the means of cultivation that capitalism offers is hard to overstate. The household is not only a site of consumption and of biological reproduction. It is also the main setting in which children are socialized, civilized, and educated, in which habits are developed that influence their subsequent fates as people and as market actors. To use the language of contemporary economics, the family is a workshop in which human capital is produced.

Over time, the family has shaped capitalism by creating new demands for new commodities. It has also been repeatedly reshaped by capitalism because new commodities and new means of production have led family members to spend their time in new ways. As new consumer goods became available at ever-cheaper prices during the eighteenth century, families devoted more of their time to market-oriented activities, with positive effects on their ability to consume. Male wages may have actually declined at first, but the combined wages of husbands, wives, and children made higher standards of consumption possible. Economic growth and expanding cultural horizons did not improve all aspects of life for everybody, however. The fact that working-class children could earn money from an early age created incentives to neglect their education, and the unhealthiness of some of the newly available commodities (white bread, sugar, tobacco, distilled spirits) meant that rising standards of consumption did not always mean an improvement in health and longevity. And as female labor time was reallocated from the household to the market, standards of cleanliness appear to have declined, increasing the chance of disease.

The late eighteenth and early nineteenth centuries saw the gradual spread of new means of production across the economy. This was the age of the machine, characterized by the increasing substitution of inorganic sources of power (above all the steam engine) for organic sources of power (human and animal), a process that increased productivity tremendously. As opposed to in a society based largely on agriculture and cottage industries, manufacturing now increasingly took place in the factory, built around new engines that were too large, too loud, and too dirty to have a place in the home. Work was therefore more and more divorced from the household, which ultimately changed the structure of the family.

At first, the owners of the new, industrialized factories sought out women and children as employees, since they were more tractable and more easily disciplined than men. But by the second half of the nineteenth century, the average British workingman was enjoying substantial and sustained growth in real wages, and a new division of labor came about within the family itself, along lines of gender. Men, whose relative strength gave them an advantage in manufacturing, increasingly worked in factories for market wages, which were high enough to support a family. The nineteenth-century market, however, could not provide commodities that produced goods such as cleanliness, hygiene, nutritious meals, and the mindful supervision of children. Among the upper classes, these services could be provided by servants. But for most families, such services were increasingly provided by wives. This caused the rise of the breadwinner-homemaker family, with a division of labor along gender lines. Many of the improvements in health, longevity, and education from the mid-nineteenth to the mid-twentieth century, de Vries has argued, can be explained by this reallocation of female labor from the market to the household and, eventually, the reallocation of childhood from the market to education, as children left the work force for school.

DYNAMISM AND INSECURITY

For most of history, the prime source of human insecurity was nature. In such societies, as Marx noted, the economic system was oriented toward stability—and stagnancy. Capitalist societies, by contrast, have been oriented toward innovation and dynamism, to the creation of new knowledge, new products, and new modes of production and distribution. All of this has shifted the locus of insecurity from nature to the economy.

Hegel observed in the 1820s that for men in a commercial society based on the breadwinner-homemaker model, one's sense of self-worth and recognition by others was tied to having a job. This posed a problem, because in a dynamic capitalist market, unemployment was a distinct possibility. The division of labor created by the market meant that many workers had skills that were highly specialized and suited for only a narrow range of jobs. The market created shifting wants, and increased demand for new products meant decreased demand for older ones. Men whose lives had been devoted to their role in the production of the old products were left without a job and without the training that would allow them to find new work. And the mechanization of production also led to a loss of jobs. From its very beginnings, in other words, the creativity and innovation of industrial capitalism were shadowed by insecurity for members of the work force.

Marx and Engels sketched out capitalism's dynamism, insecurity, refinement of needs, and expansion of cultural possibilities in *The Communist Manifesto*:

> The bourgeoisie has, through its exploitation of the world market, given a cosmopolitan character to production and consumption in every country. To the great chagrin of reactionaries, it has drawn from under the feet of industry the national ground on which it stood. All old-established national industries have been destroyed or are daily being destroyed. They are dislodged by new industries, whose introduction becomes a life and death question for all civilized nations, by industries that no longer work up indigenous raw material, but raw material drawn from the remotest zones; industries whose products are consumed, not only at home, but in every quarter of the globe. In

place of the old wants, satisfied by the production of the country, we find new wants, requiring for their satisfaction the products of distant lands and climes. In place of the old local and national seclusion and self-sufficiency, we have intercourse in every direction, universal inter-dependence of nations.

In the twentieth century, the economist Joseph Schumpeter would expand on these points with his notion that capitalism was characterized by "creative destruction," in which new products and forms of distribution and organization displaced older forms. Unlike Marx, however, who saw the source of this dynamism in the disembodied quest of "capital" to increase (at the expense, he thought, of the working class), Schumpeter focused on the role of the entrepreneur, an innovator who introduced new commodities and discovered new markets and methods.

The dynamism and insecurity created by nineteenth-century industrial capitalism led to the creation of new institutions for the reduction of insecurity, including the limited liability corporation, to reduce investor risks; labor unions, to further worker interests; mutual-aid societies, to provide loans and burial insurance; and commercial life insurance. In the middle decades of the twentieth century, in response to the mass unemployment and deprivation produced by the Great Depression (and the political success of communism and fascism, which convinced many democrats that too much insecurity was a threat to capitalist democracy itself), Western democracies embraced the welfare state. Different nations created different combinations of specific programs, but the new welfare states had a good deal in common, including old-age and unemployment insurance and various measures to support families.

The expansion of the welfare state in the decades after World War II took place at a time when the capitalist economies of the West were growing rapidly. The success of the industrial economy made it possible to siphon off profits and wages to government purposes through taxation. The demographics of the postwar era, in which the breadwinner-homemaker model of the family predominated, helped also, as moderately high birthrates created a favorable ratio of active workers to dependents. Educational opportunities expanded, as elite universities increasingly admitted students on the basis of their academic achievements and potential, and more and more people attended institutions of higher education. And barriers to full participation in society for women and minorities began to fall as well. The result of all of this was a temporary equilibrium during which the advanced capitalist countries experienced strong economic growth, high employment, and relative socioeconomic equality.

LIFE IN THE POSTINDUSTRIAL ECONOMY

For humanity in general, the late twentieth and early twenty-first centuries have been a period of remarkable progress, due in no small part to the spread of capitalism around the globe. Economic liberalization in China, India, Brazil, Indonesia, and other countries in the developing world has allowed hundreds of millions of people to escape grinding poverty and move into the middle class. Consumers in more advanced capitalist countries, such as the United States, meanwhile, have experienced a radical reduction in the price of many commodities, from clothes to televisions, and the availability of a river of new goods that have transformed their lives.

Most remarkable, perhaps, have been changes to the means of self-cultivation. As the economist Tyler Cowen notes, much of the fruit of recent developments "is in our minds and in our laptops and not so much in the revenue-generating sector of the economy." As a result, "much of the value of the internet is experienced at the personal level and so will never show up in the productivity numbers." Many of the great musical performances of the twentieth century, in every genre, are available on YouTube for free. Many of the great films of the twentieth century, once confined to occasional showings at art houses in a few metropolitan areas, can be viewed by anybody at any time for a small monthly charge. Soon, the great university libraries will be available online to the entire world, and other unprecedented opportunities for personal development will follow.

All this progress, however, has been shadowed by capitalism's perennial features of inequality and insecurity. In 1973, the sociologist Daniel Bell noted that in the advanced capitalist world, knowledge, science, and technology were driving a transformation to what he termed "postindustrial society." Just as manufacturing had previously displaced agriculture as the major source of employment, he argued, so the service sector was now displacing manufacturing. In a postindustrial, knowledge-based economy, the production of manufactured goods depended more on technological inputs than on the skills of the workers who actually built and assembled the products. That meant a relative decline in the need for and economic value of skilled and semiskilled factory workers—just as there had previously been a decline in the need for and value of agricultural laborers. In such an economy, the skills in demand included scientific and technical knowledge and the ability to work with information. The revolution in information technology that has swept through the economy in recent decades, meanwhile, has only exacerbated these trends.

One crucial impact of the rise of the postindustrial economy has been on the status and roles of men and women. Men's relative advantage in the preindustrial and industrial economies rested in large part on their greater physical strength—something now ever less in demand. Women, in contrast, whether by biological disposition or socialization, have had a relative advantage in human skills and emotional intelligence, which have become increasingly more important in an economy more oriented to human services than to the production of material objects. The portion of the economy in which women could participate has expanded, and their labor has become more valuable—meaning that time spent at home now comes at the expense of more lucrative possibilities in the paid work force.

This has led to the growing replacement of male breadwinner-female homemaker households by dual-income households. Both advocates and critics of the move of women into the paid economy have tended to overemphasize the role played in this shift by the ideological struggles of feminism, while underrating the role played by changes in the nature of capitalist production. The redeployment of female labor from the household has been made possible in part by the existence of new commodities that cut down on necessary household labor time (such as washing machines, dryers, dishwashers, water heaters, vacuum cleaners, microwave ovens). The greater time devoted to market activity, in turn, has given rise to new demand for household-oriented consumer goods that require less labor (such as packaged and prepared food) and the expansion of restaurant and fast-food eating. And it has led to the commodification of care, as the young, the elderly, and the infirm are increasingly looked after not by relatives but by paid minders.

The trend for women to receive more education and greater professional attainments has been accompanied by changing social norms in the choice of marriage partners. In the age of the breadwinner-homemaker marriage, women tended to place a premium on earning capacity in their choice of partners. Men, in turn, valued the homemaking capacities of potential spouses more than their vocational attainments. It was not unusual for men and women to marry partners of roughly the same intelligence, but women tended to marry men of higher levels of education and economic achievement. As the economy has passed from an industrial economy to a postindustrial service-and-information economy, women have joined men in attaining recognition through paid work, and the industrious couple today is more likely to be made of peers, with more equal levels of education and more comparable levels of economic achievement—a process termed "assortative mating."

INEQUALITY ON THE RISE

These postindustrial social trends have had a significant impact on inequality. If family income doubles at each step of the economic ladder, then the total incomes of those families higher up the ladder are bound to increase faster than the total incomes of those further down. But for a substantial portion of households at the lower end of the ladder, there has been no doubling at all—for as the relative pay of women has grown and the relative pay of less-educated, working-class men has declined, the latter have been viewed as less and less marriageable. Often, the limitations of human capital that make such men less employable also make them less desirable as companions, and the character traits of men who are chronically unemployed sometimes deteriorate as well. With less to bring to the table, such men are regarded as less necessary—in part because women can now count on provisions from the welfare state as an additional independent source of income, however meager.

In the United States, among the most striking developments of recent decades has been the stratification of marriage patterns among the various classes and ethnic groups of society. When divorce laws were loosened in the 1960s, there was a rise in divorce rates among all classes. But by the 1980s, a new pattern had emerged: divorce declined among the more educated portions of the populace, while rates among the less-educated portions continued to rise. In addition, the more educated and more well-to-do were more likely to wed, while the less educated were less likely to do so. Given the family's role as an incubator of human capital, such trends have had important spillover effects on inequality. Abundant research shows that children raised by two parents in an ongoing union are more likely to develop the self-discipline and self-confidence that make for success in life, whereas children—and particularly boys—reared in single-parent households (or, worse, households with a mother who has a series of temporary relationships) have a greater risk of adverse outcomes.

All of this has been taking place during a period of growing equality of access to education and increasing stratification of marketplace rewards, both of which have increased the importance of human capital. One element of human capital is cognitive ability: quickness of mind, the ability to infer and apply patterns drawn from experience, and the ability to deal with mental complexity. Another is character and social skills: self-discipline, persistence, responsibility. And a third is actual knowledge. All of these are becoming increasingly crucial for success in the postindustrial marketplace. As the economist Brink Lindsey notes in his recent book *Human Capitalism*, between 1973 and 2001, average annual growth in real income was only 0.3 percent for people in the bottom fifth of the U.S. income distribution, compared with 0.8 percent for people in the middle fifth and 1.8 percent for those in the top fifth. Somewhat similar patterns also prevail in many other advanced economies.

Globalization has not caused this pattern of increasingly unequal returns to human capital but reinforced it. The economist Michael Spence has distinguished between "tradable" goods and services, which can be easily imported and exported, and "untradable" ones, which cannot. Increasingly, tradable goods and services are imported to advanced capitalist societies from less advanced capitalist societies, where labor costs are lower. As manufactured goods and routine services are outsourced, the wages of the relatively unskilled and uneducated in advanced capitalist societies decline further, unless these people are somehow able to find remunerative employment in the untradable sector.

THE IMPACT OF MODERN FINANCE

Rising inequality, meanwhile, has been compounded by rising insecurity and anxiety for people higher up on the economic ladder. One trend contributing to this problem has been the financialization of the economy, above all in the United States, creating what was characterized as "money manager capitalism" by the economist Hyman Minsky and has been called "agency capitalism" by the financial expert Alfred Rappaport.

As late as the 1980s, finance was an essential but limited element of the U.S. economy. The trade in equities (the stock market) was made up of individual investors, large or small, putting their own money in stocks of companies they believed to have good long-term prospects. Investment capital was also available from the major Wall Street investment banks and their foreign counterparts, which were private partnerships in which the partners' own money was on the line. All of this began to change as larger pools of capital became available for investment and came to be deployed by professional money managers rather the owners of the capital themselves.

One source of such new capital was pension funds. In the postwar decades, when major American industries emerged from World War II as oligopolies with limited competition and large, expanding markets at home and abroad, their profits and future prospects allowed them to offer employees defined-benefit pension plans, with the risks involved assumed by the companies themselves. From the 1970s on, however, as the U.S. economy became more competitive, corporate profits became more uncertain, and companies (as well as various public-sector organizations) attempted to shift the risk by putting their pension funds into the hands of professional money managers, who were expected to generate significant profits. Retirement income for employees now depended not on the profits of their employers but on the fate of their pension funds.

Another source of new capital was university and other non-profit organizations' endowments, which grew initially thanks to donations but were increasingly expected to grow further based on their investment performance. And still another source of new capital came from individuals and governments in the developing world, where rapid economic growth, combined with a high propensity to save and a desire for relatively secure investment prospects, led to large flows of money into the U.S. financial system.

Spurred in part by these new opportunities, the traditional Wall Street investment banks transformed themselves into publicly traded corporations—that is to say, they, too, began to invest not just with their own funds but also with other people's money—and tied the bonuses of their partners and employees to annual profits. All of this created a highly competitive financial system dominated by investment managers working with large pools of capital, paid based on their supposed ability to outperform their peers. The structure of incentives in this environment led fund managers to try to maximize short-term returns, and this pressure trickled down to corporate executives. The shrunken time horizon created a temptation to boost immediate profits at the expense of longer-term investments, whether in research and development or in improving the skills of the company's work force. For both managers and employees, the result has been a constant churning that increases the likelihood of job losses and economic insecurity.

An advanced capitalist economy does indeed require an extensive financial sector. Part of this is a simple extension of the division of labor: outsourcing decisions about investing to professionals allows the rest of the population the mental space to pursue things they do better or care more about. The increasing complexity of capitalist economies means that entrepreneurs and corporate executives need help in deciding when and how to raise funds. And private equity firms that have an ownership interest in growing the real value of the firms in which they invest play a key role in fostering economic growth. These matters, which properly occupy financiers, have important consequences, and handling them requires intelligence, diligence, and drive, so it is neither surprising nor undesirable that specialists in this area are highly paid. But whatever its benefits and continued social value, the financialization of society has nevertheless had some unfortunate consequences, both in increasing inequality by raising the top of the economic ladder (thanks to the extraordinary rewards financial managers receive) and in increasing insecurity among those lower down (thanks to the intense focus on short-term economic performance to the exclusion of other concerns).

THE FAMILY AND HUMAN CAPITAL

In today's globalized, financialized, postindustrial environment, human capital is more important than ever in determining life chances. This makes families more important, too, because as each generation of social science researchers discovers anew (and much to their chagrin), the resources transmitted by the family tend to be highly determinative of success in school and in the workplace. As the economist Friedrich Hayek pointed out half a century ago in *The Constitution of Liberty*, the main impediment to true equality of opportunity is that there is no substitute for intelligent parents or for an emotionally and culturally nurturing family. In the words of a recent study by the economists Pedro Carneiro and James Heckman, "Differences in levels of cognitive and noncognitive skills by family income and family background emerge early and persist. If anything, schooling widens these early differences."

Hereditary endowments come in a variety of forms: genetics, prenatal and postnatal nurture, and the cultural orientations conveyed within the family. Money matters, too, of course, but is often less significant than these largely nonmonetary factors. (The prevalence of books in a household is a better predictor of higher test scores than family income.) Over time, to the extent that societies are organized along meritocratic lines, family endowments and market rewards will tend to converge.

Educated parents tend to invest more time and energy in child care, even when both parents are engaged in the work force. And families strong in human capital are more likely to make fruitful use of the improved means of cultivation that contemporary capitalism offers (such as the potential for online enrichment) while resisting their potential snares (such as unrestricted viewing of television and playing of computer games).

This affects the ability of children to make use of formal education, which is increasingly, at least potentially, available to all regardless of economic or ethnic status. At the turn of the twentieth century, only 6.4 percent of American teenagers graduated from high school, and only one in 400 went on to college. There was thus a huge portion of the population with the capacity, but not the opportunity, for greater educational achievement. Today, the U.S. high school graduation rate is about 75 percent (down from a peak of about 80 percent in 1960), and roughly 40 percent of young adults are enrolled in college.

The Economist recently repeated a shibboleth: "In a society with broad equality of opportunity, the parents' position on the income ladder should have little impact on that of their children." The fact is, however, that the greater equality of institutional opportunity there is, the more families' human capital endowments matter. As the political scientist Edward Banfield noted a generation ago in *The Unheavenly City Revisited*, "All education favors the middle- and upper-class child, because to be middle- or upper-class is to have qualities that make one particularly educable." Improvements in the quality of schools may improve overall educational outcomes, but they tend to increase, rather than diminish, the gap in achievement between children from families with different levels of human capital. Recent investigations that purport to demonstrate less intergenerational mobility in the United States today than in the past (or than in some European nations) fail to note that this may in fact be a perverse product of generations of increasing equality of opportunity. And in this respect, it is possible that the United States may simply be on the leading edge of trends found in other advanced capitalist societies as well.

DIFFERENTIAL GROUP ACHIEVEMENT

The family is not the only social institution to have a major impact on the development of human capital and eventual success in the marketplace; so do communal groupings, such as those of religion, race, and ethnicity. In his 1905 book, *The Protestant Ethic and the Spirit of Capitalism*, the sociologist Max Weber observed that in religiously diverse areas, Protestants tended to do better economically than Catholics, and Calvinists better than Lutherans. Weber presented a cultural explanation for this difference, grounded in the different psychological propensities created by the different faiths. A few years later, in *The Jews and Modern Capitalism*, Weber's contemporary Werner Sombart offered an alternative explanation for differential group success, based partly on cultural propensities and partly on racial ones. And in 1927, their younger colleague Schumpeter titled a major essay "Social Classes in an Ethnically Homogeneous Environment" because he took it for granted that in an ethnically mixed setting, levels of achievement would vary by ethnicity, not just class.

The explanations offered for such patterns are less important than the fact that differential group performance has been a perennial feature in the history of capitalism, and such differences continue to exist today. In the contemporary United States, for example, Asians (especially when disaggregated from Pacific Islanders) tend to outperform non-Hispanic whites, who in turn tend to outperform Hispanics, who in turn tend to outperform African Americans. This is true whether one looks at educational achievement, earnings, or family patterns, such as the incidence of nonmarital births.

Those western European nations (and especially northern European nations) with much higher levels of equality than the United States tend to have more ethnically homogeneous populations. As recent waves of immigration have made many advanced post-industrial societies less ethnically homogeneous, they also seem to be increasingly stratifying along communal lines, with some immigrant groups exhibiting more favorable patterns than the preexisting population and other groups doing worse. In the United Kingdom, for example, the children of Chinese and Indian immigrants tend do better than the indigenous population, whereas those of Caribbean blacks and Pakistanis tend to do worse. In France, the descendants of Vietnamese tend to do better, and those of North African origin tend to do worse. In Israel, the children of Russian immigrants tend to do better, while those of immigrants from Ethiopia tend to do worse. In Canada, the children of Chinese and Indians tend to do better, while those of Caribbean and Latin American origin tend to do worse. Much of this divergence in achievement can be explained by the differing class and educational backgrounds of the immigrant groups in their countries of origin. But because the communities themselves act as carriers and incubators of human capital, the patterns can and do persist over time and place.

In the case of the United States, immigration plays an even larger role in exacerbating inequality, for the country's economic dynamism, cultural openness, and geographic position tend to attract both some of world's best and brightest and some of its least educated. This raises the top and lowers the bottom of the economic ladder.

WHY EDUCATION IS NOT A PANACEA

A growing recognition of the increasing economic inequality and social stratification in postindustrial societies has naturally led to discussions of what can be done about it, and in the American context, the answer from almost all quarters is simple: education.

One strand of this logic focuses on college. There is a growing gap in life chances between those who complete college and those who don't, the argument runs, and so as many people as possible should go to college. Unfortunately, even though a higher percentage of Americans are attending college, they are not necessarily learning more. An increasing number are unqualified for college-level work, many leave without completing their degrees, and others receive degrees reflecting standards much lower than what a college degree has usually been understood to mean.

The most significant divergence in educational achievement occurs before the level of college, meanwhile, in rates of completion of high school, and major differences in performance (by class and ethnicity) appear still earlier, in elementary school. So a second strand of the education argument focuses on primary and secondary schooling. The remedies suggested here include providing schools with more money, offering parents more choice, testing students more often, and improving teacher performance. Even if some or all of these measures might be desirable for other reasons, none has been shown to significantly diminish the gaps between students and between social groups—because formal schooling itself plays a relatively minor role in creating or perpetuating achievement gaps.

The gaps turn out to have their origins in the different levels of human capital children possess when they enter school—which has led to a third strand of the education argument, focusing on earlier and more intensive childhood intervention. Suggestions here often amount to taking children out of their family environments and putting them into institutional settings for as much time as possible (Head Start, Early Head Start) or even trying to resocialize whole neighborhoods (as in the Harlem Children's Zone project). There are examples of isolated successes with such programs, but it is far from clear that these are reproducible on a larger scale. Many programs show short-term gains in cognitive ability, but most of these gains tend to fade out over time, and those that remain tend to be marginal. It is more plausible that such programs improve the noncognitive skills and character traits conducive to economic success—but at a significant cost and investment, employing resources extracted from the more successful parts of the population (thus lowering the resources available to them) or diverted from other potential uses.

For all these reasons, inequality in advanced capitalist societies seems to be both growing and ineluctable, at least for the time being. Indeed, one of the most robust findings of contemporary social scientific inquiry is that as the gap between high-income and low-income families has increased, the educational and employment achievement gaps between the children of these families has increased even more.

WHAT IS TO BE DONE?

Capitalism today continues to produce remarkable benefits and continually greater opportunities for self-cultivation and personal development. Now as ever, however, those upsides are coming with downsides, particularly increasing inequality and insecurity. As Marx and Engels accurately noted, what distinguishes capitalism from other social and economic systems is its "constant revolutionizing of production, uninterrupted disturbance of all social conditions, [and] everlasting uncertainty and agitation."

At the end of the eighteenth century, the greatest American student and practitioner of political economy, Alexander Hamilton, had some profound observations about the inevitable ambiguity of public policy in a world of creative destruction:

Tis the portion of man assigned to him by the eternal allotment of Providence that every good he enjoys, shall be alloyed with ills, that every source of his bliss shall be a source of his affliction—except Virtue alone, the only unmixed good which is permitted to his temporal Condition. . . . The true politician . . . will favor all those institutions and plans which tend to make men happy according to their natural bent which multiply the sources of individual enjoyment and increase those of national resource and strength—taking care to infuse in each case all the ingredients which can be devised as preventives or correctives of the evil which is the eternal concomitant of temporal blessing.

Now as then, the question at hand is just how to maintain the temporal blessings of capitalism while devising preventives and correctives for the evils that are their eternal concomitant.

One potential cure for the problems of rising inequality and insecurity is simply to redistribute income from the top of the economy to the bottom. This has two drawbacks, however. The first is that over time, the very forces that lead to greater inequality reassert themselves, requiring still more, or more aggressive, redistribution. The second is that at some point, redistribution produces substantial resentment and impedes the drivers of economic growth. Some degree of postmarket redistribution through taxation is both possible and necessary, but just how much is ideal will inevitably be contested, and however much it is, it will never solve the underlying problems.

A second cure, using government policy to close the gaps between individuals and groups by offering preferential treatment to underperformers, may be worse than the disease. Whatever their purported benefits, mandated rewards to certain categories of citizens inevitably create a sense of injustice among the rest of the population. More grave is their cost in terms of economic efficiency, since by definition, they promote less-qualified individuals to positions they would not attain on the basis of merit alone. Similarly, policies banning the use of meritocratic criteria in education, hiring, and credit simply because they have a "differential impact" on the fortunes of various communal groups or because they contribute to unequal social outcomes will inevitably impede the quality of the educational system, the work force, and the economy.

A third possible cure, encouraging continued economic innovation that will benefit everybody, is more promising. The combination of the Internet and computational revolutions may prove comparable to the coming of electricity, which facilitated an almost unimaginable range of other activities that transformed society at large in unpredictable ways. Among other gains, the Internet has radically increased the velocity of knowledge, a key factor in capitalist economic growth since at least the eighteenth century. Add to that the prospects of other fields still in their infancy, such as biotechnology, bioinformatics, and nanotechnology, and the prospects for future economic growth and the ongoing improvement of human life look reasonably bright. Nevertheless, even continued innovation and revived economic growth will not eliminate or even significantly reduce socioeconomic inequality and insecurity, because individual, family, and group differences will still affect the development of human capital and professional accomplishment.

For capitalism to continue to be made legitimate and palatable to populations at large, therefore—including those on the lower and middle rungs of the socioeconomic ladder, as well as those near the top, losers as well as winners—government safety nets that help diminish insecurity, alleviate the sting of failure in the marketplace, and help maintain equality of opportunity will have to be maintained and revitalized. Such programs already exist in most of the advanced capitalist world, including the United States, and the right needs to accept that they serve an indispensable purpose and must be preserved rather than gutted—that major government social welfare spending is a proper response to some inherently problematic features of capitalism, not a "beast" that should be "starved."

In the United States, for example, measures such as Social Security, unemployment insurance, food stamps, the Earned Income

Tax Credit, Medicare, Medicaid, and the additional coverage provided by the Affordable Care Act offer aid and comfort above all to those less successful in and more buffeted by today's economy. It is unrealistic to imagine that the popular demand for such programs will diminish. It is uncaring to cut back the scope of such programs when inequality and insecurity have risen. And if nothing else, the enlightened self-interest of those who profit most from living in a society of capitalist dynamism should lead them to recognize that it is imprudent to resist parting with some of their market gains in order to achieve continued social and economic stability. Government entitlement programs need structural reform, but the right should accept that a reasonably generous welfare state is here to stay, and for eminently sensible reasons.

The left, in turn, needs to come to grips with the fact that aggressive attempts to eliminate inequality may be both too expensive and futile. The very success of past attempts to increase equality of opportunity—such as by expanding access to education and outlawing various forms of discrimination—means that in advanced capitalist societies today, large, discrete pools of untapped human potential are increasingly rare. Additional measures to promote equality are therefore likely to produce fewer gains than their predecessors, at greater cost. And insofar as such measures involve diverting resources from those with more human capital to those with less, or bypassing criteria of achievement and merit, they may impede the economic dynamism and growth on which the existing welfare state depends.

The challenge for government policy in the advanced capitalist world is thus how to maintain a rate of economic dynamism that will provide increasing benefits for all while still managing to pay for the social welfare programs required to make citizens' lives bearable under conditions of increasing inequality and insecurity. Different countries will approach this challenge in different ways, since their priorities, traditions, size, and demographic and economic characteristics vary. (It is among the illusions of the age that when it comes to government policy, nations can borrow at will from one another.) But a useful starting point might be the rejection of both the politics of privilege and the politics of resentment and the adoption of a clear-eyed view of what capitalism actually involves, as opposed to the idealization of its worshipers and the demonization of its critics.⊛

Red White

Why a Founding Father of Postwar Capitalism Spied for the Soviets

Benn Steil

I n the wake of the 2008 financial crisis and the ensuing global economic downturn, it has become commonplace for politicians, pundits, and economists to invoke the memory of Bretton Woods. In July 1944, in the midst of World War II, representatives of 44 nations gathered in this remote New Hampshire town to create something that had never before existed: a global monetary system to be managed by an international body. The gold standard of the late nineteenth century, the organically formed foundation of the first great economic globalization, had collapsed during the previous world war. Efforts to revive it in the 1920s proved catastrophically unsuccessful. Economies and trade collapsed; cross-border tensions soared. In the 1930s, internationalists in the U.S. Treasury Department saw a powerful cause and effect and were determined to resolve the flaws in the international economic system once and for all. In the words of Harry Dexter White, a then little-known Treasury official who became the unlikely architect of the Bretton Woods system, it was time to build a "New Deal for a new world."

Working in parallel and in prickly collaboration with his British counterpart, the revolutionary economist John Maynard Keynes,

BENN STEIL is a Senior Fellow and Director of International Economics at the Council on Foreign Relations. This essay is adapted from his most recent book, *The Battle of Bretton Woods: John Maynard Keynes, Harry Dexter White, and the Making of a New World Order* (Princeton University Press, 2013).

White set out to create the economic foundations for a durable postwar global peace. Governments would be given more power over markets but fewer prerogatives to manipulate them for trade gains. Trade would in the future be harnessed to the service of political cooperation by ending shortages of gold and U.S. dollars. Speculators who stoked and profited from fears of such shortages would be shackled by strictures placed on the frenetic cross-border flows of capital. Interest rates would be set by government experts schooled in the powerful new discipline of macroeconomics, which Keynes had been instrumental in establishing. A newly created International Monetary Fund (IMF) would ensure that exchange rates were not manipulated for competitive advantage. Most important, budding dictators would never again be able to use barriers to trade and currency flows as tools of economic aggression, ruining their neighbors and fanning the flames of war.

Despite having never held any official title of importance, White had by 1944 achieved implausibly broad influence over U.S. foreign and economic policy. Grudgingly respected by colleagues at home and counterparts abroad for his gritty intelligence, attention to detail, relentless drive, and knack for framing policy, White made little effort to be liked. "He has not the faintest conception how to behave or observe the rules of civilized intercourse," Keynes groused. Arrogant and bullying, White was also nerve-ridden and insecure, always acutely conscious that his tenuous status in Washington depended wholly on his ability to keep Treasury Secretary Henry Morgenthau, a confidant of President Franklin Roosevelt with limited smarts, armed with actionable policies. White often made himself ill with stress before negotiations with Keynes, and then exploded during them. "We will try," White spat out during one particularly heated session, "to produce something which Your Highness can understand."

But as the chief architect of Bretton Woods, White outmaneuvered his far more brilliant British counterpart, distinguishing himself as an unrelenting nationalist who could extract every advantage out of the tectonic shift in geopolitical circumstances put in motion by World War II. White installed the groundwork for a dollar-centric postwar order antithetical to long-standing British interests, particularly as they related to the United Kingdom's collapsing colonial empire. Even White's closest colleagues were unaware, however, that his postwar vision involved a far more radical reordering of U.S. foreign policy, centered on the establishment of a close permanent alliance with the new rising European power— the Soviet Union. And they most surely did not know that White was willing to use extraordinary means to bring it about.

Over the course of 11 years, beginning in the mid-1930s, White acted as a Soviet mole, giving the Soviets secret information and advice on how to negotiate with the Roosevelt administration and advocating for them during internal policy debates. White was arguably more important to Soviet intelligence than Alger Hiss, the U.S. State Department official who was the most famous spy of the early Cold War.

The truth about White's actions has been clear for at least 15 years now, yet historians remain deeply divided over his intentions and his legacy, puzzled by the chasm between White's public views on political economy, which were mainstream progressive and Keynesian, and his clandestine behavior on behalf of the Soviets. Until recently, the White case has resembled a murder mystery with witnesses and a weapon but no clear motive.

Now we have one. The closest thing to a missing link between the official White and the secret White is an unpublished handwritten essay on yellow-lined notepaper that I found buried in a large folder of miscellaneous scribblings in White's archives at Princeton University. Apparently missed by his previous chroniclers, it provides a fascinating window onto the aspirations and mindset of this intellectually ambitious overachiever at the height of his power, in 1944.

In the essay, hazily titled "Political-Economic Int. of Future," White describes a postwar world in which the Soviet socialist model of economic organization, although not supplanting the American liberal capitalist one, would be ascendant. "In every case," he argues, "the change will be in the direction of increased [government] control over industry, and increased restrictions on the operations of competition and free enterprise." Whereas White believed in democracy and human rights, he consistently down-played both the lack of individual liberty in the Soviet Union ("The trend in Russia seems to be toward greater freedom of religion. . . . The constitution of [the] USSR guarantees that right") and the Soviets' foreign political and military adventurism ("The policy pursued by present day Russia [is one] of not actively supporting [revolutionary socialist] movements in other countries").

In the essay, White argues that the West is hypocritical in its demonization of the Soviet Union. He urges the United States to draw the Soviets into a tight military alliance in order to deter re-newed German and Japanese aggression. But such an alliance, White lamented, faced formidable obstacles: "rampant imperial-ism" in the United States, hiding under "a variety of patriotic cloaks"; the country's "very powerful Catholic hierarchy," which might "well find an alliance with Russia repugnant"; and groups "fearful that any alliance with a socialist country cannot but strengthen socialism and thereby weaken capitalism."

After sweeping away internal politics, religion, and foreign pol-icy as honest sources of Western opposition to the Soviet Union, White concludes that the true foundation of the conflict must be economic ideology. "It is basically [the] opposition of capitalism to socialism," he writes. "Those who believe seriously in the superior-ity of capitalism over socialism"—a group from which White ap-parently excluded himself—"fear Russia as the source of socialist ideology." He then ends his essay with what, coming from the U.S. government's most important economic strategist, can only be de-scribed as an astounding conclusion: "Russia is the first instance of a socialist economy in action. And it works!"

It turns out that the chief designer of the postwar global capital-ist financial architecture saw Soviet behavior through rose-colored glasses not simply because he believed that the Soviet Union was a vital U.S. ally but because he also believed passionately in the success of the bold Soviet experiment with socialism.

NO MERE FELLOW TRAVELER

White's admiration for the Soviet economic system is striking, coming from one of the most influential policy figures in 1940s Washington. Yet it was not out of keeping with the tenor of the times. White belonged to a generation of Russophile writers and public officials who had come of age intellectually between the two world wars, a period marked by political upheaval, the Great Depression, and the collapse of the international trade and monetary systems. The whole world order seemed to be in flux. To many observers, radical social, economic, and political change were inevitable. To some, the upheaval was also a call to action—inside and outside the traditional confines of national politics.

As a young man, White had been a passionate supporter of Robert La Follette, the firebrand who ran as the Progressive Party's first presidential candidate in 1924; La Follette called for muscular government intervention in the U.S. economy and condemned American imperialism in Latin America. White had a long-standing fascination with Soviet economic planning, having decided in 1933, shortly after becoming an economics professor at what was then Lawrence College, in Wisconsin, to try to go to the Soviet Union to study its system. He was diverted from this plan only by an invitation to work on a monetary-reform study at the Treasury Department. Soon after his arrival in Washington in 1934, White enmeshed himself in a web of fellow travelers working for the Soviet underground. Eager for influence and dismissive of bureaucratic barriers to action, White began the sort of dangerous double life that attracted many of his Washington contemporaries in the 1930s and 1940s.

According to Whittaker Chambers, a courier between Soviet intelligence agencies and their secret sources within the U.S. government, White's clandestine work began in 1935. An idealist who envisioned a future in which world affairs were managed by enlightened technocrats such as himself, White appeared to welcome the chance to hasten that future's coming by collaborating with secretive foot soldiers such as Chambers. White's official status in the U.S. government was beneath what he knew his talents merited, and he craved the recognition such operatives accorded him. Yet unlike Chambers, White would not take orders from Moscow. He worked on his own terms. He joined no underground movements. Working through intermediaries close to him, White secured official Treasury documents for Chambers, which, after Chambers photographed them in his Baltimore workshop, White returned through the same channels. White also prepared weekly or biweekly memos for Chambers summarizing what he considered useful information.

"There's no doubt that Harry was close to the Russians," White's Treasury Department colleague Edward Bernstein reflected decades after Bretton Woods. And "it was just like Harry to think he could give advice to everybody." But why would White have strayed so far beyond merely giving advice?

During World War II, a surprising number of U.S. officials provided covert assistance to the Soviets without considering themselves disloyal to the United States. "They were," in the reckoning of one famous confessed spy, Elizabeth Bentley, "a bunch of misguided idealists. They were doing it for something they believed was right. . . . They felt very strongly that we were allies with Russia, that Russia was bearing the brunt of the war, that she [Russia] must have every assistance, because the people from within the Government . . . were not giving her things that we should give her . . . [things] that we were giving to Britain and not to her. And they felt . . . it was their duty, actually, to get this stuff to Russia."

White had begun his efforts well before the war, however, in the years just after the Soviet Union secured U.S. diplomatic recognition, in 1933, and joined the League of Nations, in 1934. By all appearances, White believed that U.S. policy should and would move in the direction of deeper engagement with Moscow. His collaboration with Chambers allowed him to establish his bona

fides with the still-mysterious foreign power years before any official opportunities would present themselves.

TO RUSSIA WITH LOVE

When such opportunities did finally arise, White took full advantage of them. The most notable of these came in early 1944, when
the Treasury Department began planning a currency to be used in
postwar occupied Germany. The British agreed that the occupation
currency should be printed in the United States, but the Soviets
demanded the right to print their own notes, using a duplicate set
of American plates. This would, of course, allow them to print as
much German money as they wished. Backing the Soviets' demands before his Treasury Department colleagues, White, according to one of his aides, argued that the United States "had not been
doing enough for the Soviet Union all along and that if the Soviets
profited as a result of this transaction we should be happy to give
them this token of our appreciation of their efforts." The director
of the Bureau of Engraving and Printing, Alvin Hall, was staunchly
opposed to giving the Soviets the plates, which elicited a fierce
rebuke from White. The Soviets, he insisted, "must be trusted to
the same degree and to the same extent as the other allies."

Morgenthau had placed White in charge of such matters, and
White ensured that the Soviets got the plates. The predictable result was that they printed a lot of currency. The Allies put into
circulation a total of about 10.5 billion Allied marks between September 1944 and July 1945; the Soviets likely issued more than 78
billion. Much of this cash wound up being redeemed by the U.S.
government at the fixed exchange rate advocated by White, resulting in the Soviets effectively raiding the U.S. Treasury for $300-
$500 million, or roughly $4.0-$6.5 billion in today's dollars. White
had wanted to give the Soviets a "token of our appreciation of their
efforts," and this was indeed a generous one.

But did White's Soviet connections have any actual impact on
the outcome at Bretton Woods? Although the broad "White Plan"
for the IMF clearly bore no imprint of Soviet monetary thinking,

as there was none to speak of, White was highly solicitous of the obstructionist Soviets at the conference itself—more so than any of his American negotiating colleagues, and vastly more so than the Europeans, some of whom were angered by the effects of White's behavior. Concerned that the Soviet government might not ratify the conference agreements, White six months later proposed a low-interest U.S. reconstruction loan of $10 billion for the Soviet Union—more than three times as much as what he advocated in transitional assistance for the United Kingdom. The fact that such a credit was not ultimately offered turned out to be one of the primary reasons the Soviet government decided against joining the IMF and the World Bank, as White had feared it would.

U.S. President Harry Truman initially planned to make White the first head of the IMF. Had White gotten the job, his pro-Soviet views might have become consequential in its operations. However, the primary reason that White did not become the institution's head—and that no American has ever since become its head—was the emerging revelations of White's activities on behalf of the Soviets.

Truman nominated White to be the first American executive director of the IMF on January 23, 1946, intending to nominate him for the top job of managing director shortly thereafter. Truman did not know that White had by that time been under FBI surveillance for two months, suspected of being a Soviet spy. Two weeks later, the FBI director, J. Edgar Hoover, sent a report to the president describing White as "a valuable adjunct to an underground Soviet espionage organization" and accusing him of placing Soviet intelligence assets inside the U.S. government. Hoover warned that if White's activities became public, it could endanger the IMF. But the Senate Committee on Banking and Currency, unaware of the allegations, had approved White's nomination to become the fund's U.S. executive director on February 5, the day after Hoover's report was delivered.

In light of Hoover's report, Secretary of State James Byrnes wanted Truman to withdraw the nomination; Treasury Secretary

Frederick Vinson wanted White out of government altogether. Truman did not trust Hoover but realized that he had a potential scandal on his hands. He decided to stick with White as an IMF executive director, a huge step down from managing director. But nominating another American to a post above White's would have raised eyebrows, since the White House would have had to explain why the fund's chief architect had been passed over.

The following month, Vinson met with Keynes, now the British governor of both the IMF and the World Bank. He said that Truman had decided not to put White's name forward for the IMF's top job and would instead back an American for the World Bank post in order to secure "the confidence of the American investment market." It would not be "proper," the administration had concluded with uncharacteristic fair-mindedness, "to have Americans as the heads of both bodies."

The United States' allies were more than happy to oblige, and a Belgian, Camille Gutt, became the first head of the IMF, while an American, Eugene Meyer, became the first head of the World Bank. The United States almost surely could have put an American in charge of the IMF after Gutt left, in 1951, but by that time, the fund's role had been supplanted by the Marshall Plan, and Washington was satisfied with its control of the World Bank's top post.

It is unclear what White knew or suspected about the FBI's investigations. In any event, his tenure at the fund was short; he resigned in the spring of 1947. After 13 years in Washington, he was despondent over the state of U.S.-Soviet relations and disillusioned with a "Democratic Party [that] can no longer fight for peace and a better America." He threw his enthusiastic backing behind Henry Wallace's Progressive Party presidential run in 1948. Wallace had fallen out with Truman, whom he had served as commerce secretary, over his administration's hardening stance toward the Soviets. Along with many prominent thinkers on both sides of the Atlantic at the time, Wallace believed that the 1917 Russian Revolution had been a seminal event in the history of the human struggle for freedom. An improbable Wallace victory would have returned White to political life as treasury secretary—assuming, that is, that White's accusers did not gain the upper hand.

"MY CREED IS THE AMERICAN CREED"

In the summer of 1948, Bentley and Chambers publicly accused White of spying for the Soviets, a charge White chose to deny vigorously before the House Un-American Activities Committee (HUAC). On the morning of August 13, White entered the packed committee room with cameras flashing. Facing the committee from behind a bevy of microphones, he raised his right hand and took the required oath. In an opening statement, he set out to establish himself as a loyal American in the progressive tradition:

> My creed is the American creed. I believe in freedom of religion, freedom of speech, freedom of thought, freedom of the press, freedom of criticism, and freedom of movement. I believe in the goal of equality of opportunity. . . . I believe in the freedom of choice of one's representatives in government, untrammeled by machine guns, secret police, or a police state. I am opposed to arbitrary and unwarranted use of power or authority from whatever source or against any individual or group. . . . I consider these principles sacred. I regard them as the basic fabric of our American way of life, and I believe in them as living realities, and not as mere words on paper. . . . I am ready for any questions you may wish to ask.

The gallery broke into applause; as far as the audience was concerned, White was on friendly turf. The committee had by this time earned a reputation for unseemly grandstanding, and White played this to his advantage. Despite his well-earned reputation for prickliness, he mostly avoided confrontation with his accusers. A 35-year-old freshman Republican congressman named Richard Nixon, hoping to set White up for a perjury charge, prodded him to state categorically that he had never met Chambers. But White would not take the bait, replying only that he did not "recollect" having met Chambers.

White was directed to a list of names; suspected Soviet spies had blue checks next to them. "Red checks would be more appropriate,"

White offered acerbically. He won rounds of applause and laughter, to the annoyance of the committee members. But White's bravado performance masked the fact that he was under enormous stress. The following day, he boarded a train bound for his summer home in New Hampshire. En route, he suffered terrible chest pains. The next day, local doctors diagnosed a severe heart attack; nothing could be done. The following evening, White was dead.

Conspiracy stories began to circulate almost immediately. White had been liquidated by Soviet intelligence. His death had been elaborately faked. He had fled to Uruguay. None of the tales had the slimmest reed of evidence to back it up. HUAC naturally came in for harsh media criticism in the wake of White's fatal heart attack, as the strain of the hearings appeared to be the proximate cause. Still, on the surface at least, the case was over. But more was to emerge.

On January 25, 1950, Hiss was sentenced to five years in prison for perjury. Truman, who had publicly attacked the espionage investigations, now conceded in private that "the SOB . . . is guilty as hell." Key to the case against Hiss were papers that Chambers had squirreled away in early 1938 as a "life preserver" in preparation for his defection from the Soviet underground. The next day, Nixon revealed on the floor of the House that he had in his possession "copies of eight pages of documents in the handwriting of Mr. White which Mr. Chambers turned over to the Justice Department." The original documents composed a four-page, double-sided memorandum, written in White's hand on yellow-lined paper, with material dated from January 10 to February 15, 1938, that had been part of Chambers' life preserver. Handwriting analysis by the FBI and what was then the Veterans Administration confirmed White's authorship.

The memo is a mixture of concise information and commentary on Treasury and State Department positions related to foreign policy and military matters. It covers European economic and political developments, including details of private discussions between the U.S. ambassador to France and French political leaders over their intentions toward the Soviet Union and Germany. The memo also outlines possible U.S. actions against Japan, such as a trade embargo or an asset freeze, and describes Japan's military protection of its oil storage facilities. White also revealed personal directives from the president to the treasury secretary, making clear that he was recording confidential information: at one point, the memo states explicitly that the Treasury Department's economic warfare plan for Japan, called for by the president, "remains unknown outside of Treasury."

THE PERFECT BUREAUCRAT

The enormous discord within the government over the White and Hiss cases stemmed at least in part from the fact that U.S. counterintelligence officials actually knew much more about the systematic nature of Soviet espionage than they chose to share with the White House. Incredibly, their trove of striking evidence would remain unknown to the public until half a century after the end of World War II.

Following the outbreak of the war in 1939, the United States began collecting copies of all cables going into and out of the country, as was standard wartime practice around the world. The complex Soviet cable cipher was theoretically unbreakable. But after examining thousands of cables, American code crackers working on the top-secret Venona project were able to identify a procedural mistake in the ciphering that made the code vulnerable to cracking. By the time they successfully decoded their first message, however, it was 1946 and the war was over. Yet what they found was still important and unexpected: copious evidence of an ongoing, ambitious Soviet espionage operation within the United States.

The code cracking took place over decades, and the first Venona cable identifying White as a Soviet mole was not known to the FBI until late 1950. In total, 18 deciphered cables refer to White, by various code names, all dated between March 16, 1944, and January 8, 1946. The cables reveal that Moscow was particularly interested in gleaning information from White during the 1945 San Francisco conference that produced the UN Charter, a conference at which White served as a technical adviser to the U.S. delegation.

The KGB officer Vladimir Pravdin cabled Moscow from San Francisco reporting that White had told him, among other things, that Truman and then Secretary of State Edward Stettinius wanted "to achieve the success of the conference at any price" and that the United States would agree to grant the Soviets veto power at the UN. Another 1945 cable describes White advising an American go-between with the Soviets that Moscow could secure more favorable loan terms from Washington than it had been seeking; yet another, dated the same day, provides corroborating evidence for allegations that White used his position to secure U.S. government appointments for other Soviet sympathizers.

Pravdin had been in San Francisco working undercover as a Soviet journalist, and what White knew of Pravdin's primary occupation is unclear. But White was certainly aware that what he was telling Pravdin was not meant for the press. White's defenders have pointed to such ambiguities to argue that he might not have known that he was sharing secrets directly with Soviet intelligence. But KGB files first seen by Western scholars in the 1990s record another Soviet mole in the U.S. government telling a Soviet intelligence operative that White "knows where his info goes, which is precisely why he transmits it in the first place."

White's handlers clearly sought to provide White with a degree of plausible deniability, but the Venona cables leave little doubt that he was well aware of where his information was headed and that he realized that the stakes of the game were very high. A deciphered portion of one cable reports the following: "As regards the technique of further work with us [White] said his wife was . . . ready for any self-sacrifice." The cable also states that White "himself did not think about his personal security, but a [security] compromise . . . would lead to a political scandal and . . . therefore he would have to be very cautious."

In 1953, Chambers wrote that White's "role as a Soviet agent was second in importance only to that of Alger Hiss—if, indeed, it was second." White, he said, had been "the perfect bureaucrat," rising under the radar to a position where he was able "to shape U.S. Government policy in the Soviet government's interest." Reviewing the Venona cables over 50 years after Chambers and Bentley made their startling espionage claims, a U.S. Senate commission led by Daniel Patrick Moynihan, then a Democratic senator from New York, concluded in 1997 that White's complicity in espionage "seems settled."

RIGHT ABOUT THE IMF, WRONG ABOUT THE WORLD

White himself struggled mightily in his last years to reconcile his belief in a dollar-centric, global free-trade architecture with his belief in a Soviet socialist economic model that had no use for it. In August 1945, according to testimony given nine years later by the journalist Jonathan Mitchell before the Senate Internal Security Subcommittee, a gloomy White told Mitchell that the system of government-controlled trading that had emerged during the war would continue into the postwar period, owing to a lack of dollars and gold, which would oblige governments to maintain tight controls on cross-border private trade. The IMF would fail to rectify this problem, White stated—a stunning viewpoint for a man who could rightfully claim the fund's paternity. The United States, White continued, would, with its huge domestic market, be able to carry on a system of private enterprise for five to ten years but could not ultimately survive as a capitalist island in a world of state trading. According to Mitchell, White lavished praise on the most recent book by the British socialist Harold Laski, *Faith, Reason, and Civilization*, which argued that the Soviet Union had created a new economic system that would replace capitalism. Mitchell testified that White had called Laski's work "the most profound book which had been written in our lifetime" and one that "had foreseen with such uncanny accuracy and depth the way in which the world was going."

That proved to be nonsense, of course. But White was right about the IMF. Truman's State Department effectively mothballed the fund, dismissing the assumptions that had underwritten White's earlier belief in it: that Soviet cooperation would continue into the postwar period; that Germany's economic collapse could be safely, and indeed profitably, managed; that the British Empire could be peaceably dismantled; and that short-term IMF credits would be sufficient to reestablish global trade. These assumptions had been based on "misconceptions of the state of the world around us," Dean Acheson, Truman's final secretary of state, later reflected, "both in anticipating postwar conditions and in recognizing what they actually were when we came face to face with them. . . . Only slowly did it dawn upon us that the whole world structure and order that we had inherited from the nineteenth century was gone and that the struggle to replace it would be directed from two bitterly opposed and ideologically irreconcilable power centers."

The Truman administration's economic response to the collapse of White's vision would become what remains to this day a touchstone of bold and enlightened U.S. diplomacy: the Marshall Plan. As for the IMF, it was only after the demise of the Bretton Woods fixed-exchange-rate system in the 1970s, ironically, that it would come to play a central role in an emerging U.S.-led global economic order—an order very different from the one White had envisioned.

Generation Kill

A Conversation With Stanley McChrystal

In July 2010, General Stanley McChrystal retired from the U.S. Army after almost three and a half decades in uniform. Soon after graduating from West Point, McChrystal had joined the U.S. Special Forces, and he eventually led the Rangers, the Joint Special Operations Command, and all U.S. and international forces in Afghanistan. Author of the recently published memoir *My Share of the Task*, he spoke with *Foreign Affairs* editor Gideon Rose in December.

A knowledgeable author wrote in a recent issue of this magazine that "as head of the U.S. Joint Special Operations Command . . . , McChrystal oversaw the development of a precision-killing machine unprecedented in the history of modern warfare," one whose "scope and genius" will be fully appreciated only "in later decades, once the veil of secrecy has been removed." What did he mean?

I was part of a [special operations] effort that we can call Task Force 714. When the counterterrorist effort against al Qaeda started, it was narrowly focused and centralized; you only did occasional operations with a high degree of intelligence and a tremendous amount of secrecy. That worked well for the pre-9/11 environment, but in the post-9/11 environment—particularly the post-March 2003 environment in Iraq—the breadth of al Qaeda and associated movements exploded. This gave us an enemy network that you couldn't just react to but actually had to dismantle. It also gave us a very complex battlefield—not just terrorism but also social problems, an insurgency, and sectarian violence.

So the first thing we did when I took over in late 2003 was realize that we needed to understand the problem much better. To do that, we had to become a network ourselves—to be connected across all parts of the battlefield, so that every time something occurred and we gathered intelligence or experience from it, information flowed very, very quickly.

The network had a tremendous amount of geographical spread. At one point, we were in 27 countries simultaneously. Inside Iraq, we were in 20 and 30 places simultaneously—all connected using modern technology but also personal relationships. This gave us the ability to learn about the constantly evolving challenge.

People hear most about the targeting cycle, which we called F3EA—"find, fix, finish, exploit, and analyze." You understand who or what is a target, you locate it, you capture or kill it, you take what intelligence you can from people or equipment or documents, you analyze that, and then you go back and do the cycle again, smarter.

When we first started, those five steps were performed by different parts of our organization or different security agencies. And as a consequence, each time you passed information from one to another, it would be like a game of telephone, so that by the time information got to the end, it would be not only slow but also corrupted. We learned we had to reduce the number of steps in the process.

In 2003, in many cases we'd go after someone, we might locate them and capture or kill them, and it would be weeks until we took the intelligence we learned from that and were able to turn it into another operation. Within about two years, we could turn that cycle three times in a night. We could capture someone, gain intelligence from the experience, go after someone else, and do three of those in a row, the second two involving people we didn't even know existed at the beginning of the night.

In August 2004, in all of Iraq, our task force did 18 raids. And we thought that was breakneck speed. I mean, we really thought we had the pedal to the metal. These were great raids, very precise, a high percentage of success. But as great as those 18 raids were, they couldn't make a dent in the exploding insurgency. Two years later, in August 2006, we were up to 300 raids a month—ten a night. This meant the network now had to operate at a speed that was not even considered before, not in our wildest dreams. It had to have decentralized decision-making, because you can't centralize ten raids a night. You have to understand them all, but you have to allow your subordinate elements to operate very quickly.

But then, we had to be able to take all of that and make it mean something—because it's not just about capturing and killing people; it's about synchronizing into the wider theater campaign. And that took us longer. We really didn't mesh completely into the conventional war effort [in Iraq] until 2006, 2007.

So that was the revolution. I didn't do it. The organization I was part of became this learning organization. If I take any credit, it is for loosening the reins and yelling "Giddyup!" a lot. I allowed, encouraged, required the team to push forward. And they just rose to the occasion.

Was this a technological revolution or an intellectual and organizational one? Could you have done it a decade or two ago, with less modern information technology?

We could have done parts of it before. You could have used radio calls and faxes. But the ability to, say, pump video teleconferences everywhere enabled the change. There were cultural things to overcome, though. People weren't comfortable with it. People feel that they lose autonomy if they are constantly connected and they're pumping information out, and they like autonomy. But if you want an organization to operate as a network, connection is key.

Is your experience scalable to other organizations, either in the military or outside?

I think it's very scalable, but there is a cultural hill to climb for every organization because it seems to threaten some people's definition of their personal roles. It makes things go much faster, and if organizations aren't ready to move faster, their decision-making processes become overwhelmed by the information flow around them and they have a lot of problems.

Did the tactics of the special operators under your command change in any way?

The operational change and the mental change was by far the more significant part of it. However, tactically there were some things that changed, and part of that was technological. We started with well-trained commandos. We had always had those. They shoot well, they move well, they think brilliantly. But three things changed.

The first was global positioning systems. These allowed you to be exactly where you wanted to be without fits and starts. Navigating from point A to point B wasn't a big part of the task anymore. People take that for granted now, but as I grew up in the military, half of doing something was getting there.

The second thing was the use of night-vision goggles and night-vision equipment on aircraft and other things. These allowed you to have superiority in what you can see and do in the dark. Our entire force operated with night vision, so at night we used no visible lights. We had laser-aiming lights on our weapons and infrared illumination if it was too dark for the night vision. And as a consequence, we just dominated night firefights and night operations dramatically. That was a big deal.

The third was the use of things like the Predators—unmanned aerial vehicles—and some manned aircraft. The big breakthrough was that we could put these up and send the downlink or the video feed down to the command or the force on the ground in real time. That doesn't give you complete situational awareness, but it lets you see a bird's-eye view of the battlefield, even though you're standing on the ground in the mud or dirt.

Traditionally, if we did a raid and we thought we were going to need 20 commandos to actually be on the target, we might take 120, because we had to put security around the site to protect it from enemy reinforcements, and we might have to put a support section and a command-and-control section there, because you need all those things to account for the unexpected. But when you have very good situational awareness and good communications, you only send the 20, because your security comes from being able to see, and then you can maneuver forces if you need them. So suddenly, the 120 commandos aren't doing one raid; they're doing six raids simultaneously, and you start to get the ability to do 300 raids a month.

And that's important, because if you're going at an enemy network, you're trying to paralyze its nervous system. If you just hit it periodically, say, every other night, it not only heals itself; some would argue it gets stronger because it gets used to doing that. But if you can hit it in enough places simultaneously, it has a very difficult time regenerating. And that's when we started to have decisive effects.

So would you argue that these tactical and operational developments had a strategic effect?

I would, but you have to link it to the larger cause. Just taking special operating forces and making them very, very effective without tying them really well to what you're trying to do in the country and in the theater proves a loser. We got effectively lashed with our conventional counterparts in the wider effort later than we should have, probably about late 2005, 2006. It was a constant improvement, but I don't think we were really as synchronized as we should have been, nested within their effort, until about halfway through.

In your book, you take a somewhat contrarian view about the changeover from the Casey era to the Petraeus era in Iraq. How decisive was the change in military leadership and the "surge," and how much of it was just a natural evolution of what had been going on in Iraq for years already?

People tend to simplify things. They try to say, "It was all screwed up here and then it got all good there," or, "This decision was decisive."

I never found anything that clear. I found the move towards counterinsurgency to be one that was more gradual than sudden. It started under General Casey; he pushed it.

I will say that when the president made the decision to surge more forces, it intersected with some things which were happening. [Iraqi] Sunnis had grown disenchanted with al Qaeda, for good reason. I think the Sunnis also came to the conclusion that they were fighting the coalition, and we were beating on them pretty badly. And so I think they said to themselves, "We had better not fight the wrong war." People were exhausted, were not sure what was going on. And then suddenly, President Bush effectively says, "OK, we are going to double down." Even though people knew it couldn't be permanent, I think there was a sense that this pushes it past the tilting point.

And then, of course, there was General Petraeus, who brought a level of energy and a commitment to the counterinsurgency campaign. All of these together produced a pretty amazing result.

Eventually, you moved from Iraq to Afghanistan and ended up overseeing a counterinsurgency effort there. Did the apparent success of the surge in Iraq lead to rote implementation of the same approach in different and inappropriate circumstances? Was it folly to think that counterinsurgency could work in Afghanistan?

When I was on the Joint Staff in the fall of 2008 and spring of 2009, we did a series of big assessments of Afghanistan and Pakistan. And each assessment basically came away with the conclusion, "This is hard, this is complex." The three options were to do more, do less, or do the same. The status quo was deteriorating, so doing the same was not an option. Doing less might make it get worse faster, and doing more was not very palatable.

So by the summer of 2009, when I was placed in command in Afghanistan, we were in a difficult situation. The coalition led by the United States hadn't done nearly as much as had been needed in the few previous years; in fact, our efforts to grow the Afghan police and army had been really pretty small. Because we had not done much, they had not progressed much. Because we had a small footprint, we couldn't provide security. So the confidence of the Afghan people was sliding; there were more and more Afghans with a greater sense of frustration and pessimism for the future.

I was faced with the question, "How do you stop and reverse this?" And when we talk about the Taliban's momentum, we're really talking about momentum in the mind of the Afghan people: once you've changed their confidence level, you win. When we first did the assessment, I expected that we wouldn't need additional forces, just a different strategy and focus. But as we did the math, we found that if you couldn't provide enough security in enough places to reverse the feeling of insecurity and the impending sense of doom, you couldn't do it.

And so I went back to President Obama with the sobering assessment that said, "We have to have enough American forces for long enough to let us really get the Afghan forces in a position where they can do the share of this that they should be doing and that we want them to do." It was a reluctant recognition that sometimes, if the house is on fire, you have to put a wet blanket over it. This was just pretty traditional counterinsurgency.

But traditional counterinsurgency math would have dictated sending an even higher number of troops. So it was really a kind of counterinsurgency lite, wasn't it?
It was. To do it the right way, we would have needed more than 500,000 soldiers.

So why didn't you conclude, "Gee, if it would take that, and that's not politically feasible, we shouldn't do it at all"?
Because we did the calculation that since the insurgency wasn't everywhere in Afghanistan, we could have a lesser footprint in many of those areas not threatened, focus on the most important

areas, and get enough security there while the Afghans build their forces and their confidence until they can do it.

So focus on the swing districts in the swing states?
That's right. We went through almost like [the American political strategist] David Plouffe would do a reelection campaign. We found 80 key districts that mattered out of 364, and then we figured out what we thought it would take in those.

Counterinsurgency typically requires three things to work: a long time, a lot of troops, and a very sensitive, low-impact, politically aware mindset. Given that the American public doesn't like long wars, and given that large numbers of forces and a politically aware, sensitive approach to the use of violence seem to be at odds, when, if ever, is counterinsurgency going to be something that the United States should actually embark on?
That's a valid and difficult question, because there are also two other factors which ought to be thrown in. Successful insurgencies usually need an outside safe haven and access to the war zone. Pakistan gave the insurgents in Afghanistan that, and so they had something that we really needed to take away. But we couldn't seal the border.

And a successful counterinsurgency needs a legitimate government. You need to offer to the people an alternative to what the insurgent is offering. The Taliban don't offer a very compelling narrative or popular government, but the government of Afghanistan has huge problems with its popular legitimacy as well.

So in reality, what we had is a situation where we had been there a long time, the coalition was tired, the people of Afghanistan were scared, the insurgency was growing in confidence, the insurgency had a safe haven, and the government of Afghanistan was weak and somewhat conflicted about the war. So there were a lot of factors against it. And that is a very valid argument on why the success of the endeavor is certainly not assured.

You say in your book that when you took command in Afghanistan, you knew there were generals smarter than you (you mentioned Jean de Lattre de Tassigny and Creighton Abrams) who took over and improved efforts in the later stages of difficult wars and still couldn't succeed, so you knew this could fail. As you look back now, do you say, "This really was doomed," or do you still believe that it could actually have worked?

I still do believe that. I ask myself that a lot. But I did believe it then, and I still do believe it now.

What made you optimistic in the face of all the obstacles and so many others' skepticism?

The president gave me a mission to do this. He didn't send me to Afghanistan and say, "You can do this or not." So I didn't have a choice whether to do this. America had made policy statements through President Obama's speeches.

Were you ever asked whether you thought it was something that should be done?

I was never asked that directly.

Do you think that question was ever asked directly at the highest levels of the U.S. government?

I'm confident that it was. But to go back to whether I thought it was doable, there were some factors that made me think so. One was that the Taliban are almost remarkably unpopular. Their polling was about six percent positive. They weren't a nationalist liberation movement with a compelling narrative, and they were not the Taliban of old, with the credibility of being stalwart, religious young men out to get rid of corruption. They had the power to intimidate, but less power to inspire. The Afghan people really yearned for a chance to defeat them, and I don't see any change to that.

The challenge is in offering a viable alternative. The Afghan people have to believe that there is a stable Afghan government that can actually provide security. If the insurgency can intimidate the population at night, the population has no choice to support the government. It's suicide. And so there's no point in trying to blame the hearts and minds because they don't have the ability to give their heart to anyone. So you've got to get enough security. And that was what created the need for the additional forces.

Was impatience in the United States or incompetence in Kabul a greater threat to the overall mission?

They go hand in hand. I think much of the impatience in the United States was derived from the perception of corruption and incompetence in Kabul, some of which was very real. And the more impatient America looked, the more the Afghans thought they were going to be abandoned. And when people think they are going to be abandoned, they go into coping mechanisms— they withdraw, steal money, put it in Dubai, do things which are going to take care of you when the rainy day comes or the government falls.

You seem to have had a better relationship with President Hamid Karzai than most other commanders and U.S. officials. Why is that?

I can't judge anyone else's relationship with President Karzai. I believed that a relationship with him was critical, because the route to success in Afghanistan went through him and his government. He needed to accept responsibility for defending the sovereignty of his country. For many years, the coalition, primarily the Americans, had been fighting a war on Afghan soil, and we'd been fighting it almost by ourselves. We picked the strategy. We conducted the operations. We called the shots. And we didn't invite or require President Karzai or his forces to have a meaningful role. So as a consequence, they didn't. They stood on the sidelines. I thought if we were going to change things, we had to change that dynamic. And when you have a relationship with someone and you want them to do something, it is much easier to work with them and convince them than it is to force them.

Conversely, when people talk about civilian-military cooperation, evidenced by teams such as General Petraeus and Ambassador Crocker, they sometimes hold up your era in Afghanistan as a counterpoint, with its seeming lack of coordination between U.S. military and civilian leadership.

It's always hard to compare things because I was in Iraq for so long, and I saw the challenges of military-civilian relationships, which were exquisitely difficult during the grand percentage of that time. Ryan Crocker is an amazing individual, and he and General Petraeus formed a magical partnership in Iraq, which, of course, [Ambassador] Karl [Eikenberry] and I tried to match. But there are a lot of things that pull and push against it. In the year I was there in Afghanistan, the embassy was trying to go from, I think, 300 people to a thousand. You try to expand something that fast, that's a challenge. Plus ISAF [International Security Assistance Force] is taking a significant number of forces who were doing strategic assessment, and the whole campaign is under a fair amount of stress militarily but also stress from a policy review and whatnot. Karl Eikenberry and I maintained a great personal relationship. The relationship between the embassy and ISAF wasn't perfect, but there was a good effort made to do that.

When you took over in Afghanistan, your experience and command had been with smaller organizations doing more kinetic operations. Do you think that experience adequately prepared you for the leadership of the larger organizations doing the more politically sensitive operations of counterinsurgency in Afghanistan?

Actually, I think it did prepare me. I had been the chief of staff in Afghanistan in the early years for JTF-180 [Joint Task Force 180, the coalition military headquarters in Afghanistan]. Then I had gone back to the United States and ultimately commanded special operating forces. Although we were a focused counterterrorist force, we actually got fairly large, even just in Iraq. And in the later years of the war, really 2006 to 2008, we increasingly became enmeshed or embedded within the overall counterinsurgency campaign. That integration provided me with a lot of insights into what was happening.

I had not had the opportunity to deal with NATO before, although I didn't find that particularly difficult. I think the opportunity to work with the White House and the president directly is something that you learn in the saddle. I'm not sure anybody is prepared for that. And you go back and read Grant's memoirs as he learned to deal with Abraham Lincoln and vice versa, I think you see you learn as you go along.

You've taken pride throughout your career in being a warrior rather than a bureaucrat or a politician. You mention in the book the mistrust that ended up emerging among so many different dyads—civilian-military on the ground, military versus the White House, and so forth. Do you think that you may have been a bit naive, because of your lack of previous political experience, about what sorts of things might contribute to this lack of trust, such as the leaking of your memo [advocating troop increases] or your comments at the [October 2009] International Institute for Strategic Studies conference?

Probably so. I had loved to read history all my life. I'd studied things, and you read about that. But until you are involved in it, until a document that you and your staff has produced is leaked—not by my staff but in D.C.—until that happens, you don't expect it actually to happen.

So you didn't realize that you were dealing with a pit of vipers who would seize on anything to fight bureaucratic wars over the fundamental nature of the mission?

I didn't fully appreciate the complexities of all the different players involved, of the different forces at work—media, politics, personal positions as people wanted different roles, and so forth. As the weeks and months passed, I certainly learned from experience. But when I started, I probably was so mission focused and convinced that if two plus two equals four and that's the right answer policywise, then that's going to be a compelling argument, that I was probably slow in appreciating it completely.

What lessons did you learn in your Iraq and Afghanistan tours?

In Iraq, when we first started, the question was, "Where is the enemy?" That was the intelligence question. As we got smarter, we started to ask, "Who is the enemy?" And we thought we were pretty clever. And then we realized that wasn't the right question, and we asked, "What's the enemy doing or trying to do?" And it wasn't until we got further along that we said, "Why are they the enemy?"

Not until you walk yourself along that intellectual path do you realize that's what you have to understand, particularly in a counterinsurgency where the number of insurgents is completely independent of simple math. In World War II, the German army could produce x number of military-aged males. In an insurgency, the number of insurgents isn't determined by the population, but by how many people want to be insurgents. And so figuring out why they want to be insurgents is crucial. And that's something we had never practiced.

Second, it's all about teams. Nobody wins the war alone. We had a culture in our force, and in many forces, of excellence. It was, "How good can I be at my task? How good can I be at flying an airplane, dropping a bomb, locating an enemy target?" But that's not as important as how well those pieces mesh together. The real art is, if somebody builds a bridge, you have the people ready to drive over it and take advantage of that. It's cooperating with civilian agencies, it's cooperating with conventional forces, it's tying the pieces together. That's the art of war, and that's the hard part.

How do you think Afghanistan looks now, where is the U.S. presence there going, and what will be left behind when we leave?

Security in many parts of the country has gotten better. Places like Helmand and Kandahar, which at one point seemed to be on the brink of falling, aren't that way now. Despite things like green-on-blue killings, there is undeniable security progress in parts of the country.

There is still a great deal of uncertainty on the political future within the Afghan government. I think people within the Afghan population aren't sure exactly where it's going. But the Taliban are suffering significant internal strife, too. They don't have either the clear narrative or the clearly-wired-together command and control to be the threat that they could be or they might have otherwise been. And there are indications that the government of Pakistan is now rolling up the welcome mat.

And so maybe the approach of 2014 is forcing all the players to make a decision: "We better try to sort something out because once the American force is small, much smaller, [the responsibility is ours.]"

Wasn't that the approach adopted in the early years of the last decade, which led to all the troubles you had to fix?

I don't think it was effectively attempted. I don't think we attempted anything very effectively. We were just too small and not very well informed. We were full of good intentions but not very effective actions.

So you're optimistic about the future of Afghanistan after 2014?

I'm cautious. I certainly worry about the Afghan people. I mean, if you were to have a breakdown in order, if the Taliban were to take over, 15 million women would certainly be disadvantaged. If it were to break into civil war, children and women always pay the highest price. So I worry about that. But at the same time, the Afghan people are practical survivors. They will adapt to the situation on the ground. And after this amount of time, I think there is a very good chance that they won't opt for civil war.

Some say that the Obama administration pocketed the gains of the surge in Iraq and traded the short-term improvement in the security environment there for an easy

American withdrawal, caring less about the ultimate future of the country than they might have. And these people might charge that something not dissimilar is playing out in Afghanistan, where the gutting of al Qaeda has provided a benign enough environment for the United States to walk away from the conflict, getting withdrawal but leaving behind something less than great on the ground. Are they wrong?

Ultimately, this is going to be an Afghan problem solved by Afghans, in concert with their neighbors, like the Pakistanis, and so I think we are going to reduce our presence naturally, and that's appropriate. We don't want to leave large numbers [of forces] in countries like that for long period, because it's not the Cold War; you don't need to have bases to produce that sort of thing. We can help by being a confidence builder.

Some kind of presence, some kind of assistance to both the government and maybe the military in a training role is appropriate. I think that you navigate from where you are, not where you wish you were. I think al Qaeda is very much weakened, although clearly not gone. The greatest al Qaeda threat, arguably, may not be from western Pakistan in the next few years, as it has been, but it might be from places such as Mali and elsewhere that are struggling to maintain control of their terrain.

Anywhere you have undergoverned or ungoverned areas, organizations like al Qaeda have a tremendous opportunity to get a foothold. And when they can get a foothold, they can start to operate and spread from there.

So what do you do with places like Mali and Yemen?

Well, you can't solve all of them. You certainly don't want to put Western forces in all of these countries. The initial reaction that says, "We will simply operate by drone strikes" is also problematic, because the inhabitants of that area and the world have significant problems watching Western forces, particularly Americans, conduct drone strikes inside the terrain of another country. So that's got to be done very carefully, on occasion. It's not a strategy in itself; it's a short-term tactic.

It seems like the methods you pioneered in Iraq have been embraced by the U.S. government and the American public as a general approach to managing small-scale irregular warfare, and doing so in a way short of putting lots of boots on the ground or walking away entirely. Some would argue that this is the true legacy of Stan McChrystal—the creation of an approach to counterterrorism that is halfway between war and peace, at such a low cost and with such a light footprint that it's politically viable for the long term in a way that war and disengagement are not. Do you disagree?

I question its universal validity. If you go back to the British tactics on the North-West Frontier, the "butcher and bolt" tactics, where they would burn an area and punish the people and say, "Don't do that anymore," and simultaneously offer a stipend to the leader while saying, "If you will remain friendly for a period of time, we'll pay you"—that approach worked for a fair amount of time. It managed problems on their periphery. But it certainly didn't solve the problems.

The tactics that we developed do work, but they don't produce decisive effects absent other, complementary activities. We did an awful lot of capturing and killing in Iraq for several years before it started to have a real effect, and that came only when we were partnered with an effective counterinsurgency approach. Just the strike part of it can never do more than keep an enemy at bay. And although to the United States, a drone strike seems to have very little risk and very little pain, at the receiving end, it feels like war.

Americans have got to understand that. If we were to use our technological capabilities carelessly—I don't think we do, but there's always the danger that you will—then we should not be upset when someone responds with their equivalent, which is a suicide bomb in Central Park, because that's what they can respond with.

So it's incorrect for someone to say, "I like the Iraq Stan McChrystal of raids and drones and targeted strikes, but I don't like the Afghanistan Stan McChrystal of clear, hold, and build and counterinsurgency; I want to deploy the first but avoid the costs and difficulties of the second"?

I would argue they should like all the Stan McChrystals. If you look at the role I had in Iraq, it is sexy, it is satisfying, it is manly, it scratches an itch in the American culture that people like. But I was doing that as part of a wider effort in Iraq, and it was that wider effort that I took control of in Afghanistan. And those wider efforts were about people. The whole point of war is to take care of people, not just to kill them. You have to have a positive reason that protects people, or it's wrong. So while I did what I had to in Iraq, and did a lot of that in Afghanistan, too (because we had a significant effort along those lines there), the broader purpose is what's important, and that's what I think people need to be reminded of. The purpose is the Afghan kid. The purpose is the Afghan female. The purpose is the 50-year-old farmer who just wants to farm.

Did the success of your efforts in Iraq lead to an overemphasis on the use of direct action by Special Forces, raids and drone attacks and targeted killings, rather than indirect action, such as training and building local capacity?

My wife Annie and I are not golfers, but some years ago, we took part in a golf tournament in our unit. After having significant trouble, on one of the tees, Annie used a Kevlar driver. She hit this amazing drive straight down the fairway, and she was elated. For the rest of the afternoon, the only club she used was the Kevlar driver. She chipped with it. She putted with it. She used it for everything.

That's the danger of special operating forces. You get this sense that it is satisfying, it's clean, it's low risk, it's the cure for most ills. That's why many new presidents are initially enamored with the Central Intelligence Agency, because they are offered a covert fix for a complex problem. But if you go back in history, I can't find a covert fix that solved a problem long term. There were some necessary covert actions, but there's no "easy button" for some of these problems. That's the danger of interpreting what we did in Iraq as being the panacea for future war. It's not.

Histories of World War II had to be rewritten when the full scope of Ultra became clear after it was declassified. Will people writing 30 years from now about the "war on terror" and the conflicts in Iraq and Afghanistan be revising the stories that we tell ourselves today because of what has been declassified in the meantime?

Yeah, they will, and they won't be right. There will be a tendency to find a piece of information that says, "We had the technical or human ability to collect X or do Y." And people will write books about that, and they'll say, "That was the decisive point," and they will be grossly oversimplifying. Bits of information will come out that make people say, "Wow, we did that and got that result." But at the end of the day, there was no single thing like that. There was no single person, no mad genius in any of our intelligence agencies or forces that pulled it all together. It was this puzzle painstakingly constructed of thousands and thousands of pieces, some of which were pretty darn interesting, some of which were extraordinarily hard to make happen, but none of which was decisive by itself.

So the story we can piece together now, in broad terms, is still the accurate story we'll be telling ourselves later on, down the road?

The story coming from the people who are accurate now, yes.

There's a debate going on about the role of torture in American policy, what constitutes it and how important and necessary a tool it is in counterterrorism. What's your take?

I teach a seminar at Yale on leadership, and in one of the classes, I decided to bring up the issue of torture to rouse their indignation at the idea. And more than half the class said, "Well, if you need to do it, it's OK." And I was shocked.

I've never been in a position where I had a detainee or prisoner who knew where a nuclear weapon in New York was and if I was able to get the information out of him in three hours I could save millions of people. So for me to say I would never torture anyone under those circumstances, I don't think anyone can answer that question, particularly if my family was there or something.

That said, I think torture is an absolute mistake, and I made that clear within our organization. Whether or not torture works is an academic argument I don't even want to be a part of, because at the end of the day, I think the torturers are weakened. They're weakened internally individually, and they're weakened strategically as a cause. The thing that hurt us more than anything else in the war in Iraq was Abu Ghraib. When the pictures came out in the spring of 2004, many Americans felt our government was being honest—that we had a problem with a platoon operating in the prison mistreating prisoners. The Iraqi people viewed it very differently. Many of them felt it was proof positive that the Americans were doing exactly what Saddam Hussein had done—that it was proof [that] everything they thought bad about the Americans was true.

So what we thought of as an exception, they thought of as the rule?
That's right. They thought that was the broader reality. And there were hundreds of foreign fighters that came in [to Iraq] because they were responding to Abu Ghraib. Using torture is ultimately self-defeating. It's morally wrong, and it's a strategic mistake.

Do you have any regrets or moral qualms in retrospect about things that happened under your command in Iraq or Afghanistan or elsewhere?
Yeah. When I took over [the Special Operations] Command, we were still very new to running operations, holding detainees, and so forth. We weren't manned with the right interrogators; we didn't have the right facilities. People were doing their best, but we were doing what I'd consider an unsatisfactory job. We weren't actively torturing people, but we weren't treating people the way that we

should have been. We started cleaning that up right away, correcting that. My biggest regret is that it took us about nine months before we got it to the point where it should have been from the beginning. That's slower than it should have been.

You've spent your life in service to your country. Do you think that's something that all Americans should do?

Absolutely. I think that the act of contributing, whether it is mandatory or whether it is voluntary (I think it ought to be mandatory), does something for the individual. When you contribute to something, you put more value on it. If I made you pick up trash on the street out front, you'd be more upset with people who littered, and you would own that street more. I think paying taxes to a nation is not enough. That's too clinical. Having the opportunity to actually go and do things for the nation that are inconvenient or unpleasant or even unsafe binds you to the larger group more deeply than before.

America suffers right now from the fact that many Americans don't meet or deal with anybody outside their social or cultural circle. It may be economic, it may be geographic, it may be religion. I think one of the great things about forced national service, like World War II, was that it blended people across the different parts of our country, made us a better melting pot than we would have been otherwise. I think mandatory national service would have a huge effect to help us in that direction.

So was it a mistake to move to a volunteer army?

I'm not sure it was a mistake, because the volunteer army I served in was this extraordinary fighting machine. But having said that, I now believe we need a draft. America's defense should be performed by a representative cross section of the population. With a draftee army, there'd be some new challenges, but I think we could solve that.

What would the consequences be for American foreign and security policy if everybody had skin in the game?

Oh, I think it'd be much better, because right now, there's a sense that if you want to go to war, you just send the military. They're not us. But if you wanted to go to war and your son or your daughter had a very high chance of going, you'd be more invested. It wouldn't be just tax money; it would be emotional.

So we'd go to war less often and take it more seriously when we did?
I think that would be the outcome.🌐

The Rise of Big Data

How It's Changing the Way We Think about the World

Kenneth Neil Cukier and
Viktor Mayer-Schoenberger

Everyone knows that the Internet has changed how businesses operate, governments function, and people live. But a new, less visible technological trend is just as transformative: "big data." Big data starts with the fact that there is a lot more information floating around these days than ever before, and it is being put to extraordinary new uses. Big data is distinct from the Internet, although the Web makes it much easier to collect and share data. Big data is about more than just communication: the idea is that we can learn from a large body of information things that we could not comprehend when we used only smaller amounts.

In the third century BC, the Library of Alexandria was believed to house the sum of human knowledge. Today, there is enough information in the world to give every person alive 320 times as much of it as historians think was stored in Alexandria's entire collection—an estimated 1,200 exabytes' worth. If all this information were placed

KENNETH CUKIER is Data Editor of *The Economist*. **VIKTOR MAYER-SCHOENBERGER** is Professor of Internet Governance and Regulation at the Oxford Internet Institute. They are the authors of *Big Data: A Revolution That Will Transform How We Live, Work, and Think* (**Houghton Mifflin Harcourt, 2013**), from which this essay is adapted. Copyright © by Kenneth Cukier and Viktor Mayer-Schoenberger. Reprinted by permission of Houghton Mifflin Harcourt.

The Rise of Big Data

on CDs and they were stacked up, the CDs would form five separate piles that would all reach to the moon.

This explosion of data is relatively new. As recently as the year 2000, only one-quarter of all the world's stored information was digital. The rest was preserved on paper, film, and other analog media. But because the amount of digital data expands so quickly—doubling around every three years—that situation was swiftly inverted. Today, less than two percent of all stored information is nondigital.

Given this massive scale, it is tempting to understand big data solely in terms of size. But that would be misleading. Big data is also characterized by the ability to render into data many aspects of the world that have never been quantified before; call it "datafication." For example, location has been datafied, first with the invention of longitude and latitude, and more recently with GPS satellite systems. Words are treated as data when computers mine centuries' worth of books. Even friendships and "likes" are datafied, via Facebook.

This kind of data is being put to incredible new uses with the assistance of inexpensive computer memory, powerful processors, smart algorithms, clever software, and math that borrows from basic statistics. Instead of trying to "teach" a computer how to do things, such as drive a car or translate between languages, which artificial-intelligence experts have tried unsuccessfully to do for decades, the new approach is to feed enough data into a computer so that it can infer the probability that, say, a traffic light is green and not red or that, in a certain context, *lumière* is a more appropriate substitute for "light" than *léger*.

Using great volumes of information in this way requires three profound changes in how we approach data. The first is to collect and use a lot of data rather than settle for small amounts or samples, as statisticians have done for well over a century. The second is to shed our preference for highly curated and pristine data and instead accept messiness: in an increasing number of situations, a bit of inaccuracy can be tolerated, because the benefits of using vastly more data of variable quality outweigh the costs of using smaller amounts of very exact data. Third, in many instances, we will need to give up our quest to discover the cause of things, in return for accepting correlations. With big data, instead of trying to understand precisely why an engine breaks down or why a drug's side effect disappears, researchers can instead collect and analyze massive quantities of information about such events and everything that is associated with them, looking for patterns that might help predict future occurrences. Big data helps answer what, not why, and often that's good enough.

The Internet has reshaped how humanity communicates. Big data is different: it marks a transformation in how society processes information. In time, big data might change our way of thinking about the world. As we tap ever more data to understand events and make decisions, we are likely to discover that many aspects of life are probabilistic, rather than certain.

APPROACHING "N=ALL"

For most of history, people have worked with relatively small amounts of data because the tools for collecting, organizing, storing, and analyzing information were poor. People winnowed the information they relied on to the barest minimum so that they could examine it more easily. This was the genius of modern-day statistics, which first came to the fore in the late nineteenth century and enabled society to understand complex realities even when little data existed. Today, the technical environment has shifted 179 degrees. There still is, and always will be, a constraint on how much data we can manage, but it is far less limiting than it used to be and will become even less so as time goes on.

The way people handled the problem of capturing information in the past was through sampling. When collecting data was costly and processing it was difficult and time consuming, the sample was a savior. Modern sampling is based on the idea that, within a certain margin of error, one can infer something about the total population from a small subset, as long the sample is chosen at random.

Hence, exit polls on election night query a randomly selected group of several hundred people to predict the voting behavior of an entire state. For straightforward questions, this process works well. But it falls apart when we want to drill down into subgroups within the sample. What if a pollster wants to know which candidate single women under 30 are most likely to vote for? How about university-educated, single Asian American women under 30? Suddenly, the random sample is largely useless, since there may be only a couple of people with those characteristics in the sample, too few to make a meaningful assessment of how the entire subpopulation will vote. But if we collect all the data—"n = all," to use the terminology of statistics—the problem disappears.

This example raises another shortcoming of using some data rather than all of it. In the past, when people collected only a little data, they often had to decide at the outset what to collect and how it would be used. Today, when we gather all the data, we do not need to know beforehand what we plan to use it for. Of course, it might not always be possible to collect all the data, but it is getting much more feasible to capture vastly more of a phenomenon than simply a sample and to aim for all of it. Big data is a matter not just of creating somewhat larger samples but of harnessing as much of the existing data as possible about what is being studied. We still need statistics; we just no longer need to rely on small samples.

There is a tradeoff to make, however. When we increase the scale by orders of magnitude, we might have to give up on clean, carefully curated data and tolerate some messiness. This idea runs counter to how people have tried to work with data for centuries. Yet the obsession with accuracy and precision is in some ways an artifact of an information-constrained environment. When there was not that much data around, researchers had to make sure that the figures they bothered to collect were as exact as possible. Tapping vastly more data means that we can now allow some inaccuracies to slip in (provided the data set is not completely incorrect), in return for benefiting from the insights that a massive body of data provides.

Consider language translation. It might seem obvious that computers would translate well, since they can store lots of information and retrieve it quickly. But if one were to simply substitute words from a French-English dictionary, the translation would be atrocious. Language is complex. A breakthrough came in the 1990s, when IBM delved into statistical machine translation. It fed Canadian parliamentary transcripts in both French and English into a computer and programmed it to infer which word in one language is the best alternative for another. This process changed the task of translation into a giant problem of probability and math. But after this initial improvement, progress stalled.

Then Google barged in. Instead of using a relatively small number of high-quality translations, the search giant harnessed more data, but from the less orderly Internet—"data in the wild," so to speak. Google inhaled translations from corporate websites, documents in every language from the European Union, even translations from its giant book-scanning project. Instead of millions of pages of texts, Google analyzed billions. The result is that its translations are quite good—better than IBM's were—and cover 65 languages. Large amounts of messy data trumped small amounts of cleaner data.

FROM CAUSATION TO CORRELATION

These two shifts in how we think about data—from some to all and from clean to messy—give rise to a third change: from causation to correlation. This represents a move away from always trying to understand the deeper reasons behind how the world works to simply learning about an association among phenomena and using that to get things done.

Of course, knowing the causes behind things is desirable. The problem is that causes are often extremely hard to figure out, and many times, when we think we have identified them, it is nothing more than a self-congratulatory illusion. Behavioral economics has shown that humans are conditioned to see causes even where none exist. So we need to be particularly on guard to prevent our cognitive biases from deluding us; sometimes, we just have to let the data speak.

Take UPS, the delivery company. It places sensors on vehicle parts to identify certain heat or vibrational patterns that in the past have been associated with failures in those parts. In this way, the company can predict a breakdown before it happens and replace the part when it is convenient, instead of on the side of the road. The data do not reveal the exact relationship between the heat or the vibrational patterns and the part's failure. They do not tell UPS why the part is in trouble. But they reveal enough for the company to know what to do in the near term and guide its investigation into any underlying problem that might exist with the part in question or with the vehicle.

A similar approach is being used to treat breakdowns of the human machine. Researchers in Canada are developing a big-data approach to spot infections in premature babies before overt symptoms appear. By converting 16 vital signs, including heartbeat, blood pressure, respiration, and blood-oxygen levels, into an information flow of more than 1,000 data points per second, they have been able to find correlations between very minor changes and more serious problems. Eventually, this technique will enable doctors to act earlier to save lives. Over time, recording these observations might also allow doctors to understand what actually causes such problems. But when a newborn's health is at risk, simply knowing that something is likely to occur can be far more important than understanding exactly why.

Medicine provides another good example of why, with big data, seeing correlations can be enormously valuable, even when the underlying causes remain obscure. In February 2009, Google created a stir in health-care circles. Researchers at the company published a paper in *Nature* that showed how it was possible to track outbreaks of the seasonal flu using nothing more than the archived records of Google searches. Google handles more than a billion searches in the United States every day and stores them all. The company took the 50 million most commonly searched terms between

2003 and 2008 and compared them against historical influenza data from the Centers for Disease Control and Prevention. The idea was to discover whether the incidence of certain searches coincided with outbreaks of the flu—in other words, to see whether an increase in the frequency of certain Google searches conducted in a particular geographic area correlated with the CDC's data on outbreaks of flu there. The CDC tracks actual patient visits to hospitals and clinics across the country, but the information it releases suffers from a reporting lag of a week or two—an eternity in the case of a pandemic. Google's system, by contrast, would work in near-real time.

Google did not presume to know which queries would prove to be the best indicators. Instead, it ran all the terms through an algorithm that ranked how well they correlated with flu outbreaks. Then, the system tried combining the terms to see if that improved the model. Finally, after running nearly half a billion calculations against the data, Google identified 45 terms—words such as "headache" and "runny nose"—that had a strong correlation with the CDC's data on flu outbreaks. All 45 terms related in some way to influenza. But with a billion searches a day, it would have been impossible for a person to guess which ones might work best and test only those.

Moreover, the data were imperfect. Since the data were never intended to be used in this way, misspellings and incomplete phrases were common. But the sheer size of the data set more than compensated for its messiness. The result, of course, was simply a correlation. It said nothing about the reasons why someone performed any particular search. Was it because the person felt ill, or heard sneezing in the next cubicle, or felt anxious after reading the news? Google's system doesn't know, and it doesn't care. Indeed, last December, it seems that Google's system may have overestimated the number of flu cases in the United States. This serves as a reminder that predictions are only probabilities and are not always correct, especially when the basis for the prediction—Internet searches—is in a constant state of change and vulnerable to outside influences, such as media reports. Still, big data can hint at the general direction of an ongoing development, and Google's system did just that.

BACK-END OPERATIONS

Many technologists believe that big data traces its lineage back to the digital revolution of the 1980s, when advances in microprocessors and computer memory made it possible to analyze and store ever more information. That is only superficially the case. Computers and the Internet certainly aid big data by lowering the cost of collecting, storing, processing, and sharing information. But at its heart, big data is only the latest step in humanity's quest to understand and quantify the world. To appreciate how this is the case, it helps to take a quick look behind us.

Appreciating people's posteriors is the art and science of Shigeomi Koshimizu, a professor at the Advanced Institute of Industrial Technology in Tokyo. Few would think that the way a person sits constitutes information, but it can. When a person is seated, the contours of the body, its posture, and its weight distribution can all be quantified and tabulated. Koshimizu and his team of engineers convert backsides into data by measuring the pressure they exert at 360 different points with sensors placed in a car seat and by indexing each point on a scale of zero to 256. The result is a digital code that is unique to each individual. In a trial, the system was able to distinguish among a handful of people with 98 percent accuracy.

The research is not asinine. Koshimizu's plan is to adapt the technology as an antitheft system for cars. A vehicle equipped with it could recognize when someone other than an approved driver sat down behind the wheel and could demand a password to allow the car to function. Transforming sitting positions into data creates a viable service and a potentially lucrative business. And its usefulness may go far beyond deterring auto theft. For instance, the aggregated data might reveal clues about a relationship between drivers' posture and road safety, such as telltale shifts in position prior to accidents. The system might also be able to sense when a driver slumps slightly from fatigue and send an alert or automatically apply the brakes.

Koshimizu took something that had never been treated as data—or even imagined to have an informational quality—and transformed it into a numerically quantified format. There is no good term yet for this sort of transformation, but "datafication" seems apt. Datafication is not the same as digitization, which takes analog content—books, films, photographs—and converts it into digital information, a sequence of ones and zeros that computers can read. Datafication is a far broader activity: taking all aspects of life and turning them into data. Google's augmented-reality glasses datafy the gaze. Twitter datafies stray thoughts. LinkedIn datafies professional networks.

Once we datafy things, we can transform their purpose and turn the information into new forms of value. For example, IBM was granted a U.S. patent in 2012 for "securing premises using surface-based computing technology"—a technical way of describing a touch-sensitive floor covering, somewhat like a giant smartphone screen. Datafying the floor can open up all kinds of possibilities. The floor could be able to identify the objects on it, so that it might know to turn on lights in a room or open doors when a person entered. Moreover, it might identify individuals by their weight or by the way they stand and walk. It could tell if someone fell and did not get back up, an important feature for the elderly. Retailers could track the flow of customers through their stores. Once it becomes possible to turn activities of this kind into data that can be stored and analyzed, we can learn more about the world—things we could never know before because we could not measure them easily and cheaply.

BIG DATA IN THE BIG APPLE

Big data will have implications far beyond medicine and consumer goods: it will profoundly change how governments work and alter the nature of politics. When it comes to generating economic growth, providing public services, or fighting wars, those who can harness big data effectively will enjoy a significant edge over others. So far, the most exciting work is happening at the municipal level, where it is easier to access data and to experiment with the information. In an effort spearheaded by New York City Mayor Michael Bloomberg (who made a fortune in the data business), the city is using big data to improve public services and lower costs. One example is a new fire-prevention strategy.

Illegally subdivided buildings are far more likely than other buildings to go up in flames. The city gets 25,000 complaints about overcrowded buildings a year, but it has only 200 inspectors to respond. A small team of analytics specialists in the mayor's office reckoned that big data could help resolve this imbalance between needs and resources. The team created a database of all 900,000 buildings in the city and augmented it with troves of data collected by 19 city agencies: records of tax liens, anomalies in utility usage, service cuts, missed payments, ambulance visits, local crime rates, rodent complaints, and more. Then, they compared this database to records of building fires from the past five years, ranked by severity, hoping to uncover correlations. Not surprisingly, among the predictors of a fire were the type of building and the year it was built. Less expected, however, was the finding that buildings obtaining permits for exterior brickwork correlated with lower risks of severe fire.

Using all this data allowed the team to create a system that could help them determine which overcrowding complaints needed urgent attention. None of the buildings' characteristics they recorded caused fires; rather, they correlated with an increased or decreased risk of fire. That knowledge has proved immensely valuable: in the past, building inspectors issued vacate orders in 13 percent of their visits; using the new method, that figure rose to 70 percent—a huge efficiency gain.

Of course, insurance companies have long used similar methods to estimate fire risks, but they mainly rely on only a handful of attributes and usually ones that intuitively correspond with fires. By contrast, New York City's big-data approach was able to examine many more variables, including ones that would not at first seem to have any relation to fire risk. And the city's model was cheaper and faster, since it made use of existing data. Most important, the big-data predictions are probably more on target, too.

Big data is also helping increase the transparency of democratic governance. A movement has grown up around the idea of "open data," which goes beyond the freedom-of-information laws that are now commonplace in developed democracies. Supporters call on governments to make the vast amounts of innocuous data that they hold easily available to the public. The United States has been at the forefront, with its Data.gov website, and many other countries have followed.

At the same time as governments promote the use of big data, they will also need to protect citizens against unhealthy market dominance. Companies such as Google, Amazon, and Facebook—as well as lesser-known "data brokers," such as Acxiom and Experian—are amassing vast amounts of information on everyone and everything. Antitrust laws protect against the monopolization of markets for goods and services such as software or media outlets, because the sizes of the markets for those goods are relatively easy to estimate. But how should governments apply antitrust rules to big data, a market that is hard to define and that is constantly changing form? Meanwhile, privacy will become an even bigger worry, since more data will almost certainly lead to more compromised private information, a downside of big data that current technologies and laws seem unlikely to prevent.

Regulations governing big data might even emerge as a battleground among countries. European governments are already scrutinizing Google over a raft of antitrust and privacy concerns, in a scenario reminiscent of the antitrust enforcement actions the European Commission took against Microsoft beginning a decade ago. Facebook might become a target for similar actions all over the world, because it holds so much data about individuals. Diplomats should brace for fights over whether to treat information flows as similar to free trade: in the future, when China censors Internet searches, it might face complaints not only about unjustly muzzling speech but also about unfairly restraining commerce.

BIG DATA OR BIG BROTHER?

States will need to help protect their citizens and their markets from new vulnerabilities caused by big data. But there is another potential dark side: big data could become Big Brother. In all countries, but particularly in nondemocratic ones, big data exacerbates the existing asymmetry of power between the state and the people.

The asymmetry could well become so great that it leads to big-data authoritarianism, a possibility vividly imagined in science-fiction movies such as *Minority Report*. That 2002 film took place in a near-future dystopia in which the character played by Tom Cruise headed a "Precrime" police unit that relied on clairvoyants whose visions identified people who were about to commit crimes. The plot revolves around the system's obvious potential for error and, worse yet, its denial of free will.

Although the idea of identifying potential wrongdoers before they have committed a crime seems fanciful, big data has allowed some authorities to take it seriously. In 2007, the Department of Homeland Security launched a research project called FAST (Future Attribute Screening Technology), aimed at identifying potential terrorists by analyzing data about individuals' vital signs, body language, and other physiological patterns. Police forces in many cities, including Los Angeles, Memphis, Richmond, and Santa Cruz, have adopted "predictive policing" software, which analyzes data on previous crimes to identify where and when the next ones might be committed.

For the moment, these systems do not identify specific individuals as suspects. But that is the direction in which things seem to be heading. Perhaps such systems would identify which young people are most likely to shoplift. There might be decent reasons to get so specific, especially when it comes to preventing negative social outcomes other than crime. For example, if social workers could tell with 95 percent accuracy which teenage girls would get pregnant or which high school boys would drop out of school, wouldn't they be remiss if they did not step in to help? It sounds tempting. Prevention is better than punishment, after all. But even an intervention that did not admonish and instead provided assistance could be construed as a penalty—at the very least, one might be stigmatized in the eyes of others. In this case, the state's actions would take the form of a penalty before any act were committed, obliterating the sanctity of free will.

Another worry is what could happen when governments put too much trust in the power of data. In his 1999 book, *Seeing Like a State*, the anthropologist James Scott documented the ways in which governments, in their zeal for quantification and data collection, sometimes end up making people's lives miserable. They use maps to determine how to reorganize communities without first learning anything about the people who live there. They use long tables of data about harvests to decide to collectivize agriculture without knowing a whit about farming. They take all the imperfect, organic ways in which people have interacted over time and bend them to their needs, sometimes just to satisfy a desire for quantifiable order.

This misplaced trust in data can come back to bite. Organizations can be beguiled by data's false charms and endow more meaning to the numbers than they deserve. That is one of the lessons of the Vietnam War. U.S. Secretary of Defense Robert McNamara became obsessed with using statistics as a way to measure the war's progress. He and his colleagues fixated on the number of enemy fighters killed. Relied on by commanders and published daily in newspapers, the body count became the data point that defined an era. To the war's supporters, it was proof of progress; to critics, it was evidence of the war's immorality. Yet the statistics revealed very little about the complex reality of the conflict. The figures were frequently inaccurate and were of little value as a way to measure success. Although it is important to learn from data to improve lives, common sense must be permitted to override the spreadsheets.

HUMAN TOUCH

Big data is poised to reshape the way we live, work, and think. A worldview built on the importance of causation is being challenged by a preponderance of correlations. The possession of knowledge, which once meant an understanding of the past, is coming to mean an ability to predict the future. The challenges posed by big data will not be easy to resolve. Rather, they are simply the next step in the timeless debate over how to best understand the world.

Still, big data will become integral to addressing many of the world's pressing problems. Tackling climate change will require analyzing pollution data to understand where best to focus efforts and find ways to mitigate problems. The sensors being placed all over the world, including those embedded in smartphones, provide a wealth of data that will allow climatologists to more accurately model global warming. Meanwhile, improving and lowering the cost of health care, especially for the world's poor, will make it necessary to automate some tasks that currently require human judgment but could be done by a computer, such as examining biopsies for cancerous cells or detecting infections before symptoms fully emerge.

Ultimately, big data marks the moment when the "information society" finally fulfills the promise implied by its name. The data take center stage. All those digital bits that have been gathered can now be harnessed in novel ways to serve new purposes and unlock new forms of value. But this requires a new way of thinking and will challenge institutions and identities. In a world where data shape decisions more and more, what purpose will remain for people, or for intuition, or for going against the facts? If everyone appeals to the data and harnesses big-data tools, perhaps what will become the central point of differentiation is unpredictability: the human element of instinct, risk taking, accidents, and even error. If so, then there will be a special need to carve out a place for the human: to reserve space for intuition, common sense, and serendipity to ensure that they are not crowded out by data and machine-made answers.

This has important implications for the notion of progress in society. Big data enables us to experiment faster and explore more leads. These advantages should produce more innovation. But at times, the spark of invention becomes what the data do not say. That is something that no amount of data can ever confirm or corroborate, since it has yet to exist. If Henry Ford had queried big-data algorithms to discover what his customers wanted, they would have come back with "a faster horse," to recast his famous line. In a world of big data, it is the most human traits that will need to be fostered—creativity, intuition, and intellectual ambition—since human ingenuity is the source of progress.

Big data is a resource and a tool. It is meant to inform, rather than explain; it points toward understanding, but it can still lead to misunderstanding, depending on how well it is wielded. And however dazzling the power of big data appears, its seductive glimmer must never blind us to its inherent imperfections. Rather, we must adopt this technology with an appreciation not just of its power but also of its limitations. 🌐

The Road to D-Day

Behind the Battle That Won the War

Rick Atkinson

A killing frost struck the United Kingdom in the middle of May 1944, stunting the plum trees and the berry crops. Stranger still was a persistent drought. Hotels posted admonitions above their bathtubs: "The Eighth Army crossed the desert on a pint a day. Three inches only, please." British newspapers reported that even King George VI kept "quite clean with one bath a week in a tub filled only to a line which he had painted on it." Gale winds from the north grounded most Allied bombers flying from East Anglia and the Midlands, although occasional fleets of Boeing Flying Fortresses could still be seen sweeping toward the continent, their contrails spreading like ostrich plumes.

Nearly five years of war had left British cities as "bedraggled, unkempt and neglected as rotten teeth," according to one visitor from the United States, who found that "people referred to 'before the war' as if it were a place, not a time." The country was steeped in heavy smells, of old smoke and cheap coal and fatigue. Wildflowers took root in bombed-out lots from Birmingham to Plymouth. Less bucolic were the millions of rats swarming through 3,000 miles of London sewers; exterminators scattered 60 tons of sausage poisoned with zinc phosphate and stale bread dipped in barium carbonate.

RICK ATKINSON is an author and military historian. His most recent book is *The Guns at Last Light: The War in Western Europe, 1944–1945* (Henry Holt, 2013), from which this essay is adapted. Copyright © 2013 by Rick Atkinson. Reprinted by arrangement with Henry Holt and Company, LLC. All rights reserved.

Privation lay on the land like another odor. The British government allowed men to buy a new shirt every 20 months. Housewives twisted pipe cleaners into hair clips. Iron railings and grillwork had long been scrapped for the war effort; even cemeteries stood unfenced. Few shoppers could find a fountain pen or a wedding ring, or bed sheets, vegetable peelers, or shoelaces. Posters discouraged profligacy with depictions of the Squander Bug, a cartoon rodent with swastika-shaped pockmarks. Classified advertisements included pleas in *The Times* of London for "unwanted artificial teeth" and for cash donations to help wounded Russian warhorses. An ad for Chez-Vous household services promised "bombed upholstery and carpets cleaned."

Government placards advised, "Food is a munition. Don't waste it." Rationing had begun in June 1940 and would not end completely until 1954. The monthly cheese allowance stood at two ounces per citizen. Many children had never seen a lemon; vitamin C came from "turnip water." The Ministry of Food promoted "austerity bread," with a whisper of sawdust, and "victory coffee," brewed from acorns. "Woolton pie," a concoction of carrots, potatoes, onions, and flour, was said to sit "like cement upon the chest." For those with strong palates, no ration limits applied to sheep's heads, or to eels caught in local reservoirs, or to roast cormorant, a stringy substitute for poultry.

More than 50,000 British civilians had died in German air raids since 1940, including many in the resurgent "Baby Blitz," begun in January 1944 and just now petering out. Luftwaffe spotter planes illuminated their targets with clusters of parachute flares, bathing buildings and low clouds in rusty light before the bombs fell. One diarist described "great steady swords of searchlights" probing for enemy aircraft as flak fragments spattered across rooftops like hailstones. Even the Wimbledon tennis club had been assaulted in a recent raid that had left center court pitted; a groundskeeper patched the shredded nets with string. Tens of thousands sheltered at night in the underground tunnels of the Tube. The cots standing in tiers along the platforms of 79 designated stations were so fetid that the sculptor Henry Moore likened wartime life in these underground rookeries to "the hold of a slave ship." It was said that some young children born in London had never spent a night in their own beds.

Even during these short summer nights, the mandatory blackout, which in London in mid-May lasted from 10:30 PM to 5:22 AM, was so intense that one writer found the city "profoundly dark, like a mental condition." Darkness also cloaked an end-of-days concupiscence, fueled by some 3.5 million soldiers now crammed into a country smaller than Oregon. At dusk, Hyde Park and Green Park were said by a Canadian soldier to resemble "a vast battlefield of sex." A chaplain reported that American GIs and streetwalkers often copulated standing up after wrapping themselves in a trench coat, a position known as "Marble Arch style," after the famous monument across the street from Hyde Park. "Piccadilly Circus is a madhouse after dark," an American lieutenant wrote his mother, "and a man can't walk without being attacked by dozens of women." Prostitutes—"Piccadilly Commandos"—sidled up to men in the blackout and felt for their rank insignia on shoulders and sleeves before tendering a price: 10 shillings ($2) for enlisted men, a pound ($4) for officers.

By day, pubs and street corners showcased the exotic military plumage of Norwegians and Indians, Belgians and Czechs, Yorkshiremen and Welshmen, and more Yanks than lived in all of Nebraska. Savile Row tailors offered specialists for every article of a bespoke uniform, from tunic to trousers, and a well-heeled officer could still buy an English military raincoat at Burberry or a silver pocket flask at Dunhill. Even soldiers recently arrived from the Mediterranean theater added a poignant splash of color, thanks to the antimalarial pills that turned their skin a pumpkin hue.

OVERLORDS

Nowhere were the uniforms more impressive on Monday morning, May 15, than at St. Paul's School on Hammersmith Road, in western London. Here, the greatest Anglo-American military conclave of World War II gathered on the war's 1,720th day to rehearse the deathblow intended to destroy Adolf Hitler's Third Reich. Admirals, generals, field marshals, logisticians, and staff wizards by the score climbed from their limousines and marched into a Gothic building of red brick and terra cotta, where American military police—known as "Snowdrops" for their white helmets, pistol belts, leggings, and gloves—scrutinized the 146 engraved invitations and security passes that had been distributed a month earlier. Then, six uniformed ushers escorted the guests, later described as "big men with the air of fame about them," into the Model Room, a cold and dimly lit auditorium with black columns and hard, narrow benches reputedly designed to keep young schoolboys awake.

Top-secret charts and maps now lined the Model Room. Since January, the school had served as the headquarters for the British 21st Army Group, and here the detailed planning for Operation Overlord, the Allied invasion of France, had gelled. As more senior officers found their seats in Rows B through J, some spread blankets across their laps or cinched their greatcoats against the chill. Row A, 14 armchairs arranged elbow to elbow, was reserved for the highest of the mighty, and now these men began to take their seats. The British prime minister, Winston Churchill, dressed in a black frock coat and puffing his usual Havana cigar, entered with the supreme allied commander, General Dwight Eisenhower. Neither cheers nor applause greeted them, but the assembly stood as one when George VI strolled down the aisle to sit on Eisenhower's right. Churchill bowed to his monarch, then resumed puffing his cigar.

As they waited to begin at the stroke of 10 AM, these men, with their airs of eminence, had reason to rejoice in their joint victories and to hope for greater victories still to come. Nearly all the senior commanders had served together in the Mediterranean—they called themselves "Mediterraneanites"—and they shared Eisenhower's sentiment that "the Mediterranean theater will always be in my blood." There they had indeed been bloodied, beginning with the invasion of North Africa in November 1942, when Anglo-American forces had swept aside feeble Vichy French defenders and then pivoted east through the wintry Atlas Mountains into Tunisia. Joined by the British Eighth Army, which had pushed west from Egypt after a signal victory at El Alamein, these forces had battled German and Italian legions for five months before a quarter of a million Axis prisoners surrendered in mid-May 1943.

The British and the Americans pounced on Sicily two months later, overrunning the island in six weeks before invading the Italian mainland in early September. The fascist regime of Benito Mussolini had collapsed, and the new government in Rome had renounced the Axis Pact of Steel to make common cause with the Allies. But a death struggle at Salerno, south of Naples, foreshadowed another awful winter campaign, as Allied troops struggled up the Italian boot for 200 miles in one sanguinary brawl after another with entrenched, recalcitrant Germans at places such as San Pietro, Ortona, the Rapido River, Cassino, and Anzio. Led by Eisenhower, many of the Mediterraneanites had left for the United Kingdom mid-campaign to begin planning Overlord, and they could only hope that the spring offensive—launched on May 11 and code-name Diadem—would break the stalemate in central Italy and carry the long-suffering Allied ranks into Rome and beyond.

By this point, the collapse of Berlin's vast empire in eastern Europe was well advanced. Germany had invaded the Soviet Union in 1941 with more than three million men, but by the beginning of 1944, German casualties exceeded 3.5 million, even as Soviet losses were quadruple that figure. The tide had turned red in all senses, and Soviet campaigns to recapture the Crimea, western Ukraine, and the territory between Leningrad and Estonia chewed up German strength. The Third Reich now had 193 divisions on the eastern front and in southeastern Europe, compared with 28 in Italy, 18 in Norway and Denmark, and 59 in France and the Low Countries. Nearly two-thirds of German combat strength remained tied up in eastern Europe, although the Wehrmacht still mustered almost 2,000 tanks and other armored vehicles in northwestern Europe. Yet the Reich was ever more vulnerable to air assault: in May 1944, Allied planes flying from the United Kingdom dropped 70,000 tons of high explosives on Axis targets, more than four times the monthly tonnage of a year earlier. Although they paid a staggering cost in airplanes and aircrews, the British Royal Air Force and the U.S. Army Air Forces had won mastery of the European skies. At last, after wresting air and naval superiority from the Germans, the Allies could make a plausible case for a successful invasion of the continent by the ground forces currently gathering in the United Kingdom.

In 1941, when the United Kingdom, the United States, and the Soviet Union first formed their grand alliance against the Axis, "the only plan was to persevere," as Churchill put it. Perseverance had brought them to this brink: a chance to close with the enemy and destroy him in his European citadel, four years after Germany had overrun France and the Low Countries. The Americans had long advocated confronting the main German armies as soon as possible, a muscle-bound pugnacity decried as "iron-mongering" by British strategists, whose preference for reducing the enemy gradually by attacking the Axis periphery had led to 18 months of Mediterranean fighting. Now, as the great hour approached, the arena would shift north, and the British and the Americans would monger iron together.

AN UGLY PIECE OF WATER

Cometh the hour, cometh the man: at 10 AM, Eisenhower rose to greet the 145 comrades who would lead the assault on "Fortress Europe." Behind him in the cockpit of the Model Room lay an immense plaster relief map of the Normandy coast, where the river Seine spilled into the Atlantic. Thirty feet wide and set on a tilted platform visible from the back benches, this apparition depicted, in bright colors and on a scale of six inches to the mile, the rivers, villages, beaches, and uplands of what would become the world's most famous battlefield. A brigadier wearing skid-proof socks and armed with a pointer stood at port arms, ready to indicate locales soon to achieve household notoriety: Cherbourg, Saint-Lo, Caen, Omaha Beach.

With only a hint of his famous grin, Eisenhower spoke briefly, a man "at peace with his soul," in the estimate of a U.S. admiral in attendance. He hailed king and comrades alike "on the eve of a great battle," welcoming them to the final vetting of an invasion blueprint two years in the making. A week earlier, he had chosen June 5 as D-Day. "I consider it to be the duty of anyone who sees a flaw in the plan not to hesitate to say so," Eisenhower said, his voice booming. "I have no sympathy with anyone, whatever his station, who will not brook criticism. We are here to get the best possible results." The supreme commander would remain preoccupied for some weeks with the sea and air demands of Operation Overlord, as well as with sundry political distractions, so he had delegated the planning and conduct of this titanic land battle in Normandy to a British officer, General Bernard Montgomery.

A wiry, elfin figure in immaculate battle dress and padded shoes, Montgomery popped to his feet, pointer in hand. His narrow vulpine face was among the British Empire's most recognizable, a visage to be gawked at in Claridge's or huzzahed on the Strand. But before he could utter a syllable, a sharp rap sounded. The rap grew bolder; a Snowdrop flung open the Model Room door, and in swaggered Lieutenant General George Patton, a ruddy, truculent American Mars, newly outfitted by those Savile Row artisans in a bespoke overcoat, bespoke trousers, and bespoke boots. Never reluctant to stage an entrance, Patton had swept through London in a huge black Packard, bedizened with three-star insignia and sporting dual Greyhound bus horns. Ignoring Montgomery's scowl, Patton found his seat in the second row and sat down, eager to take part in a war he condemned, without conviction, as "goddamned son-of-bitchery." "It is quite pleasant to be famous," Patton had written his wife, Beatrice. "Probably bad for the soul."

With a curt swish of his pointer, Montgomery stepped to the great floor map. Glancing at his notes—20 brief items, written in his tidy cursive on unlined stationery—Montgomery began in his reedy voice, each syllable as sharply creased as his trousers. "There are four armies under my command," he said, two composing the assault force into Normandy and two more to follow in exploiting the beachhead. "We must blast our way on shore and get a good lodgement before the enemy can bring sufficient reserves to turn us out," he continued. "Armored columns must penetrate deep inland, and quickly, on D-Day. This will upset the enemy plans and tend to hold him off while we build up strength. We must gain space rapidly, and peg out claims well inland."

The Bay of the Seine, which lay within range of almost 200 fighter airfields in the United Kingdom, had been designated as the invasion site more than a year earlier for its flat, sandy beaches and its proximity to Cherbourg, a critical French port needed to supply the invading hordes. True, the Pas-de-Calais coastline was closer, but it had been deemed "strategically unsound" because the small beaches there not only were exposed to storms in the English Channel but also had become the most heavily defended strands in France. Planners under the capable British lieutenant general Frederick Morgan had scrutinized other possible landing sites, from the French region of Brittany to the Netherlands, and found them wanting. Secret missions to inspect the Overlord beaches, launched from tiny submarines during the dark of the moon in what the Royal Navy called "impudent reconnaissance," had dispelled anxieties about quicksand bogs and other perils. As proof, commandos brought back Norman sand samples in buckets, test tubes, and Durex condoms.

The location of the landings was crucial, for if Overlord failed, the entire Allied enterprise faced abject collapse. But before the invading force could take any territory, it would have to contend with "an ugly piece of water called the Channel," as the official U.S. Army history of the invasion would later describe it. The English Channel was only 21 miles wide at its narrowest point. Yet for nearly a thousand years, invading armies facing a hostile shore across it had found more grief than glory. "The only solution," one British planner had quipped, "is to tow the beaches over already assaulted." The U.S. War Department had even pondered tunneling beneath the seabed: a detailed study deemed the project "feasible," requiring one year and 15,000 men to excavate 55,000 tons of spoil. Wiser heads questioned "the strategic and functional" complexities, such as the inconvenience of the entire German Seventh Army waiting for the first tunneler to emerge. The study was shelved.

Montgomery's presentation focused mostly on the technical details of the landings, but the general closed it on a different note. "We shall have to send the soldiers into this party seeing red," he declared, eyes aglint. "Nothing must stop them. If we send them into battle this way, then we shall succeed." After lunch and a number of briefings by other officers, Eisenhower stood for a few words of thanks, noting that Hitler had "missed his one and only chance of destroying with a single well-aimed bomb the entire high command of the Allied forces." Churchill gave a brief valedictory, grasping his coat lapels in both hands. "Let us not expect all to go according to plan. Flexibility of mind will be one of the decisive factors," he said. "Risks must be taken." He bade them all Godspeed. "I am hardening on this enterprise. I repeat, I am now hardening toward this enterprise."

Never would they be more unified, never more resolved. They came to their feet, shoulders squared, tramping from the hall to the limousines waiting on Hammersmith Road to carry them to command posts across the United Kingdom. Ahead lay the most prodigious undertaking in the history of warfare.

"RAMMING OUR FEET IN THE STIRRUPS"

Shortly after 6 PM, Eisenhower sped southwest through London in his chauffeured Cadillac, drawing deeply on a cigarette. In these fraught times, he often smoked 80 Camels a day, aggravating the throat and respiratory infections that had plagued him all spring. He also suffered from high blood pressure, headaches, and ringing in one ear; he had even begun placing hot compresses on his inflamed eyes. "Ike looks worn and tired," his naval aide, Commander Harry Butcher, noted in mid-May. "The strain is telling on him.

He looks older now than at any time since I have been with him." The supreme commander was 53 years old.

As the dreary suburbs rolled past, Churchill's final remark at St. Paul's gnawed at Eisenhower: "I am now hardening toward this enterprise." The tentative commitment and implicit doubt seemed vexing, although Churchill had never concealed either his reluctance to risk calamity in a cross-channel attack or his dismay at the cautionary experience of Anzio, where four months after that invasion a large Anglo-American force remained bottled up and was shelled daily in a pinched beachhead. Yet for Overlord, the die was cast, spelled out in a 30-word order to Eisenhower from the Combined Chiefs of Staff, his superiors in Washington and London: "You will enter the continent of Europe and, in conjunction with the other united nations, undertake operations aimed at the heart of Germany and the destruction of her armed forces." Now was the time, as Eisenhower put it, for "ramming our feet in the stirrups."

For years, he had pondered just how to successfully enter the continent of Europe—first as a War Department planner; next as the senior American soldier in London in the spring and summer of 1942; then as the general superintending the invasions of North Africa, Sicily, and mainland Italy; and now as the commander of what was officially known as the Supreme Headquarters Allied Expeditionary Force. No one knew the risks better. No one was more keenly aware that three times the Germans had nearly driven Allied landings back into the sea—on Sicily, at Salerno, and at Anzio.

Growing in stature and confidence, Eisenhower had become the indispensable man, so renowned that a Hollywood agent had recently offered $150,000 for the rights to his life (plus $7,500 each to his wife, Mamie; his mother; and his in-laws). "He has a generous and lovable character," Montgomery would tell his diary before the invasion, "and I would trust him to the last gasp." Other comrades considered him clubbable, articulate, and profoundly fair. His senior naval subordinate, Admiral Sir Bertram Ramsay, asserted simply, "He is a very great man." U.S. President Franklin Roosevelt had chosen him to command Operation

Overlord in part because he considered him to be "the best politician among the military men." In a memorandum, Roosevelt described Eisenhower as "a natural leader who can convince other men to follow him."

Yet he had not convinced everyone that he was a great captain, a commander with the ability to see the field both spatially and temporally, intuiting the enemy's intent and subordinating all resistance to an iron will. Montgomery, whose ambivalence toward Eisenhower's generalship would only intensify, offered private complaints as well as praise: "When it comes to war," he told a colleague, "Ike doesn't know the difference between Christmas and Easter." Field Marshal Sir Alan Brooke, chief of the Imperial General Staff, confided to his diary an assessment of the supreme commander's role at St. Paul's: "No real director of thought, plans, energy or direction! Just a coordinator—a good mixer, a champion of inter-allied cooperation, and in those respects few can hold a candle to him. But is that enough? Or can we not find all the qualities of a commander in one man?"

Eisenhower sensed such doubts, and perhaps harbored a few himself. In his own diary, he lamented the depiction of him in British newspapers as an administrator rather than a battlefield commander. "They dislike to believe that I had anything particularly to do with campaigns. They don't use the words 'initiative' and 'boldness' in talking of me," he wrote. "It wearies me to be thought of as timid, when I've had to do things that were so risky as to be almost crazy. Oh, hum."

He had indeed taken risks, crazy risks, but more lay dead ahead. Eisenhower was neither a philosopher nor a military theorist. But he believed that too few commanders grappled with what he called "subjects that touch the human soul—aspirations, ideals, inner beliefs, affection, hatreds." On such broken ground during the coming weeks and months, his captaincy and his cause would be assayed. For more than any other human enterprise, war revealed the mettle of men's souls.

Rick Atkinson

"BRITAIN IS NOW OCCUPIED TERRITORY"

By the tens of thousands, souls in olive drab poured into the United Kingdom. Since January, the number of GIs had doubled to 1.5 million, a far cry from the first paltry tranche of 4,000 in early 1942. Of the U.S. Army's 89 divisions, 20 now could be found in the United Kingdom, with 37 more either en route or earmarked for the European theater. Through Liverpool they arrived, and through Swansea, Cardiff, Belfast, Avonmouth, Newport. But most came into Glasgow and adjacent Greenock, more than 100,000 in April alone, 15,000 at a time on the two *Queens—Elizabeth* and *Mary*—each of which could haul an entire division and outrun German U-boats to make the crossing from New York in five days.

Down the gangplanks they tromped, names checked from a clipboard, each soldier wearing his helmet, his field jacket, and a large celluloid button color-coded by the section of the ship to which he had been confined during the passage. Soldiers carried four blankets apiece to save cargo space, while deluded officers could be seen lugging folding chairs, pillowcases, and tennis rackets. A brass band and Highland pipers greeted them on the dock; Scottish children raised their arms in a *V* for "Victory." Combat pilots who had fulfilled their mission quotas and were waiting to board ship for the return voyage bellowed, "Go back before it's too late!" or "What's your wife's telephone number?"

Just over eight million men had been inducted into the U.S. Army and Navy during the past two years—11,000 every day. The average GI was 26 years old, born the year that "the war to end all wars" ended, but manpower demands in this global struggle meant the force was growing younger: henceforth, nearly half of all U.S. troops arriving to fight in Europe in 1944 would be teenagers. One in three GIs had only a grade school education, one in four held a high school diploma, and slightly more than one in ten had attended college for at least a semester. *War Department Pamphlet 21-13* would assure them that they were "the world's best paid soldiers." A private earned $50 a month, a staff sergeant $96. Any valiant GI awarded the Medal of Honor would receive an extra $2 each month.

The typical U.S. soldier stood five feet eight inches tall and weighed 144 pounds, but physical standards had been lowered with respect to defects that once would have kept many young men out of uniform. A man with 20/400 vision could now be conscripted if his sight was correctable to at least 20/40 in one eye; toward that end, the armed forces would make 2.3 million pairs of eyeglasses for the troops. The old jest that the army no longer examined eyes but instead just counted them had come true. A man could be drafted if he had only one eye, or was completely deaf in one ear, or had lost both external ears, or was missing a thumb or three fingers on either hand—including a trigger finger. Earlier in the war, a draftee had had to possess at least 12 of his original 32 teeth, but now he could be utterly toothless. After all, the government had drafted a third of all the civilian dentists in the United States; collectively, they would extract 15 million teeth, fill 68 million more, and make 2.5 million sets of dentures, enabling each GI to meet the minimum requirement of "masticating the Army ration."

A revision of mental and personality standards was also under way. In April 1944, the U.S. War Department decreed that inductees need have only a "reasonable chance" of adjusting to military life, although psychiatric examiners were advised to watch for two dozen "personality deviations," including silly laughter, sulkiness, resentfulness of discipline, and other traits that would seemingly disqualify every teenager in the United States. In addition, the army began drafting "moderate" obsessive-compulsives, as well as stutterers. Men with malignant tumors, leprosy, or certifiable psychosis still were deemed "nonacceptable," but by early 1944, 12,000 venereal disease patients, most of them syphilitic, were inducted each month and rendered fit for service with a new miracle drug called penicillin.

Nearly 400,000 prefabricated huts and 279,000 tents had been erected to accommodate the Yank horde, supplementing 112,000 borrowed British buildings and 20 million square feet of storage space. GIs called this new world "Spamland," but the prevailing odor came from the burning feces in the army's coal-fired incinerators.

No alliance in the war proved more vital or enduring than that of the English-speaking peoples, but this vast American encampment strained the fraternal bond. "You may think of them as enemy Redcoats," each arriving GI was advised in a War Department brochure, "but there is no time today to fight old wars over again or bring up old grievances." Detailed glossaries translated English into English: chemist/druggist, geyser/hot-water heater, tyre/tire. Disparities in pay caused resentment; a GI private earned triple what his tommy counterpart drew, and the U.S. staff sergeant's $96 monthly salary was equivalent to a British captain's. The U.S. Army tried to blur the difference by paying GIs twice a month. But British penury was as obvious as the pubs that required patrons to bring their own beer glasses, or the soap shortage that caused GIs to call the unwashed United Kingdom "Goatland," or the fact that British quartermasters stocked only 18 shoe sizes, compared with the 105 provided by the U.S. Army.

American authorities urged tolerance and gratitude. "It is always impolite to criticize your hosts," a guide to the United Kingdom advised GIs. "It is militarily stupid to insult your allies." Not least important, British producers stocked the American larder and supply depot with 240 million pounds of potatoes, a thousand cake pans, 2.4 million tent pegs, 15 million condoms, 260,000 grave markers, 80 million packets of cookies, and 54 million gallons of beer.

The British displayed forbearance despite surveys revealing that less than half viewed the Americans favorably. "They irritate me beyond words," one housewife complained. "Loud, bombastic, bragging, self-righteous, morals of the barnyard, hypocrites"— these were among the terms Britons commonly used to described the GIs, according to one survey. *Meet the Americans*, a manual published in London, included chapters titled "Drink, Sex and Swearing" and "Are They Our Cousins?" An essay written for the British army by the anthropologist Margaret Mead sought to explain "why Americans seem childish." George Orwell groused in a newspaper column that "Britain is now Occupied Territory."

Occasional bad behavior reinforced the stereotype of boorish Yanks. GIs near Newcastle killed and ate the royal swans at the king's summer palace. Paratroopers from the 101st Airborne used grenades to fish in a private pond, and bored soldiers sometimes set haystacks ablaze with tracer bullets. Despite War Department assurances that "men who refrain from sexual acts are frequently stronger, owing to their conservation of energy," so many GIs impregnated British women that the U.S. government agreed to give local courts jurisdiction in "bastardy proceedings"; child support was fixed at a pound per week until the little Anglo-American turned 13, and 5 to 20 shillings weekly for teenagers. Road signs cautioned, "To all GIs: please drive carefully, that child may be yours."

Both on the battlefield and in the rear, the transatlantic relationship would remain, in one British general's description, "a delicate hothouse growth that must be carefully tended lest it wither away." Nothing less than Western civilization depended on it. As American soldiers by the boatload continued to swarm into their Spamland camps, a British major spoke for many of his countrymen: the Yanks were "the chaps that [matter]. . . . We couldn't possibly win the war without them."

GEARS OF WAR

On Tuesday, May 23, a great migration of assault troops swept toward the English seaside and into a dozen marshaling areas—Americans on the southwest coast, British and Canadians in the south—where the final staging began. Marching rates called for each convoy to travel 25 miles in two hours, vehicles 60 yards apart, with a ten-minute halt before every even-numbered hour. Military police wearing armbands specially treated to detect poison gas waved traffic through intersections and thatched-roof villages. Soldiers snickered nervously at the new road signs reading "One Way." "We sat on a hilltop and saw a dozen roads in the valleys below jammed with thousands of vehicles, men, and equipment moving toward the south," wrote Sergeant Forrest Pogue, a U.S. Army historian.

Mothers held their children aloft from the curb to watch the armies pass. An old man "bent like a boomerang" and pushing a cart outside London yelled, "Good luck to yer all, me lads!" a British captain reported. On tanks and trucks, the captain added, men chalked the names of sweethearts left behind so that nearly every vehicle had a "patron girl-saint," or perhaps a patron girl-sinner. Almost overnight, the bright plumage of military uniforms in London dimmed as the capital thinned out. "Restaurants and night clubs were half empty, taxis became miraculously easier to find," one account noted. A pub previously used by U.S. officers for assignations was rechristened the Whore's Lament.

By late in the week, all marshaling camps were sealed, with sentries ordered to shoot absconders. "Do not loiter," signs on perimeter fences warned. "Civilians must not talk to army personnel." GIs wearing captured German uniforms and carrying enemy weapons wandered through the bivouacs so that troops grew familiar with the enemy's aspect. The invasion had begun to resemble "an overrehearsed play," complained the newspaper correspondent Alan Moorehead. Fantastic rumors swirled: that British commandos had taken Cherbourg, that Berlin intended to sue for peace, that a particular unit would be sacrificed in a diversionary attack, that the Wehrmacht possessed both a death beam capable of incinerating many acres instantly and a vast refrigerating apparatus to create icebergs in the English Channel. The U.S. military newspaper *Stars and Stripes* tried to calm jumpy soldiers with an article promising that "shock kept the wounded from feeling much pain." Another column in the paper advised, "Don't be surprised if a Frenchman steps up to you and kisses you. That doesn't mean he's queer. It just means he's emotional."

Security remained paramount. Planners had concluded that Overlord had scant chance of success if the enemy received even 48 hours' advance notice, and "any longer warning spells certain defeat." As part of Churchill's demand that security measures be "high, wide, and handsome," the British government imposed a ban in early April that kept the usual 600,000 monthly visitors from approaching coastal stretches along the North Sea, the Bristol Channel, and the English Channel. Two thousand counterintelligence agents sniffed about for leaks. Censors fluent in 22 languages, including Ukrainian and Slovak, and armed with X-Acto knives scrutinized soldiers' letters for indiscretions until, on May 25, all outgoing mail was impounded for ten days as an extra precaution.

Camouflaged inspectors roamed through southern England to ensure that the invasion assembly remained invisible to German surveillance planes. Thousands of tons of cinders and sludge oil darkened new road cuts. Garnished nets concealed tents and huts— the British alone used one million square yards—and even medical stretchers and surgical hampers were slathered with "tone-down paint," either Standard Camouflage Color 1A (dark brown) or SCC 15 (olive drab). Any vehicle stopped for more than ten minutes was to be draped with a net "propped away from the contours of the vehicle."

Deception complemented the camouflage. The greatest prevarication of the war, originally known as "Appendix Y," until given the code name Fortitude, tried "to induce the enemy to make faulty strategic dispositions of forces," as the Combined Chiefs of Staff requested. Fifteen hundred Allied deceivers used phony radio traffic to suggest that a fictional army with eight divisions in Scotland would attack Norway in league with the Soviets, followed by a larger invasion of France in mid-July through the Pas-de-Calais, 150 miles northeast of the actual Overlord beaches. More than 200 eight-ton "Bigbobs"—decoy landing craft fashioned from canvas and oil drums—had been conspicuously deployed beginning on May 20 around the Thames estuary. Dummy transmitters broadcast the radio hubbub of a spectral, 150,000-man First U.S. Army Group, notionally poised to pounce on the wrong coast in the wrong month.

The British genius for deception furthered the ruse by passing misinformation through more than a dozen German agents, all of whom had been discovered, arrested, and flipped by British intelligence officers. A network of British double agents with code names such as Garbo and Tricycle embellished the deception, and some 500 false radio reports were sent from London to enemy spymasters in Madrid and thence to Berlin. The Operation Fortitude deception spawned a German hallucination: enemy analysts now detected 79 Allied divisions staging in the United Kingdom, when in fact there were only 52. By late May, Allied intelligence, including Ultra, information gathered through the British ability to intercept and decipher most coded German radio traffic, had uncovered no evidence suggesting "that the enemy has accurately assessed the area in which our main assault is to be made," as Eisenhower learned to his relief. In a final pre-invasion fraud, Lieutenant Clifton James of the Royal Army Pay Corps, after spending time studying the many tics of Montgomery, whom he strikingly resembled, flew to Gibraltar on May 26 and then to Algiers. Fitted with a black beret, he strutted about in public for days in hopes that Berlin would conclude that no attack across the channel was imminent if "Monty" was swanning through the Mediterranean.

As May slid toward June, the invasion preparations grew febrile. Every vehicle to be shoved onto the French coast required waterproofing to a depth of 54 inches with a gooey compound of grease, lime, and asbestos fibers and outfitting with a vertical funnel from the exhaust pipe that "stuck up like a wren's tail," to keep the engine from flooding. A single Sherman tank took 300 man-hours to waterproof, occupying a five-man crew for a week. On May 29, Eisenhower also ordered all 11,000 Allied planes to display three broad white stripes on each wing as recognition symbols. A frantic search for 100,000 gallons of whitewash and 20,000 brushes required mobilizing the British paint industry, and workers toiled through the weekend. Some aircrews slathered on the white stripes with push brooms.

Soldiers were provided with seasickness pills, vomit bags, and life belts, incidentals that brought the average rifleman's combat load to 68.4 pounds, far beyond the 43 pounds recommended for assault troops. A company commander in Dorset with the 116th Infantry, bound for Omaha Beach, reported that his men were "loping and braying about the camp under their packs, saying that as long as they were loaded like jackasses they may as well sound like them." On June 2, the men donned "skunk suits," stiff and malodorous uniforms heavily impregnated against poison gas. Each soldier placed his personal effects into a quartermaster box 12 inches long, eight inches wide, and four inches deep, for storage at a depot in Liverpool. Like shedding an old skin or a past life, troops bound for France would fill 500 rail boxcars with such accoutrements of peace every week for the rest of the summer.

"THE TRICK IS TO KEEP MOVING"

Across the fleet, the war cry sounded: "Up anchor!" In the murky, fretful dawn of Monday, June 5, from every English harbor and estuary spilled the great effluent of liberation, from Salcombe and Poole, Dartmouth and Weymouth, in tangled wakes from the Thames past the Black Deep and the Whalebone Marshes, all converging on the white-capped channel: nearly 200,000 seamen and merchant mariners crewing 59 convoys carrying 130,000 soldiers, 2,000 tanks, and 12,000 vehicles.

The early light revealed cutters, corvettes, frigates, freighters, ferries, trawlers, tankers, subchasers: ships for channel marking, cable laying, and smoke making; ships for refrigerating, towing, and hauling food. Leading the fleet was the largest minesweeping operation in naval history. Some 255 vessels began by clearing Area Z, a circular swatch of sea below the Isle of Wight that was ten miles in diameter and soon dubbed Piccadilly Circus. From there, the minesweepers sailed through eight corridors that angled toward a German minefield in the middle of the channel, where a week earlier Royal Navy launches had secretly planted underwater sonic beacons. Electronically dormant until Sunday, the beacons now summoned the sweepers to the entrances of ten channels, each of which was 400 to 1,200 yards wide; these channels would be cleared for 350 miles to five beaches on the Bay of the Seine, in

Normandy. Seven-foot waves and a cross-tidal current of nearly three knots bedeviled helmsmen who fought their wheels, the wind, and the sea to keep station. As the sweepers swept, more boats followed to lay a lighted buoy every mile on either side of each channel. The effect, one reporter observed, was "like street lamps across to France."

As the invasion convoys swung toward Area Z, the churlish open English Channel tested the seaworthiness of every landing vessel. The flat-bottomed LST (landing ship, tank) showed what one observer called "a capacity for rolling all ways at once," and the smaller lci (landing craft, infantry) revealed why it was widely derided as a "Lousy Civilian Idea." Worse yet was the LCT (landing craft, tank), capable of only six knots in perfectly calm waters and half that when faced with oncoming waves or currents. Even the U.S. Navy acknowledged that "the LCT is not an ocean-going craft due to poor sea-keeping facilities, low speed, and structural weakness"; the last quality included being bolted together in three sections so that the vessel "gave an ominous impression of being liable to buckle in the middle." Miserable passengers traded seasickness nostrums, such as one sailor's advice to "swallow a pork chop with a string, then pull it up again."

For those who could eat, pork chops were in fact served to the 16th Infantry, with ice cream. Aboard the *Thomas Jefferson*, 116th Infantry troops ate what one officer described as "bacon and eggs on the edge of eternity." Soldiers primed grenades, sharpened blades, and field-striped their rifles; a U.S. Navy physician recommended that soldiers wash themselves well, sponging away skin bacteria, "in case you stop one." Some Yanks sang "Happy D-Day, dear Adolf, happy D-Day to you," but tommies preferred "Jerusalem," based on William Blake's bitter poem set to music: "Bring me my bow of burning gold." Sailors broke out their battle ensigns, stripped each bridge to fighting trim, and converted mess tables into operating theaters.

To inspirit the men, officers read stand-tall messages from Eisenhower and Montgomery, then offered their own prognostications and advice. "The first six hours will be the toughest," Colonel George Taylor of the 16th Infantry told reporters on the USS *Samuel Chase*. "They'll just keep throwing stuff onto the beaches until something breaks. That is the plan." Brigadier General Norman Cota told officers aboard the USS *Charles Carroll*, "You're going to find confusion. The landing craft aren't going in on schedule and people are going to be landed in the wrong place. Some won't be landed at all. . . . We must improvise, carry on, not lose our heads. Nor must we add to the confusion." A tank battalion commander was more succinct: "The government paid $5 billion for this hour. Get to hell in there and start fighting."

Far inland, at more than a dozen airfields scattered across the United Kingdom, some 20,000 parachutists and glider troops also made ready. Soldiers from the British Sixth Airborne Division blackened their faces with teakettle soot, then chalked bosomy girls and other graffiti on aircraft fuselages while awaiting the order to enplane. "I gave the earth by the runway a good stamp," one private reported.

American paratroopers smeared their skin with cocoa and linseed oil or with charcoal raked from campfires along the taxiways. A few company clowns imitated the singer Al Jolson's minstrel act and joked about the imminent "$10,000 jump"—$10,000 being the maximum death benefit paid by government insurance policies. When a chaplain in the 101st Airborne began to pray aloud, one GI snapped, "I'm not going to die. Cut that crap out." Every man was overburdened, from the burlap strips woven into the helmet net to the knife with a brass-knuckle grip tucked into the jump boots. Also: parachute, reserve chute, life jacket, entrenching tool, rations, fragmentation and smoke grenades, blasting caps, TNT blocks, brass pocket compass, raincoat, blanket, bandoliers, rifle, cigarette carton, and morphine doses ("one for pain and two for eternity"). Carrier pigeons were stuffed into extra GI socks—their heads poking out of little holes cut in the toe—and fastened to paratroopers' jackets. Some officers trimmed the margins from their maps in order to carry a few more rounds of ammunition.

"We look all pockets, pockets and baggy pants. The only visible human parts are two hands," wrote Louis Simpson, the poet who belonged to the 101st Airborne Division. "The letter writers are at it again," he continued, "heads bowed over their pens and sheets of paper." Among the scribblers and the map trimmers was the 37-year-old assistant commander of the 82nd Airborne, Brigadier General James Gavin, who confessed in a note to his young daughter, "I have tried to get some sleep this afternoon but to no avail." The impending jump likely would be "about the toughest thing we have tackled," added Gavin, whose exploits in Sicily were among the most storied in the Mediterranean. In his diary, he was more explicit: "Either this 82nd Division job will be the most glorious and spectacular episode in our history or it will be another Little Big Horn. There is no way to tell now. . . . It will be a very mean and nasty fight."

The prospect of "another Little Big Horn" gnawed at Eisenhower in these final hours. After watching British troops board their lcis from South Parade Pier, in Portsmouth, he sat down to compose a contrite note of responsibility, just in case. "Our landings in the Cherbourg-Havre area have failed to gain a satisfactory foothold and I have withdrawn the troops," he wrote. "If any blame or fault attaches to the attempt it is mine alone." Misdating the paper July 5—symptomatic of exhaustion and anxiety—he slipped it into his wallet, for use as needed.

Just after 6 PM, Eisenhower climbed into his Cadillac. Leading a three-car convoy, he rolled north for 90 minutes on narrow roads clogged with military trucks. "It's very hard really to look a soldier in the eye when you fear that you are sending him to his death," he told his driver, Kay Summersby. At the Greenham Common airfield, in the Berkshire Downs, outside the eleventh-century town of Newbury, he strolled among the C-47s newly striped with white paint. Troopers with blackened faces and heads shaved or clipped Mohawk style wiggled into their parachute harnesses and sipped a final cup of coffee. "The trick is to keep moving. If you stop, if you start thinking, you lose your focus," Eisenhower told a young soldier from Kansas. "The idea, the perfect idea, is to keep moving."

When he returned to the manor house at his headquarters, in a royal preserve outside London, Eisenhower climbed to the roof to get a final glimpse of his men. "The light of battle was in their eyes," he would write George Marshall, the U.S. Army chief of staff. To Summersby, he confessed, "I hope to God I know what I'm doing."

Red and green navigation lights twinkled across the downs as the sun set at 10:06 PM. Singing voices drifted in the gloaming—"Give me some men who are stout-hearted men / Who will fight for the right they adore"—punctuated by a guttural roar from paratroopers holding their knives aloft in homicidal resolve. Into the airplane bays they heaved themselves, with a helpful shove from behind. Many knelt on the floor to rest their cumbersome gear and chutes on a seat, faces bathed by the soft glow of cigarette embers and red cabin lights. "Give me guts," one trooper prayed. "Give me guts." Engines coughed and caught, the feathered propellers popping as crew chiefs slammed the doors. "Flap your wings, you big-assed bird!" a soldier yelled.

From the west, the last gleam of a dying day glinted off the aluminum fuselages. "Stay, light," a young soldier murmured, "stay on forever, and we'll never get to Normandy."

The light faded and was gone. Deep into the English Channel, 59 darkened convoys went to battle stations as they pushed past the parallel rows of dim buoys: red to starboard, white to port. "This is like trying to slip into a room where everyone is asleep," an officer on the USS *Quincy* observed.

Small craft struggled in the wind and chop. "Men sick, waves washed over deck," an LCT log recorded. "Stove went out, nothing to eat, explosives wet and could not be dried out." Short seas snapped tow ropes, flooded engine rooms, and sloshed through troop compartments. Some helmsmen held their wheels 30 degrees off true to keep course. Several heaving vessels blinked a one-word message: "Seasick. Seasick. Seasick."

Down the ten channels they plunged, two designated for each of the five forces steaming toward the five beaches to which planners had given the code names Utah, Omaha, Gold, Juno, and Sword. Wakes braided and rebraided. The amber orb of a full moon rose through a thinning overcast off the port bow, and the sea sang as swells slipped along every hull bound for a better world. Hallelujah, sang the sea. Hallelujah. Hallelujah.

Lesser Israel

How Jewish Extremism Threatens Zionism

Jeffrey Goldberg

The War Within: Israel's Ultra-Orthodox Threat to Democracy and the Nation. BY YUVAL ELIZUR AND LAWRENCE MALKIN. Overlook Press, 2013, 224 pp. $26.95.

The Triumph of Israel's Radical Right. BY AMI PEDAHZUR. Oxford University Press, 2012, 296 pp. $29.95.

The highlight of U.S. President Barack Obama's visit in March to Israel—the highlight, at least, for Obama, although probably not for his host, Israeli Prime Minister Benjamin Netanyahu—was an emotional speech he delivered to a surprisingly enthusiastic crowd of Israelis at Jerusalem's International Convention Center. Obama gave an eloquent defense of the dream and promise of Zionism and simultaneously pleaded with Israelis to understand the predicament of the Palestinians.

The audience was made up mostly of college students, who were clearly delighted by the speech. By contrast, the scattering of right-wing Israeli political leaders in attendance appeared rather miserable. They, however, were not the audience members who seemed most out of place. That distinction went to a handful of ultra-Orthodox men, or *haredim* (Hebrew for "those who tremble before God"), as they are commonly called in Israel.

JEFFREY GOLDBERG is a columnist for *Bloomberg View* and a national correspondent for *The Atlantic*.

A couple of these men showed up in my row. They were quite well dressed, which is to say that their black coats and black hats were of a finer quality than one usually sees on the streets of ultra-Orthodox enclaves. I was seated with friends of mine, a married couple: committed secularists, politically liberal, and—this is important, given what followed—very genteel, particularly for Israel, where politesse is not a valued trait.

One of the two *haredi* men in our row found himself seated next to a woman. He appeared agitated by this: *haredi* men scrupulously avoid any contact with, even close proximity to, women who are not family members. He turned to my male friend and asked to switch seats. Doing so would have moved my friend away from me and away from his wife. But for the sake of *shalom bayit* (peace at home), my friend—the compromising sort—appeared ready to move.

That is when I objected. "He's not moving," I said in Hebrew. I'm not sure what prompted this reaction. Perhaps it was the years of built-up resentment I have felt about the assertive public-square fundamentalism of the *haredim*, who are trying to turn Jerusalem, a city I adore, into a kind of Jewish Riyadh. Or perhaps it was the fact that on a recent flight to Israel, I had witnessed a *haredi* man sternly rebuke a female flight attendant for inadvertently, and fleetingly, brushing her arm against his shoulder.

The *haredi* man in our row was taken aback. "What?" he replied.

I answered, "I don't tell you how to sit in your synagogue, so don't try to arrange seating in a public space."

He became righteous and angry: "If a Muslim asked you to move, you would move!" he said.

"No," I replied, "I wouldn't. This is a public gathering. You come to the civic center with everyone; you can't make it segregated."

"Why are you so prejudiced?" he asked.

"Why are you so afraid of women?" I shot back.

I may have won this awkward skirmish (which horrified my friends), but as Yuval Elizur and Lawrence Malkin demonstrate in *The War Within*, the *haredim* are dominating the larger campaign.

Elizur and Malkin write that since the founding of the state in 1948, "the ultra-Orthodox have been allowed to fashion a privileged community that enfolds, protects and isolates its adherents in a bizarre culture with a cloistered and often strangely skewed view of the world." Israel, the "start-up nation," of high-tech companies and world-renowned universities, is now also home to an unconscionably large number of state-subsidized rabbis who reject the theory of evolution and believe that teaching mathematics is a sin.

The consequences have been profound: an ever-expanding community of ever more radical fundamentalists has formed into a partisan bloc able to manipulate the Israeli political system even as it makes little effort to hide its contempt for secular democracy. Elizur and Malkin do not adequately explain the risk this poses, which should be made clear: if the numbers and power of the *haredim* continue to increase, the brightest and most talented secular Israelis—the descendants of the men and women who actually built the state—will leave, abandoning the country to the rule of rabbis whose interpretation of Jewish law is pinched, misogynistic, and antediluvian.

David Ben-Gurion, the George Washington of Israel, was a brilliant statesman who understood the value of compromise. But Israel today is haunted by the compromise Ben-Gurion made in 1948 with leaders of what was then a tiny haredi community. Ben-Gurion, motivated in large part by sentiment, granted haredi yeshiva students an exemption from Israel's universal military draft. There was a certain logic to the exemption: the Holocaust had destroyed most of Europe's ultra-Orthodox Jews, and the 400 students who received the first exemptions were, in the minds of Israel's secular leaders, an endangered remnant, people whose beliefs and folkways would soon enough be swamped by modern culture anyway.

But ultra-Orthodoxy, like fundamentalism all across the Middle East, made a comeback. How could it not, when the commandment *haredim* observe above all others is "Be fruitful and multiply"? They have multiplied very well: although it is hard to pin down the precise number of *haredim* who lived in Israel at its founding, they likely represented only around one percent of the population. Today, they make up roughly ten percent. And the political parties that represent them have adeptly exploited Israel's parliamentary system to squeeze subsidies and welfare support from the successive governing coalitions they have joined. Today, at any given moment, roughly 60,000 yeshiva students are allowed to avoid the draft, and many of these students stay in the yeshiva system their whole lives. (The fight over these exemptions is fierce, and it contributed to the breakup of Netanyahu's last governing coalition.) Only a minority of *haredi* men are currently employed (the rest study Talmud full time). The result, no surprise, is an immense drain on the country's resources.

As the *haredim* have come to play an outsized role in Israeli civic and political life, their rise has abetted the dominance of a different form of Jewish religious extremism: the settlement movement, which is the core of the political faction referred to in the title of Ami Pedahzur's *The Triumph of Israel's Radical Right*. Although they subscribe to distinct visions of Jewish identity, a political alliance between the *haredim* and Israel's settlers has shaped decision-making on almost every major foreign and domestic issue the country has faced during the past two decades.

THE BLACK-HAT BRIGADE

The *haredim*'s influence on civic life in Israel can hardly be overstated. The most ostentatious manifestation of their retrograde vision is an intermittent campaign to have public buses segregated by gender. But their influence is even more pernicious and enduring in the spheres of family law and Jewish religious practice. Because of the *haredim*'s influence in the Knesset and in the state-funded rabbinate, Jews who wish to have their marriages recognized by the government cannot use non-Orthodox rabbis, and non-Jews who wish to convert to Judaism under the auspices of non-Orthodox movements cannot do so. (It is a continual, and often losing, struggle to gain recognition in Israel for non-Orthodox conversions performed abroad; although the state says it accepts the conversions, the Orthodox rabbinate does not.)

The *haredim* hold deep prejudices against modern interpretations of Judaism. This view was perhaps best summed up by Rabbi Ovadia Yosef, the spiritual mentor of Shas (a major ultra-Orthodox political party), who once said that "Reform Jews have no place within Israel. They are a nation apart. We should vomit out these people. . . . They are essentially dead."

Such contempt is common among the ultra-Orthodox rank and file, and it finds expression in acts of hysterical intolerance, such as the recent verbal and physical attacks by *haredim* on women seeking to pray as equals at the Western Wall in Jerusalem, Judaism's holiest site. Even more disturbing than the wrath poured out on these women is the *haredim*'s ability to manipulate the state into doing their bidding. Members of the group Women of the Wall, which seeks to make it legal for women to pray aloud, read from the Torah, and wear religious attire at the wall, have been arrested by the police for simply wearing prayer shawls at the holy site. The *haredim* insist that such shawls are meant only for men, but some liberal Jews disagree. Official behavior endorsing the Orthodox view is hard to square with the belief held by most Israelis that they live in a nontheocratic representative democracy. This is not the Israel the country's founders imagined.

Elizur and Malkin do a serviceable job outlining the many ways in which the *haredim* have succeeded in forcing Israel to underwrite their lifestyle and condone their theological and cultural predispositions. They also argue that it is not too late to reverse the trend. Indeed, the secular Israeli center has begun to object with increasing vehemence to the special dispensations offered to the *haredim*. In elections in January, many Israelis fed up with the state's coddling of the ultra-Orthodox voted for Yesh Atid (There Is a Future), the party led by the popular television presenter Yair Lapid, a vocal opponent of draft exemptions for the *haredim*. Lapid's party stunned Israel's political class by capturing almost 15 percent of the vote, coming in second at the polls and forcing Netanyahu to exclude the *haredi* parties from his new coalition government, in which Lapid now serves as the finance minister. The draft exemption for the *haredim* was ruled unconstitutional by Israel's Supreme Court last year, and the army and the Knesset are now searching for ways to increase the number of yeshiva students drafted without upending society.

There are also signs of a loosening of sorts within some *haredi* communities, motivated in part by simple necessity. Ultra-Orthodox men have begun seeking gainful employment in greater numbers than ever before, because even with government subsidies, many *haredi* families—for whom it is not unusual to have as many as ten children—are finding it difficult to survive. And reformers have arisen within the ranks of the ultra-Orthodox, including rabbis who have demanded that their schools teach secular subjects as well as religious ones.

But such modest steps have not changed the fact that secularists and the *haredim* appear to be on a collision course. And as Elizur and Malkin warn, "Unless the quarrels between religious and secular extremes are resolved in a spirit of tolerance, the Jewish foundations of the Israeli state will crumble and the state itself risks fragmentation."

FOR GOD AND COUNTRY

Israel, of course, has always been a high achiever when it comes to existential threats. Most countries cruise through history without facing any such intense perils. Israel, a young country, has already dealt with a few, and it faces several more today. In fact, the rise of the *haredim* is not even at the top of Israel's list. That distinction goes to the threat that Israel's most dire enemy, Iran, might soon develop a nuclear weapon. Israel's main internal threat, meanwhile, is posed by a different variant of religious extremism: the religious-nationalist ideology that drives the settlement movement. Although centrists and secularists may yet stem the civic influence of the *haredim*, as Elizur and Malkin contend, it may already be too late to reverse the damage the settlement movement has caused.

That, at least, is what the political scientist Pedahzur argues in *The Triumph of Israel's Radical Right*. Intended as a follow-up to the late Israeli political scientist Ehud Sprinzak's groundbreaking 1991 book, *The Ascendance of Israel's Radical Right*, Pedahzur's book suggests that the religious nationalists have come to dominate Israeli politics so thoroughly that the settlement project has become irreversible and that, therefore, the dream of an equitable two-state solution is dead.

Pedahzur devotes a good deal of his book to retelling a now familiar story. Orthodox Jews were marginal to Israel's early development, but Israel's immense victory in its 1967 war against its Arab neighbors, which led to the conquest of the West Bank, was seen by the very religious—and, to be fair, even by many secularists—as a sign from God. Many Israelis succumbed to a messianic urge and devoted themselves to the cause of making permanent Israel's possession of this newly acquired land, which is at the center of Jewish history. Successive governments allowed pioneers, many of them graduates of Orthodox youth movements, to settle in the West Bank, and Menachem Begin's Likud Party made colonization a priority. Along the way, the religious-nationalist movement co-opted some *haredim*, building towns in the occupied territories exclusively for their use. This helped create another crucial political constituency for the movement.

Others, including Sprinzak, the journalist Gershom Gorenberg, and the historian Gadi Taub, have told this story before in electrifying books about the settlements and their political and moral consequences. Pedahzur's book is nowhere near as bracing as those works and sheds little new light on the subject. Still, Pedahzur makes some important points about the methods the settlers and their supporters have used to capture important branches of the Israeli bureaucracy. He tells the stories of such organizations as Elad, which has spent the past several years buying up properties in the Arab neighborhoods of East Jerusalem, reportedly with funding from wealthy American donors. Elad's leaders believe that Jews have a right to live anywhere in greater Jerusalem, but they also know that these pocket settlements will, over time, make it more difficult to cleave Jerusalem in two, thereby blocking the creation of a Palestinian capital in East Jerusalem. They also know that the Palestinians will never agree to a two-state solution without a capital in East Jerusalem.

Pedahzur also details the ways in which the advocates for the settlers have infiltrated key government bureaucracies, making it far easier for Israel, a nation of laws, to circumvent international law. But in his effort to prove that Israel has become wholly illiberal, Pedahzur also puts forward some tendentious arguments. He suggests, for instance, that opposition to illegal immigration from Africa to Israel is motivated by a sort of fascistic tendency among Israelis. It is true that several politicians in Israel have argued against unimpeded immigration in ugly ways. But the immigration debate in Israel is not so different from the one in the United States, and yet I doubt that Pedahzur would condemn Obama as a fascist because he has overseen the deportation of almost 1.5 million undocumented immigrants over the past four years.

Pedahzur had already finished writing this obituary for liberal Israel by the time of Lapid's surprising success at the polls, which confirmed the existence of a sizable Israeli center that is not ready to cede permanent power to either the *haredim* or the settlers. Its struggles against religious nationalism and against *haredi* hegemony are linked—and leading figures on the right know this. Avigdor Lieberman, Israel's once and possibly future foreign minister and one of the country's most powerful right-wing revanchists, acknowledged as much when he said in 2008, according to Pedahzur, that "newcomers, residents of development towns"—a coded reference to Jews of Middle Eastern origin, who tend to support right-wing parties—"settlers, Chabad Hasidim [followers of the late Lubavitcher rebbe], and the ultra-Orthodox: we are the majority and we will change the division [of power] between the religious and the irreligious."

FEAR AND TREMBLING

Seated just behind me at Obama's speech in Jerusalem was a man named Dani Dayan, the former head of the Yesha Council, the governing body of the settlement movement. I was not too busy fuming at my *haredi* row-mates to notice that Dayan was also fuming, although about something very different. Although he seemed pleased by Obama's strong defense of the Zionist idea and equally strong condemnation of Iran's nuclear ambitions, he sat scowling, his arms folded, when Obama asked Israelis to imagine what life must be like for the Palestinians who live under Israeli occupation.

Afterward, I asked Dayan what he thought of Obama's speech. "He wants a two-state solution," he answered. "He doesn't know that the two-state solution is dead: dead and buried. And then he tells us we're occupying our own land. How can we occupy what is ours?" If that were the case, I asked, then why did so many in the audience of 2,000 Israelis cheer Obama's message of reconciliation and territorial compromise? "They are naive," he replied. "They are naive about what is important for the future of the state."

On the contrary: I would argue, as Pedahzur, Elizur, and Malkin undoubtedly would as well, that it is the religious camp—both its nationalist and its ultra-Orthodox wings—that is naive about the future. Israel's strength comes from its democracy and its openness to the world. The *haredim* want to turn Israel into a Jewish Saudi Arabia. The settlers, if left unimpeded, would turn the country into the Jim Crow South. Each vision is fatally flawed. The only question is, can the Israeli center move the country off these paths? I believe it is not too late. The strong performance of Lapid's Yesh Atid party supports a notion that many polls, over many years, have shown to be true: a majority of Israelis object to the power of the *haredim*, and a majority still support a negotiated two-state solution with the Palestinians, which would lead to the dismantling of many of the most of religiously extreme settlements.

But Pedahzur, along with many left-leaning academics, fails to coherently account for why the settlement movement thrives even

Jeffrey Goldberg

though most Israelis support a hypothetical peace agreement that would doom it. Contrary to Pedahzur's view, the growth of the settlements is not solely the result of a radical right-wing takeover of Israeli politics, and the unsustainable status quo is not solely the result of Jewish chauvinism. Like many left-of-center commentators on the Middle East, Pedahzur rarely acknowledges that it is not irrational for Israelis to question the wisdom of territorial concessions when confronted with the activities of Hamas and Hezbollah (groups that have murdered thousands of Israeli civilians and that most definitely do not seek an equitable two-state solution); the rhetoric and actions of the Iranians; and the weakness of the Palestinian Authority and the venality that its founder, the late Yasir Arafat, demonstrated in prior peace talks. Israel is plagued by fundamentalism, but the country does not exist in a vacuum: extremism is a disease that has infected its whole neighborhood, and the countries surrounding Israel suffer from far worse cases of it. It is true that the Israeli right exploits the public's fears of those external threats for political gain. But it is also true that from the mainstream Israeli perspective, there is much in the Middle East to legitimately fear.

The trick for the Israelis is to properly balance their fears about such dangers against their fears of threats that originate even closer to home. Although it is not unreasonable to worry what might happen if Israel were to withdraw from large swaths of the West Bank—the 2005 withdrawal from Gaza, which added considerably to Hamas' power and influence, is an object lesson—it is also not irrational for Israelis to fear what would happen to their country if it did not withdraw. If Israel were to make permanent its hold over the West Bank, it would either cease to be a democracy (by permanently disenfranchising the Palestinians) or cease to be a "Jewish state" (by granting full citizenship to the Palestinians and thus becoming more like a binational state, one that would stand a chance of quickly devolving into civil war).

It is difficult, on a day-to-day basis, to understand which frightens Israelis more: an Israel without the West Bank or an Israel with it. But it seems clear that the settlement movement and its allies have not yet convinced the majority of Israelis that the right-wing vision of the future—a majority-Jewish state ruling over disenfranchised Arab cantons—is the best possible outcome.⊕

Who Is Ali Khamenei?

The Worldview of Iran's Supreme Leader

Akbar Ganji

In June, Hassan Rouhani was elected president of the Islamic Republic of Iran. Rouhani ran as a reform candidate, and many have interpreted his victory as a harbinger of a possible liberalization or rationalization of Iranian domestic and foreign policy. But the dominant figure in Iranian politics is not the president but rather the supreme leader, Ayatollah Ali Khamenei. The Iranian constitution endows the supreme leader with tremendous authority over all major state institutions, and Khamenei, who has held the post since 1989, has found many other ways to further increase his influence. Formally or not, the executive, legislative, and judicial branches of the government all operate under his absolute sovereignty; Khamenei is Iran's head of state, commander in chief, and top ideologue. His views are what will ultimately shape Iranian policy, and so it is worth exploring them in detail.

Khamenei was born in the northeastern Iranian city of Mashhad in 1939. His father was a religious scholar of modest means, and Khamenei, the second of eight children, followed his father's path to seminary. (Two of his brothers are also clerics.) He studied in Qom from 1958 to 1964, and while there, he joined the religious

AKBAR GANJI is an Iranian journalist and dissident. He was imprisoned in Tehran from 2000 to 2006, and his writings are currently banned in Iran. This article was translated from the Farsi by Evan Siegel.

opposition movement of Ayatollah Ruhollah Khomeini, in 1962. He played an important role in the 1979 Iranian Revolution and went on to become Iran's president, from 1981 to 1989, and then Khomeini's successor as supreme leader.

Khamenei has always been in contact with the world of Iranian intellectuals, and the basic outlines of his thinking were laid down in his youth and young adulthood, during the 1950s and 1960s. Iran was then a monarchy and an ally of the United States; according to the Iranian opposition at the time, the shah was nothing but an American puppet. Unlike many other Islamists, Khamenei had contact with the most important secular opposition intellectuals and absorbed their prerevolutionary discourse. But he was also a seminary student, whose chief focus was learning sharia, Islamic law. He became acquainted with the theoreticians of the Muslim Brotherhood and was influenced by the works of Sayyid Qutb, some of which Khamenei himself translated into Persian.

As a young man, Khamenei saw a tension between the West and the Third World, and these views hardened during his dealings with the United States after the Iranian Revolution. He concluded that Washington was determined to overthrow the Islamic Republic and that all other issues raised by U.S. officials were nothing more than smoke screens. Even today, he believes that the U.S. government is bent on regime change in Iran, whether through internal collapse, democratic revolution, economic pressure, or military invasion.

Khamenei has always been critical of liberal democracy and thinks that capitalism and the West are in inevitable long-term decline. Moreover, he sees Washington as inherently Islamophobic. Nevertheless, he is not reflexively anti-Western or anti-American. He does not believe that the United States and the West are responsible for all of the Islamic world's problems, that they must be destroyed, or that the Koran and sharia are by themselves sufficient to address the needs of the modern world. He considers science and progress to be "Western civilization's truth," and he wants the Iranian people to learn this truth. He is not a crazy, irrational, or reckless zealot searching for opportunities for aggression. But his deep-rooted views and intransigence are bound to make any negotiations with the West difficult and protracted, and any serious improvement in the relationship between Iran and the United States will have to be part of a major comprehensive deal involving significant concessions on both sides.

A PORTRAIT OF THE SUPREME
LEADER AS A YOUNG MAN

To understand Khamenei's worldview, it helps to start by looking at the history of U.S. intervention in Iran. In 1953, the Eisenhower administration helped engineer a coup against the democratically elected government of Mohammad Mosaddeq, and Washington was the chief supporter of Mohammad Reza Shah Pahlavi's authoritarian regime, until its overthrow in 1979. This helped shape the discourse of all of the regime's opponents; opposition to the shah went hand in hand with opposition to the United States, since the shah was considered Washington's gendarme.

Khamenei was 40 when the revolution occurred; before then, he had been a seminary student and cleric, but one engaged with the broader world as well as his narrow religious circles. As he said in a meeting with ulama (Muslim scholars) and young clergymen in May 2012, "I participated in intellectual circles before the revolution and had close relations with political groups. I got to know them all, and got into discussions and debates with many of them." He was a man of music, poetry, and novels as well as religious law. No other present-day *marja* (senior ayatollah) or prominent *faqih* (Islamic jurist) has such a cosmopolitan past.

Khamenei's widespread relationships with secular intellectuals in Iran radicalized his views about the United States, since these circles became increasingly anti-American after the 1953 coup and the U.S. backing of the shah and his subsequent repression of dissidents. As Khamenei's friend Mehdi Akhavan Sales, a poet, put it in one of his verses, "I will not forget: that we were a flame, and they doused us with water." Khamenei has spoken about the U.S.

role in the 1953 coup several times, and the memory continues to resonate with him today. As he said just last year in a meeting with university students in Tehran,

> It is interesting to realize that America overthrew his government even though Mosaddeq had shown no animosity toward them. He had stood up to the British and trusted the Americans. He had hoped that the Americans would help him; he had friendly relations with them, he expressed an interest in them, perhaps he [even] expressed humility toward them. And [still] the Americans [overthrew] such a government. It was not as if the government in power in Tehran had been anti-American. No, it had been friendly toward them. But the interests of Arrogance [a term Khamenei often uses to symbolize the United States] required that the Americans ally with the British. They gathered money and brought it here and did their job. Then, when they brought their coup into fruition and had returned the shah, who had fled, they had the run of the country.

Khamenei had strong ties to Jalal Al-e Ahmad and Ali Shariati, the two most influential intellectuals of the prerevolutionary period. They were important contributors to the theory of "Westoxication." But anti-imperialism seems to have been the strand of secular intellectual thought that shaped Khamenei the most.

In prerevolutionary Iranian opposition intellectual circles, Western culture and civilization were not only disparaged as a model but considered to be in crisis and decline. The Third World was its rising alternative; as the Iranian writer Daryush Ashuri, a contemporary of Khamenei, put it, "The Third World is composed of the poor and colonized nations, which are at the same time revolutionary." Iran was ostensibly independent, but colonialism was seen as taking a new form there, with native ruling political elites serving as agents of imperialism and working to secure its interests. The Western world, led by the United States, moreover, was thought to be laying the groundwork for its political and economic expansion by destroying indigenous cultures. Under such circumstances, it was easy to see Islam as not simply a religion but also a cultural and ideological weapon in the struggle against imperialism.

As a young man, Khamenei loved novels. He read such Iranian writers as Muhammad Ali Jamalzadah, Sadeq Chubak, and Sadeq Hedayat but came to feel that they paled before classic Western writers from France, Russia, and the United Kingdom. He has praised Leo Tolstoy and Mikhail Sholokhov and likes Honoré de Balzac and Michel Zévaco, but he considers Victor Hugo supreme. As he told some officials of Iran's state-run television network in 2004,

> In my opinion, Victor Hugo's *Les Misérables* is the best novel that has been written in history. I have not read all the novels written throughout history, no doubt, but I have read many that relate to the events of various centuries. I have read some very old novels. For example, say, I've read *The Divine Comedy*. I have read *Amir Arsalan*. I have also read *A Thousand and One Nights*. . . . [But] *Les Misérables* is a miracle in the world of novel writing. . . . I have said over and over again, go read *Les Misérables* once. This *Les Misérables* is a book of sociology, a book of history, a book of criticism, a divine book, a book of love and feeling.

Khamenei felt that novels gave him insight into the deeper realities of life in the West. "Read the novels of some authors with leftist tendencies, such as Howard Fast," he advised an audience of writers and artists in 1996. "Read the famous book *The Grapes of Wrath*, written by John Steinbeck, . . . and see what it says about the situation of the left and how the capitalists of the so-called center of democracy treated them." He is also a fan of *Uncle Tom's Cabin*, which he recommended in March 2002 to high-level state managers for the light it sheds on U.S. history: "Isn't this the government that massacred the original native inhabitants of the land of America? That wiped out the American Indians? Wasn't it this system and its agents who seized millions of Africans from their houses and carried them off into slavery and kidnapped their young sons and daughters to become slaves and inflicted on them for long years the most severe tragedies? Today, one of the most tragic works of art is *Uncle Tom's Cabin*. . . . This book still lives after almost 200 years."

THE BUDDING ISLAMIST

Yet if Khamenei frequented prerevolutionary secular intellectual circles and was a student of Western culture more generally, he was first and foremost a seminarian, devoted to pursuing social change in accordance with the teachings of religion. And in this regard, it was Qutb, the Egyptian intellectual, activist, and chief theoretician of the Muslim Brotherhood, who stole Khamenei's heart as a young man.

Qutb, who was executed by Egyptian President Gamal Abdel Nasser's regime in 1966, propagated the idea of an Islamic state. As he wrote in *The Battle between Islam and Capitalism*,

> If you want Islam to be an agent of salvation, you must rule and must understand that this religion has not come for one to sit in houses of worship; it hasn't come to make a nest in hearts. Rather, it has come to govern and run life in a proper fashion; it has come to build a progressive and complete society. . . . If we want Islam to answer social, ethnic, and other problems and solve our problems and show a way to cure them, we must think about government and its formation and bring our decisions to implementation. . . . Islam without government and a Muslim nation without Islam are meaningless.

The pillars of Qutb's idea of Islamic government were justice, equality, and the redistribution of wealth. "True Islam," he wrote in *Social Justice in Islam*, "is a liberation movement that frees the hearts of individuals and then of human societies from fear of the bonds of the powerful."

Qutb's ideas would go on to become the template for the modern Salafi movement, eventually influencing radical Islamists such as Osama bin Laden and Ayman al-Zawahiri. They were also very appealing for Iranian seminary students. Khamenei read them, was attracted to Qutb's personality and to some of his ideas, and went so far as to translate some of the master's works into Persian himself.

As Khamenei wrote in the introduction to his 1967 translation of Qutb's *The Future of This Religion*, "This lofty and great author has tried in the course of the chapters of this book . . . to first introduce the essence of the faith as it is and then, after showing that it is a program for living . . . [confirm] with his eloquent words and his particular world outlook that ultimately world government shall be in the hands of our school and 'the future belongs to Islam.'"

Qutb revived the classic Muslim concepts of the House of Islam and the House of War but gave them a new meaning: "There is only one House of Islam, and that is precisely the one in which an Islamic state has been founded, and God's sharia rules, and the divine punishments are applied, and in which Muslims support each other. Aside from this, everything is the House of War, and the relationship of the Muslim with it is either war or peace based on a treaty with it."

Qutb also offered Khamenei a perspective on the United States as something of a licentious society, ideas Qutb had picked up during his sojourn there in the late 1940s. Qutb came to feel that Americans were prepared to accept Islam, but not in its true, non-subservient incarnation:

> These days, the Americans have come to think about Islam once more. They need Islam to fight against communism in the Middle East and the Islamic countries of Asia and Africa. . . . Of course, the Islam that America and the Western imperialists and their allies in the Middle East want is not the same Islam that fights imperialism and struggles against absolutism; rather, it is that Islam that struggles against the Communists. Thus, they do not want the Islam that rules and definitely do not want an Islamic government, since when Islam rules, it sets up another *ummah* [Islamic community] and teaches the nations that it is obligatory to become strong, and that rejecting imperialism is a necessity, and that the Communists, too, are like the imperialist pests, and that both are enemies and aggressive.

AFTER THE REVOLUTION

In the early days of the Iranian Revolution, after Washington announced that it was letting the ailing shah into the United States for medical treatment, a group of radical Iranian students seized the U.S. embassy in Tehran and held its occupants hostage, creating a new crisis in U.S.-Iranian relations. Not all the members of the new ruling elite had known about the plan or agreed with it. According to former Iranian President Ali Akbar Hashemi Rafsanjani, neither he nor Khamenei supported the move:

> Ayatollah Khamenei and I were in Mecca when we heard news of the seizure of the American embassy over the radio at night, when we were on the roof of our domicile preparing to sleep. We were shocked, since we had no expectation of such an event. It was not our politics. Even early into the revolution's victory, when political groups shouted very extreme anti-American slogans, the officials helped Americans who were in Iran return to their country uninjured, and many of them even carried their property with them. Once, when an armed group attacked the American embassy and occupied it, a representative came on behalf of the provisional government and settled the problem. Thus, it is clear that neither the revolutionary council nor the provisional government was inclined to take such measures.

But after Khomeini came out in support of the embassy takeover, the other rulers of the Islamic Republic followed his lead. As Khamenei put it in April 1999,

> I, along with Mr. Hashemi and another individual, met with Imam [Khomeini] after traveling from Tehran to Qom to ask, 'What are we finally going to do with these spies?' Should they remain, or should we not keep them, particularly since there was an amazing tumult in the provisional government over what we were to do with them? When we came into the imam's presence and our friends explained the situation and said what the [foreign] radio stations were saying, what America was saying, what government officials were saying, he thought and then answered in the form of a question: "Are you afraid of America?" We said, "No." He said, "Then keep them."

During his tenure as supreme leader, Khamenei has always defended the seizure. Revolutionary regimes often maintain their relationships with former colonial powers and suffer as a result, he argues. In the Iranian case, the embassy takeover helped make that impossible: "The matter of the den of spies [the revolutionaries' term for the U.S. embassy] cut the last possible thread connecting the revolution and America," he noted in a speech in 1993. The embassy takeover, he said, "was a great and valuable service performed for our revolution."

Khomeini appointed Khamenei as a member of the Council of the Islamic Revolution, and before becoming president of the republic in 1981, he served as deputy defense minister, acting chair of the Islamic Revolutionary Guard Corps, and Khomeini's representative in the Supreme Defense Council. His work on security issues brought him face-to-face with Washington's cold realpolitik. In August 1980, Saddam Hussein launched a military attack on Iran, trying to take advantage of the new regime's disarray. Still stinging from the fall of the shah and the ongoing hostage crisis, the United States refused to criticize Iraq's actions, first protecting Iraq from censure at the United Nations and then actually supporting the Iraqi war effort against Iran. By the late 1980s, the U.S. military was increasingly engaging Iran directly, including attacking Iranian oil rigs in the Persian Gulf in 1987 and shooting down an Iranian passenger plane in 1988.

In 1987, Khamenei took his only trip to date to the United States, in order to participate as Iran's president in a session of the UN General Assembly. In his speech, he addressed the relationship between Iran and the United States:

> The history of our nation is in a black, bitter, and bloody chapter, mixed with varieties of hostility and spite from the American regime. [That regime] is culpable in 25 years of support of the Pahlavi dictatorship, with all the crimes it committed against our people. The looting of this nation's wealth with the shah's help, the intense confrontation with the revolution during the last months of the shah's regime, its encouragement in crushing the demonstrations of millions of people, its sabotage of the revolution through various means in the first years of its victory, the American embassy in Tehran's provocative contacts with counterrevolutionary elements, the aid to coup plotters and terrorist and counterrevolutionary elements

outside the country, the blockading of Iranian cash and property and refusal to transfer goods whose payment had long been received or assets that the shah had taken from the national wealth and deposited in his own name in American banks, the striving to enforce an economic embargo and the creation of a united Western front against our nation, the open and effective support of Iraq in its war against us, and, finally, an irrational, thuggish invasion of the Persian Gulf that seriously threatened the region's security and tranquility—all this is only part of our nation's indictment against the regime in the United States of America.

In a public speech the following year, he related an experience he'd had while staying in New York: "A high-ranking official of a European country came to meet me and said, 'You should finally solve your problem with America!' They thought that [with my] having come to New York and being in America, they might be able to warm their bread in this oven. I said, 'Impossible. The issue of the UN is another story. I have come to the UN to speak with the people of the world, and this has nothing to do with America. The issue of America is another story.'"

FROM KHOMEINI TO KHAMENEI

Since becoming supreme leader in 1989, Khamenei has sharpened his views of U.S. policy. His position now is clear and simple: Western governments, led by Washington, wish to overthrow the Islamic Republic and destroy the Islamic revolution, just as they did to the Soviet Union.

At a meeting with Iranian government officials in 2000, he put it this way: "An all-encompassing American plan has been arranged to collapse the Islamic Republican system, and all its aspects have been weighed. This plan is reconstructed from the collapse of the Soviet Union. . . . They have, in their own imaginings, revived the plan for the collapse of the Soviets in accordance with the conditions in Iran." Khamenei noted that there had been domestic factors responsible for the Soviet Union's collapse, including poverty, repression, corruption, and ethnic and nationalist tensions. But the Americans capitalized on these, he argued, to push the Soviet state to collapse—partly by manipulating the media and staging a "cultural invasion," and partly by using political and economic pressure. However, such efforts would not work in Iran, he argued, because the Islamic Republic was not like the Soviet Union—not least because, unlike communism, Islam was not a newly adopted ideology imposed by a ruling party after winning a civil war. Iran, moreover, had a long history of unified statehood. Its constituent elements had not been yoked together through imperialist expansion and wars of conquest over recent centuries, as was the case with the Russian empire that the Soviet system inherited. He also noted that the Islamic Republic was the product of a popular revolution and enjoyed considerable religious legitimacy.

Khamenei thinks several measures can ensure that the Islamic Republic does not meet the Soviet Union's fate. First, potential political insurgents—the local Iranian versions of Boris Yeltsin—must be identified and checked. Second, sensible reforms must be announced clearly, so they cannot be misunderstood or perverted. Reform measures must, as he has described, "be led by a powerful and restraining center so that they don't get out of control." Third, the media must not be allowed to undermine the government. And fourth, interference by outside powers, such as the United States and Israel, must be kept at bay.

Khamenei also thinks that the United States, the West more generally, and Israel want to use elections to various Iranian offices (city councils, the legislature, the judiciary, the Assembly of Experts) to create, through their "internal allies," a situation of "dual sovereignty." The aim is, according to Khamenei, to create a split between the supreme leader and elected officials of the government. Just as the British, who once had absolute rulers, eventually turned the position of their monarch into a merely ceremonial office, so Iran's enemies, Khamenei believes, want to turn the absolute rule of the *faqih*, or "guardianship of the jurist," into a meaningless shell. Iran's chief reformist strategist, Saeed Hajjarian, used the concept of dual sovereignty as an analytic tool to describe the changing balance of power in Iran following the victory of Mohammad Khatami in the May 1997 presidential election. In response, Khamenei loyalists tried to assassinate Hajjarian in March 1999. He survived, but he has been paralyzed ever since. Khamenei mentioned the concept of dual sovereignty as a subversive idea in a public speech in 2004, as the Khatami administration limped through its final year in office: "You have heard the slogan 'dual sovereignty'! A number of irrational people have even repeated these words within the country. . . . Dual sovereignty is not desirable but damaging and a deadly poison! This is what [Iran's enemies] want."

After Iran's presidential election in June 2009, hundreds of thousands of people poured out into the streets of Tehran and held peaceful demonstrations against the manipulated outcome. As the demonstrations spread, Khamenei, in a Friday prayer speech, compared the protests to the "color revolutions," particularly the one in Georgia, which he claimed the Americans and the British had launched. Khamenei emphasized that during the previous weeks, the speeches of American and European statesmen had become harsher, and that after the Tehran protests, they set aside their "masks" and showed their "true features."

In a public speech in June 2011, Khamenei called the protests, which came to be known as the Green Movement, a continuation of the regime-change policy of United States and its allies and contrasted it with a true revolution, such as the one that led to the founding of the Islamic Republic: "A revolution that cannot defend itself in an age of sedition, against various political or military coup attempts and other such acts, is not alive. This revolution is alive, for it defends itself and indeed prevails and wins. This is certain, as you saw happen [following the protests] in 2009."

A frequent Khamenei theme is the constant presence of foreign threats to the Islamic Republic and the regime's ability to withstand them. The United States and the Western bloc, he argues, want to overthrow the system in Iran and have launched a variety of attempts to do so, including Iraq's military invasion in 1980, the manipulation of ethnic tensions, and economic sanctions. As he put it in another public speech in August 2010,

> They want to bring the revolution down. One of the important means they have employed has been these economic sanctions. They say that [the sanctions] are not targeting the Iranian people, but they are lying! The sanctions are meant to cripple the Iranian nation. They are designed to exhaust the Iranian people and make them say, "We are under the pressure of the sanctions because of the [policies of] the Islamic Republican state." They want to sever the ties between the people and the Islamic Republican system. This is the true aim of the sanctions. They are exerting economic pressure by means of sanctions.

He repeatedly claims that the stated rationales for U.S. policies are meant to mask more sinister motives. As he put it in yet another public speech in August 2011, "Although the excuse for the sanctions is the issue of nuclear energy, they are lying. . . . Perhaps you recall that the first sanctions against this country were enacted at a time when the nuclear issue absolutely did not exist. . . . Thus, the enemy's goal is to hurl the Islamic Republic to the ground."

Khamenei bases such arguments partly on what he sees as two failed attempts by Iran to compromise with the United States. The first was during Khatami's term as president, when the government suspended its uranium enrichment for two years as a trust-building measure. Khamenei believes the Western governments were not interested in trust building, only in making the pause in enrichment permanent. The two-year suspension resulted in no achievements for Iran—not the lifting of sanctions, nor the release of frozen Iranian assets in the United States, nor any other reward. In a speech in January 2008, Khamenei noted,

> Today, to whomever comes to us and says, "Sir, suspend temporarily," we say, "We have already had a temporary suspension, for two years!" We had a two-year temporary suspension. How did it benefit us? . . . We, for our part, imagined that it was temporary and imagined that it was voluntary. Then, when we talked of resuming work, they started this media frenzy and tumult in political circles, saying,

"Woe! Iran wants to end the suspension!" The suspension became a sacred issue that Iran had absolutely no right to approach. . . . Finally, they said, "This temporary suspension isn't enough; you must completely pack the whole atomic project in." This was a setback for us. [The Khatami government] accepted the retreat. But this retreat had a positive effect for us. We learned a lesson from that experience. World public opinion learned from the experience, too. . . . I said if this process of adding new demands is to go on, I will intervene. And I did. I said . . . we should go on the offensive [and resume enrichment].

Khamenei then went on to remind his audience that despite Khatami's willingness to compromise, his kind words for Americans, his cooperation in toppling the Taliban and in the subsequent Bonn negotiations to install a pro-American government in Afghanistan, U.S. President George W. Bush had still included Iran in his "axis of evil."

The second experience he draws on is Libya's 2003 decision to give up its nuclear ambitions, which nevertheless did not prevent Muammar al-Qaddafi's violent removal through NATO military involvement. "In Libya," Khamenei said in his annual Iranian New Year speech in March 2011, "although Qaddafi had shown an anti-Western tendency during his first years in power, in later years, he performed a great service to the West. . . . This gentleman gathered up his nuclear program, . . . gave it to the Westerners, and said, 'Take it away!' . . . [Yet he was overthrown.]" Khamenei suspects that even if all of Iran's nuclear facilities were closed down, or opened up to inspections and monitoring, Western governments would simply pocket the concessions and raise other issues—such as terrorism, human rights, or Israel—as excuses for maintaining their pressure and pursuing regime change. To Khamenei, when it comes to nuclear weapons, the Iraqi and Libyan cases teach the same lesson. Saddam and Qaddafi opened their facilities up to inspections by the West, ended up having no nuclear weapons, and were eventually attacked, deposed, and killed. Major compromises by Iran on the nuclear front without significant concessions by the

West, he believes, could end up leading to similar consequences for the Iranian regime.

SANCTITIES

Another important issue for Khamenei is what he sees as actions that amount to insults to Islam. After the announcement of a possible burning of the Koran by a pastor in Florida in 2010, he asked in one of his public speeches, "What and who is behind the scenes of these evil deeds?" He went on to say that "a careful study of this evil occurrence, which came along with criminal deeds in Afghanistan, Iraq, Palestine, Lebanon, and Pakistan, leaves no doubt that the planning and the operational command of these acts are in the hands of the system of hegemony and Zionist planning centers, which enjoy the greatest influence over the American government and its security and military agencies, as well as the British and some European governments." Similarly, after the release of the film *Innocence of Muslims* in 2012, he published a statement citing the American and Israeli governments as "prime suspects for this crime." He said that "if they had not supported the previous links in this rotten chain—that is, Salman Rushdie, the Danish cartoonist, the American Koran-burning pastor—and did not order dozens of anti-Islamic films from the cliques linked with Zionist capitalists, things would not have reached the point of this great and unforgivable crime."

At the same time, he tries hard to avoid casting this issue as a conflict between Islam and Christianity. "The goal of these infuriating measures [Koran burnings]," he argued in a public speech in September 2010, "is to bring the confrontation with Islam and Muslims into the mainstream of Christian societies and to give it a religious coloration and zeal." But "we must all realize," he said, that this "has nothing to do with churches or Christianity, and the puppet deeds of a few idiotic and mercenary clerics must not be laid at the feet of Christians and their clergy. We Muslims will never commit similar acts in regard to the sanctities of other religions. The struggle between Muslims and Christians on a general level is what the enemies and plotters of these insane displays want, and the Koran instructs us to take the opposite position."

THE DECLINE OF THE WEST

Khamenei does not deny the astonishing progress of the West over the past century. As he said in a public speech in June 2004, "In America, you see the pinnacle of the rise of materialist civilization from the perspective of science, wealth, military power, and political and diplomatic efforts. America is a country that has legendary wealth and military power and extraordinary political mobility." He accepts Western science and technology and laments the fact that despotic regimes in Iran and elsewhere in the developing world are responsible for these countries' underdevelopment. Khamenei admires certain aspects of Western societies. Meeting with youth and cultural affairs workers in the Caspian city of Rasht in 2001, for example, he noted that "one good quality in European people is their willingness to take risks. This is the chief source of their successes. . . . Another of their good qualities is perseverance and keeping at hard work. . . . The greatest and most talented Western inventors and scholars are those who for long years live a hard life sitting in a garret and discover something. When one reads their biographies, one sees what a hard life they lived. . . . These are the good parts of Western culture."

"Western culture," he noted in a discussion with Iranian youths in February 1999, on the occasion of the anniversary of the revolution, "is a combination of beautiful and ugly things. No one can say that Western culture is completely ugly. No, like any other culture, it surely has beautiful manifestations. . . . A sensible nation and a group of sensible people will take the good and add it to their own culture, thus enriching it, and reject the bad." He believes that Islamic civilization is superior, however, because Western civilization is overly materialistic. "The West looks at only one dimension, one feature—the material feature," he said during a recent meeting with youths devoted to the topic of socioeconomic development. He added that the Western outlook considers "progress first and foremost, composed of progress in wealth, science, military affairs, and technology. . . . But in Islamic logic, progress has other dimensions: progress in science, in justice, in public welfare, in economics, in international grandeur and status, in political independence, in prayer and approaching the exalted God—in other words, it has a spiritual aspect, a divine aspect."

Khamenei is not a fan of liberal democracy. He argues that its supposed majoritarian legitimacy is undermined by the fact that actual governments in the West have received the votes of only a small fraction of the total possible electorate. He claims, moreover, that liberal democracies, such as the United States, have repeatedly violated their own principles by supporting despotic governments elsewhere, and have even worked to overthrow democratic regimes (such as with the 1953 coup in Iran). He sees liberal democratic governments as being interested in ruling the world at large, pushing globalization as a route toward Americanization, and attacking other countries at will (such as Afghanistan and Iraq).

The Islamic Republic has its own form of democracy, Khamenei believes, one that is rooted in religion. "The foundations of religious democracy are different from those of Western democracy," he argued in June 2005 in a speech on the anniversary of Khomeini's death. "Religious democracy, which is the basis we have voted for and which arises from the divine rights and duties of man, is not just a contract. All humans have the right to vote and the right to self-determination. This is what lends meaning to elections in the Islamic Republic. [What we have here] is much more advanced and meaningful and deeply rooted than what exists today in Western liberal democracy."

In practice, Khamenei believes that liberal democracy yields not freedom but domination, aggression, and imperialism, and this is what makes it unacceptable. "We believe in democracy," he said in a meeting with members of the Basij militia in northwestern Iran in October 2011. "We believe in freedom, too. But we do not accept liberal democracy. . . . We don't want to use that name for our pure, sound, righteous, and clean meaning. We say Islamic democracy, or the Islamic Republic." For all his criticisms of liberalism, however, he has not prevented the translation into Persian and the publication during his term of the works of liberal authors, such as Karl Popper, Milton Friedman, Ronald Dworkin, Isaiah Berlin, John Rawls, Richard Rorty, Martha Nussbaum, Robert Putnam, Amartya Sen, and many others.

Khamenei believes that Western governments and capitalism in general are suffering from incurable structural problems and face inevitable decline. In June 1992, in a message to pilgrims to Mecca, he said,

> The Western capitalist system is sunk to its neck in human problems. Despite the copious wealth that it has at its disposal, it is completely incapable of establishing social justice. The recent riots of blacks in America showed that the American system treats not only the nations of Asia, Africa, and Latin America with injustice but also its own people, and answers protest with violence and repression just like in those other countries. It is true that the communist camp collapsed and vanished, but its rival, the capitalist camp, . . . particularly plagued by the arrogance that has affected it after the disappearance of its powerful rival, will vanish too, sooner or later.

He has argued that the financial crisis that began in 2008 is evidence in support of his pessimistic view of the West's prospects. He saw the Occupy Wall Street protests as the beginning of a major crisis in capitalism. "The people in these meetings and demonstrations of several thousand in New York," he noted at a large gathering of people in the city of Kermanshah in October 2011, "put up a poster on which it was written, 'We are the 99 percent.' In other words, 99 percent of the American people—the majority of the American people—are ruled by a dominant one percent. . . . Today, the capitalist system has reached a complete dead end. Perhaps it will take years for the consequences of this dead end to reach their final conclusion. But the crisis of the West has begun in earnest."

For Khamenei, world history is "turning a corner," and "a new age in the entire world" is beginning. The Marxist, liberal, and nationalist creeds have lost their attraction, and only Islam has kept its. The Arab Spring—or, as he calls it, "the Islamic Awakening"—is a prelude to a worldwide uprising against the United States and international Zionism. In his view, the fact that routine materialistic calculations make such an outcome unlikely is unimportant, because divine providence will bring it about. He sees the survival of the Islamic Republic in the face of more than three decades of international opposition as evidence of this heavenly support and counts on it continuing in the future. Khamenei believes that the historic turn he anticipates will lead to the victory of spiritual and divine values in the world. Contrary to Max Weber's diagnosis that modern science has disenchanted the world and the realm of power, Khamenei still relies on esoteric notions and divine beings in his approach to politics. He is re-enchanting the world.

TALKING ABOUT TALKS

In August 1989, two months after being elected supreme leader, Khamenei announced to the United States,

> No one in the Islamic Republic has ever negotiated with you, nor will they. . . . As long as American policy is based on lies, deception, and duplicity and supports corrupt regimes, like that of Israel, and perpetuates oppression against the weak and poor nations, and as long as crimes and transgressions of the American rulers, such as the downing of the passenger plane and the impounding of Iran's property, remain in our nation's memory, there is no possibility of our holding negotiations with the American government or establishing diplomatic relations with it. We completely reject relations between them and us.

The following year, in a meeting with a group of students on the anniversary of the embassy takeover, he elaborated his thinking on this front:

> Those who think that we must negotiate with . . . America are either simple-minded or frightened. . . . What would negotiations mean? Would all problems be solved if only you go and sit with America and talk and negotiate? This is not the case. Negotiations with America mean trading with America. Trade means you get something and you

give something. What will you give to America from the Islamic revolution for which you will get something? . . . Do you know what it wants? By God, America is not upset with the Iranian nation for anything more than its being Muslim, its standing firm with Muhammad's pure Islam. It wants you to stop being so firm. It wants you to not be proud. Are you ready for that?

Seventeen years later, in December 2007, at a gathering of students in the central city of Yazd, he returned to the topic:

One of our fundamental policies is cutting relations with America. Yet we have never said that we will cut these relations forever. No, there is no reason to cut relations forever with any state. . . . [But] relations with America are harmful to us. First, establishing relations will not reduce the danger posed by America. America attacked Iraq while the countries had diplomatic relations. . . . Second, having relations with the Americans is a way for them to increase their influence within certain strata . . . in Iran. . . . They need a base that they don't have now. This is what they want. They want their intelligence officers to be able to travel to Iran without restrictions. . . . Some people brag about the harm that results from the absence of [diplomatic] relations. No, gentlemen! Not having relations with America is good for us. The day when relations with America will be beneficial, I will be the first one to say that relations should be established.

In August 2010, in a meeting with high-level officials of the government under President Mahmoud Ahmadinejad, Khamenei offered his interpretation of "two recent cases of negotiations with the United States, one of which was related to problems in Iraq." This was at a time when Ahmadinejad had stated that he was ready to negotiate with the United States. Khamenei described his understanding of the U.S. negotiating style:

When the Americans don't have strong arguments, when they cannot present an argument that is acceptable and logical, they resort to bullying. And since bullying has no effect on the Islamic Republic, they unilaterally declare the end of negotiations! Fine, what kind of negotiation is that? This is our experience in both cases. So, when people like Mr. President [Ahmadinejad] say that we are ready to negotiate, I say yes, we are ready to negotiate, but not with the United States. The reason is that America does not enter the field honestly, like an ordinary negotiator; it enters into negotiations like a superpower. . . . Let them set aside threats, let them set aside sanctions, let them not insist that the negotiations must end in a specific conclusion. [Then there can be negotiations.]

In February 2013, attending a security conference in Munich, U.S. Vice President Joseph Biden said that in its efforts to prevent Iran from acquiring nuclear weapons, the United States had imposed "the most robust sanctions in history" and that Iran's leaders were punishing their own people through economic deprivation and international isolation. Biden indicated that diplomacy still had a chance but that direct talks would be possible only "when the Iranian leadership, the supreme leader, is serious."

Khamenei responded quickly and directly. In a speech to the commanders of the Iranian air force, he said that since U.S. President Barack Obama's election in 2008, he had announced that the Iranian leadership would take an unprejudiced look at the new government's behavior and then make a decision. But what had been the results of Obama's first term? Washington had supported the "internal rebellion" (the Green Movement); it had imposed crippling sanctions that, he claimed, U.S. Secretary of State Hillary Clinton said were intended to foment a popular uprising against the Islamic Republic; it had turned a blind eye to Israel's assassinations of Iran's nuclear scientists and perhaps even backed them; and it had supported the same terrorists in Syria that they had overthrown in Afghanistan in 2001. He then addressed Biden's call for talks:

Whom did you want to cripple [with sanctions]? Did you want to paralyze the Iranian people? Is there any goodwill in this? . . . I am not a diplomat. I am a revolutionary and talk in a clear and forthright manner. . . .

Diplomats say something, and they mean something else. We talk in honest and clear terms. . . . Negotiations are meaningful when the other side shows its goodwill. When the other side does not show any goodwill, when you yourselves say pressure and negotiations, these two don't go together. You want to point a gun at the Iranian people and say, "Negotiate, or I'll fire." . . . You should know that the Iranian people will not be frightened as a result of such acts.

Khamenei claimed that the Islamic Republic was ready for direct negotiations with Washington but that there were several necessary preconditions. He wants the United States to give up what he sees as its attempts to overthrow the Islamic Republic, enter into negotiations in a spirit of mutual respect and equality, and abandon its simultaneous efforts to pressure Iran, such as with military threats and economic sanctions. He argues that on these matters, contrary to what Biden said in Munich, the ball is in Washington's court, not Tehran's.

Khamenei rejects the notion that the differences between Iran and the United States center on the nuclear program. "If we wanted to make nuclear weapons," he said in a public meeting with a delegation of ulama and martyrs' families from the Iranian region of Azerbaijan this past February,

how could you prevent it? If Iran was determined to have nuclear weapons, America could not prevent it in any way. We do not want to make nuclear weapons. Not because America is upset over this, but because it's our own belief. We believe that nuclear weapons are a crime against humanity and must not be produced and that those that already exist in the world must be eliminated. This is our belief. It has nothing to do with you. If we did not have this belief and decided to make nuclear weapons, no power could prevent us, just as they were not able to prevent it in other places—not in India, not in Pakistan, not in North Korea.

The key to successful negotiations, he claims, is for Washington to change its attitude and sense of entitlement. "The Americans must confirm their good intentions and show that they are not interested in bullying. If they demonstrate this, then they will see that the Iranian nation will respond in kind. Let them not make trouble, let them not intervene, let them not bully, let them recognize the Iranian nation's rights. Then they will receive a commensurate response from Iran."

Every year, Khamenei gives his most important speech in Mashhad on the first day of spring, the beginning of the Iranian New Year. This year's address was striking, however, for what seemed to be a slight softening of his position on talks. For the first time, even while expressing his lack of optimism about direct negotiations with the United States, he explicitly said, "But I don't oppose them." And while noting that Washington seems to have no inclination to complete the nuclear negotiations and resolve the issue, he nevertheless said that the solution to the conflict "is very near and very simple." Iran's only demand, he said, was recognition of its right to enrich uranium for peaceful purposes, and it would be "very simple" to eliminate foreigners' concerns. "They can implement the nuclear agency's legal regulations; from the start, we, for our part, have had no opposition to implementing these supervisions and regulations."

What is noteworthy about the road traveled by the supreme leader during these tumultuous past three decades is the change in the manner of his discourse. He has shifted away from absolute ideological notions of "the West," "world arrogance," and the United States as a totally homogenous other and moved toward accepting a more nuanced conception of the West as a complex social reality—one with not only an inherent drive to ruthless market competition, capitalist exploitation and foreign policy expansion but also dynamic artistic products, literature, science and technology, risk taking and institutional innovations, and religious and spiritual diversity. The discourse depicting the United States as an absolute enemy with which it would be absurd and naive even to think about negotiating has given way to a discourse about the United States as a potential interlocutor with which it might be possible to discuss acceptable terms of negotiations over such issues as the nuclear program and security in Iraq. It appears that for Khamenei, the United States has gone from being the monstrous absolute other to a powerful regional presence with a domestic political system plagued by the painful consequences of two recent failed military adventures in the Middle East.

WHAT COMES NEXT?

Given Khamenei's control over Iranian policy and his deeply rooted suspicion of U.S. intentions toward the Islamic Republic, improving the relationship between Iran and the United States will be difficult, especially if long-standing U.S. policies, such as constantly escalating sanctions, remain in place. Yet improved relations are not impossible, because the most important interests of both Tehran and Washington can indeed be accommodated simultaneously.

What Khamenei needs to know is that Washington is not determined to cripple or overthrow the Islamic Republic, and what the United States needs to know is that the Iranian nuclear project is peaceful, that Iran will not block free access to energy resources and regional sea-lanes, and that Israel can enjoy peace and security within its internationally recognized borders (which, some still hope, will be determined in a final settlement with the Palestinians). Iran can reassure Western governments that its nuclear project is peaceful by making it transparent and by ratifying and implementing the International Atomic Energy Agency's Additional Protocols on proliferation safeguards in exchange for its guaranteed right under the Nuclear Nonproliferation Treaty to enrich uranium for peaceful purposes. The West, in turn, can reassure Iran that it is not bent on regime change by taking tangible practical measures in exchange for Iranian adherence to security and peace in the Persian Gulf and the wider Middle East—and it will have to do so in order to make significant progress on the nuclear front.

Washington would be well advised to lift the economic sanctions, since whatever their aims, sanctions inflict damage on populations at large, not only or even primarily on the government officials who are their ostensible targets. This is as true in Iran as it is elsewhere, and it means that outside powers, and the United States in particular, are currently responsible for widespread unemployment, soaring inflation, and a massive increase in poverty. Under these circumstances, more and more middle-class families will join the ranks of the poor, and more children of the poor will fall victim to malnutrition, disease, and violence. Problems of daily survival will become the public's main concern, issues of democracy and human rights will be marginalized, and Iran's social fabric will be destroyed from within—just as happened in Iraq during the 1990s. That is not something the United States should want to see for any number of reasons.

Khamenei, for his part, must accept that in the long run, the only way to make the Islamic Republic truly powerful and sustainable is to legitimize his regime through the people's free votes. The Soviet Union had the largest army in the world and amassed thousands of nuclear weapons, but it eventually collapsed. Even if Western governments forswear any intentions of regime change, Iran's domestic problems will never be solved without democracy, freedom, and human rights.

If the Obama administration is serious about pursuing a solution to the problems between Tehran and Washington, it would be well advised to develop a road map that specifies the unresolved issues in the Iranian nuclear file in a clear manner and sets out a timeline for investigating, resolving, and closing the cases one by one. Step-by-step progress on the nuclear front should be linked to step-by-step progress on lifting the sanctions. The administration would also be well advised to take a comprehensive approach to the region and embed discussions of the Iranian nuclear program in a broader framework of regional security, bringing Washington's allies on board and minimizing those allies' desire to play the spoiler. This would mean building a consensus around a set of rules for regional politics, guaranteeing borders and abjuring regime change as a policy, achieving real results in ending the impasse in the Israeli-Palestinian peace process, working toward the eventual removal of weapons of mass destruction from the region, and supporting human rights across the Middle East.

This is obviously a very tall order, but there is no other way to avoid the continuation, or even escalation, of the existing conflicts in the region. Confrontational policies on all sides over the last decade have yielded little except stalemate and misery. The election of Rouhani as president showed the desire of the Iranian people to put a decisive end to the Ahmadinejad era, and it has created an opportunity for both Iran and the international community to move forward toward more constructive relations. That opportunity should be seized rather than ignored.☯

Biology's Brave New World

The Promise and Perils of the Synbio Revolution

Laurie Garrett

In May 2010, the richest, most powerful man in biotechnology made a new creature. J. Craig Venter and his private-company team started with DNA and constructed a novel genetic sequence of more than one million coded bits of information known as nucleotides. Seven years earlier, Venter had been the first person in history to make a functioning creature from information. Looking at the strings of letters representing the DNA sequence for a virus called phi X174, which infects bacteria, he thought to himself, "I can assemble real DNA based on that computer information." And so he did, creating a virus based on the phi X174 genomic code. He followed the same recipe later on to generate the DNA for his larger and more sophisticated creature. Venter and his team figured out how to make an artificial bacterial cell, inserted their man-made DNA genome inside, and watched as the organic life form they had synthesized moved, ate, breathed, and replicated itself.

As he was doing this, Venter tried to warn a largely oblivious humanity about what was coming. He cautioned in a 2009 interview, for example, that "we think once we do activate a genome that yes, it probably will impact people's thinking about life."

LAURIE GARRETT is Senior Fellow for Global Health at the Council on Foreign Relations.

Venter defined his new technology as "synthetic genomics," which would "start in the computer in the digital world from digitized biology and make new DNA constructs for very specific purposes. . . . It can mean that as we learn the rules of life we will be able to develop robotics and computational systems that are self-learning systems." "It's the beginning of the new era of very rapid learning," he continued. "There's not a single aspect of human life that doesn't have the potential to be totally transformed by these technologies in the future."

Today, some call work such as Venter's novel bacterial creation an example of "4-D printing." 2-D printing is what we do everyday by hitting "print" on our keyboards, causing a hard copy of an article or the like to spew from our old-fashioned ink-printing devices. Manufacturers, architects, artists, and others are now doing 3-D printing, using computer-generated designs to command devices loaded with plastics, carbon, graphite, and even food materials to construct three-dimensional products. With 4-D printing, manufacturers take the next crucial step: self-assembly or self-replication. What begins as a human idea, hammered out intellectually on a computer, is then sent to a 3-D printer, resulting in a creation capable of making copies of and transforming itself. In solid materials, Skylar Tibbits of the Massachusetts Institute of Technology creates complex physical substances that he calls "programmable materials that build themselves." Venter and hundreds of synthetic biologists argue that 4-D printing is best accomplished by making life using life's own building blocks, DNA.

When Venter's team first created the phi X174 viral genome, Venter commissioned a large analysis of the implications of synthetic genomics for national security and public health. The resulting report warned that two issues were impeding appropriate governance of the new science. The first problem was that work on synthetic biology, or synbio, had become so cheap and easy that its practitioners were no longer classically trained biologists. This meant that there were no shared assumptions regarding the new field's ethics, professional standards, or safety. The second problem was that existing standards, in some cases regulated by government agencies in the United States and other developed countries, were a generation old, therefore outdated, and also largely unknown to many younger practitioners.

Venter's team predicted that as the cost of synthetic biology continued to drop, interest in the field would increase, and the ethical and practical concerns it raised would come increasingly to the fore. They were even more prescient than they guessed. Combined with breakthroughs in another area of biology, "gain-of-function" (GOF) research, the synthetic genomics field has spawned a dizzying array of new possibilities, challenges, and national security threats. As the scientific community has started debating "human-directed evolution" and the merits of experiments that give relatively benign germs dangerous capacities for disease, the global bioterrorism and biosecurity establishment remains well behind the curve, mired in antiquated notions about what threats are important and how best to counter them.

In the United States, Congress and the executive branch have tried to prepare by creating finite lists of known pathogens and toxins and developing measures to surveil, police, and counter them; foreign governments and multilateral institutions, such as the UN and the Biological Weapons Convention, have been even less ambitious. Governance, in short, is focused on the old world of biology, in which scientists observed life from the outside, puzzling over its details and behavior by tinkering with its environment and then watching what happened. But in the new biology world, scientists can now create life themselves and learn about it from the inside. As Venter put it back in 2009, "What we have done so far is going to blow your freakin' mind."

CODING LIFE

Shortly after Venter's game-changing experiment was announced, the National Academy of Sciences' Institute of Medicine convened a special panel aimed at examining the brave new biology world's ethical, scientific, and national security dimensions. Andrew Ellington and

Jared Ellefson of the University of Texas at Austin argued that a new breed of biologists was taking over the frontiers of science—a breed that views life forms and DNA much the way the technology wizards who spawned IBM, Cisco, and Apple once looked at basic electronics, transistors, and circuits. These two fields, each with spectacular private-sector and academic engagement, are colliding, merging, and transforming one another, as computer scientists speak of "DNA-based computation" and synthetic biologists talk of "life circuit boards." The biologist has become an engineer, coding new life forms as desired.

Gerald Joyce of the Scripps Research Institute in La Jolla, California, frets that as the boundaries blur, biologists are now going to be directing evolution and that we are witnessing "the end of Darwinism." "Life on Earth," Joyce has noted, "has demonstrated extraordinary resiliency and inventiveness in adapting to highly disparate niches. Perhaps the most significant invention of life is a genetic system that has an extensible capacity for inventiveness, something that likely will not be achieved soon for synthetic biological systems. However, once informational macromolecules are given the opportunity to inherit profitable variation through self-sustained Darwinian evolution, they just may take on a life of their own."

This is not hyperbole. All the key barriers to the artificial synthesis of viruses and bacteria have been overcome, at least on a proof-of-principle basis. In 2002, researchers at SUNY Stony Brook made a living polio virus, constructed from its genetic code. Three years later, scientists worried about pandemic influenza decided to re-create the devastating 1918 Spanish flu virus for research purposes, identifying key elements of the viral genes that gave that virus the ability to kill at least 50 million people in less than two years. What all this means is that the dual-use dilemma that first hit chemistry a century ago, and then hit physics a generation later, is now emerging with special force in contemporary biology.

Between 1894 and 1911, the German chemist Fritz Haber figured out how to mass-produce ammonia. This work revolutionized agriculture by generating the modern fertilizer industry. But the same research helped create chemical weapons for German use during World War I—and Haber was crucial to both the positive and the negative efforts. Three years after Haber won the Nobel Prize in Chemistry, his compatriot Albert Einstein won a Nobel Prize for his contributions to physics. Einstein's revolutionary theories of relativity, gravity, mass, and energy helped unravel the secrets of the cosmos and paved the way for the harnessing of nuclear energy. They also led to the atom bomb.

The problem of "dual-use research of concern" (DURC)—work that could have both beneficial and dangerous consequences—was thus identified long ago for chemistry and physics, and it led to international treaties aimed at limiting the most worrisome applications of problematic work in each field. But in this respect, at least, biology lagged far behind, as the United States, the Soviet Union, and many other countries continued to pursue the development of biological weapons with relatively few restrictions. These efforts have not yielded much of military consequence, because those who aspire to use bioweapons have not found ways to transmit and disperse germs rapidly or to limit their effects to the intended targets alone. That could now be changing.

Dual-use concerns in biology have gained widespread publicity in the last couple of years thanks to GOF research, which attempts to start combating potential horrors by first creating them artificially in the lab. On September 12, 2011, Ron Fouchier of the Erasmus Medical Center, in Rotterdam, took the stage at a meeting in Malta of the European Scientific Working Group on Influenza. He announced that he had found a way to turn H5N1, a virus that almost exclusively infected birds, into a possible human-to-human flu. At that time, only 565 people were known to have contracted H5N1 flu, presumably from contact with birds, of which 331, or 59 percent, had died. The 1918 influenza pandemic had a lethality rate of only 2.5 percent yet led to more than 50 million deaths, so H5N1 seemed potentially catastrophic. Its saving grace was that it had not yet evolved into a strain that could readily spread directly from one human to another. Fouchier told the scientists in Malta that his

Dutch group, funded by the U.S. National Institutes of Health, had "mutated the hell out of H5N1," turning the bird flu into something that could infect ferrets (laboratory stand-ins for human beings). And then, Fouchier continued, he had done "something really, really stupid," swabbing the noses of the infected ferrets and using the gathered viruses to infect another round of animals, repeating the process until he had a form of H5N1 that could spread through the air from one mammal to another.

"This is a very dangerous virus," Fouchier told Scientific American. Then he asked, rhetorically, "Should these experiments be done?" His answer was yes, because the experiments might help identify the most dangerous strains of flu in nature, create targets for vaccine development, and alert the world to the possibility that H5N1 could become airborne. Shortly after Fouchier's bombshell announcement, Yoshihiro Kawaoka, a University of Wisconsin virologist, who also received funding from the National Institutes of Health, revealed that he had performed similar experiments, also producing forms of the bird flu H5N1 that could spread through the air between ferrets. Kawaoka had taken the precaution of altering his experimental H5N1 strain to make it less dangerous to human beings, and both researchers executed their experiments in very high-security facilities, designated Biosafety Level (BSL) 3+, just below the top of the scale.

Despite their precautions, Fouchier and Kawaoka drew the wrath of many national security and public health experts, who demanded to know how the deliberate creation of potential pandemic flu strains could possibly be justified. A virtually unknown advisory committee to the National Institutes of Health, the National Science Advisory Board for Biosecurity, was activated, and it convened a series of contentious meetings in 2011–12. The advisory board first sought to mitigate the fallout from the H5N1 experiments by ordering, in December 2011, that the methods used to create these new mammalian forms of H5N1 never be published. *Science* and *Nature* were asked to redact the how-to sections of Fouchier's and Kawaoka's papers, out of a stated concern on the part of some advisory board members that the information constituted a cookbook for terrorists.

Michael Osterholm, a public health expert at the University of Minnesota and a member of the advisory board, was particularly concerned. He felt that a tipping point had been reached and that scientists ought to pause and develop appropriate strategies to ensure that future work of this sort was safely executed by people with beneficial intentions. "This is an issue that really needs to be considered at the international level by many parties," Osterholm told journalists. "Influenza is virtually in a class by itself. Many other agents worked on within BSL-4 labs don't have that transmissibility that we see with influenza. There are many agents worked on in BSL-4 that we wouldn't want to escape. But I can't think of any that have the potential to be transmitted around the world as with influenza."

Paul Keim, a microbiologist at Northern Arizona University who was chair of the National Science Advisory Board for Biosecurity, had played a pivotal role in the FBI's pursuit of the culprit behind the 2001 anthrax mailings, developing novel genetic fingerprinting techniques to trace the origins of the spores that were inserted into envelopes and mailed to news organizations and political leaders. Keim shared many of Osterholm's concerns about public safety, and his anthrax experience gave him special anxiety about terrorism. "It's not clear that these particular [experiments] have created something that would destroy the world; maybe it'll be the next set of experiments that will be critical," Keim told reporters. "And that's what the world discussion needs to be about."

In the end, however, the December 2011 do-not-publish decision settled nothing and was reversed by the advisory board four months later. It was successfully challenged by Fouchier and Kawaoka, both papers were published in their entirety by *Science* and *Nature* in 2012, and a temporary moratorium on dual-use research on influenza viruses was eventually lifted. In early 2013, the National Institutes of Health issued a series of biosafety and clearance guidelines for GOF research on flu viruses, but the restrictions applied only to work on influenza. And Osterholm, Keim, and most of the vocal opponents of the work retreated, allowing the advisory board to step back into obscurity.

A GLOBAL REMEDY?

In the last two years, the World Health Organization has held two summits in the hopes of finding a global solution to the Pandora's box opened by the H5N1 experiments. The WHO's initial concern was that flu scientists not violate the delicately maintained agreements among nations regarding disease surveillance and the sharing of outbreak information—a very real concern, given that the 2005 International Health Regulations, which assign the WHO authority in the event of an epidemic and compel all nations to monitor infectious diseases and report any outbreaks, had taken 14 years to negotiate and had been challenged by some developing countries, such as Indonesia, from the day of their ratification.

Jakarta resisted sharing viral samples on the grounds that Western pharmaceutical companies would seek to patent products derived from them and ultimately reap large profits by selling vaccines and drugs back to poor countries at high prices. So Indonesia refused to share samples of the H5N1 flu virus that was spreading inside its borders; made wild accusations about the global health community in general, and the United States in particular; and even expelled the U.S. negotiator working on the issue. Eventually, a special pandemic-prevention agreement was hammered out and approved by the World Health Assembly (the decision-making body of the WHO) in 2011, serving as a companion to the International Health Regulations. But by 2012, fewer than 35 countries had managed to comply with the safety, surveillance, and research requirements of the regulations, and many samples of H5N1 and other pathogens of concern had yet to be shared with global authorities and databases. Public health experts worried that a pandemic might unfold before authorities knew what they were up against.

The WHO knew that Egypt's primary public health laboratory in Cairo had been raided during the riots that ultimately toppled the Mubarak regime in early 2011 and that vials of germs had gone missing—including samples of the H5N1 virus. Egypt has a robust H5N1 problem, with the second-largest number of human cases of the disease (behind, you guessed it, Indonesia). Although it was assumed that the rioters had no idea what was in the test tubes and were merely interested in looting the lab's electronics and refrigeration equipment, nobody can say with certainty whether the flu vials were destroyed or taken.

From the WHO's perspective, the Egyptian episode demonstrated that the extensive security precautions taken by the Dutch to ensure the security of Fouchier's work and the ones that the Americans had adhered to regarding Kawaoka's were not going to be followed in biology labs in many other countries. Margaret Chan, the WHO's director general, and Keiji Fukuda, an assistant director general, remembered the SARS epidemic of 2003, during which Chinese leaders dissembled and dragged their feet for months, allowing the disease to spread to 29 countries. They knew that even in countries that claimed to have met all the standards of the International Health Regulations, there were no consistent dual-use safety regulations. Across most of Asia, the very concept of biosafety was a new one, and a source of confusion. Even in Europe, there were no consistent guidelines or definitions for any aspects of dual-use research, biosafety, or biosecurity. European countries were far more concerned about genetically modified food products than about pathogens and microbes; they were preoccupied with enforcing the 2000 Cartagena Protocol on Biosafety, which despite its name has nothing to do with terrorism, national security, or the sorts of issues raised by dual-use research; its focus is genetically modified organisms.

The WHO's first dual-use summit, in February 2012, pushed Fouchier and Kawaoka to reveal the details of their experimental procedures and outcomes to their scientific colleagues. Fouchier's boasting about mutations seemed less worrying when the scientist indicated that he had not used synthetic biological techniques and that although his virus had spread between caged ferrets, it had not killed any of them. The technical consultation on H5N1, which was dominated by flu virologists, led the scientists to decide that the work was less dangerous than previously thought and that the moratorium on it could soon be lifted.

An exasperated Osterholm told the New York Academy of Sciences that the United States and the WHO had no clear protocols for DURC, no standards for determining safety, and no plans for a coordinated global response. But many other scientists engaged in the debate were less concerned, and they complained that the potential public health benefits of GOF research might be held back by excessive worries about its potential risks. In meeting after meeting, they claimed, the FBI, the CIA, and other intelligence agencies had proved unable to characterize or quantify the risk of bioweapons terrorism, GOF work, or synthetic biological research.

I BELIEVE THE CHILDREN ARE OUR FUTURE

Advocates for open, fast-paced synthetic biological research, such as Drew Endy of Stanford University and Todd Kuiken of the Wilson Center, the latter one of the leaders of a growing do-it-yourself international biology movement, insist that attention should be paid not just to the dangers of synthetic biology but also to its promise. Endy reckons that two percent of the U.S. economy is already derived from genetic engineering and synthetic biology and that the sector is growing by 12 percent annually. His bioengineering department at Stanford operates on a budget of half a billion dollars a year, and Endy predicts that synthetic biology will in the near future lead to an economic and technological boom like that of Internet and social media technologies during the earlier part of this century.

Many biology students these days see the genetic engineering of existing life forms and the creation of new ones as the cutting edge of the field. Whether they are competing in science fairs or carrying out experiments, they have little time for debates surrounding dual-use research; they are simply plowing ahead. The International Genetically Engineered Machine contest, in which teams of college students compete to build new life forms, began at MIT in 2004; it was recently opened to high school teams as well. Last year's contest drew more than 190 entries by youngsters from 34 countries. What sounds like science fiction to one generation is already the norm for another.

In just a few years, synthetic biological research has become relatively cheap and easy. In 2003, the Human Genome Project completed the first full sequencing of human DNA. It cost several billion dollars, involved thousands of scientists and technicians toiling in more than 160 labs, and took more than ten years. A decade later, it was possible to buy a sequencing device for several thousand dollars and sequence one's entire genome at home in less than 24 hours. For even less, a private company will sequence your genome for you, and prices are still dropping. Sequencing costs have plummeted so far that the industry is no longer profitable in the developed world and has largely been outsourced to China. In vast lab warehouses outside Beijing, Shanghai, and Shenzhen, automated sequencers now decipher, and massive computers store, more genetic information every month than the sum total of the information amassed from James Watson and Francis Crick's 1953 discovery of DNA to Venter's 2003 synthesis of the phi X174 genome.

To understand how the field of synthetic biology works now, it helps to use a practical example. Imagine a legitimate public health problem—say, how to detect arsenic in drinking water in areas where ground-water supplies have been contaminated. Now imagine that a solution might be to create harmless bacteria that could be deposited in a water sample and would start to glow brightly in the presence of arsenic. No such creature exists in nature, but there are indeed creatures that glow (fireflies and some fish). In some cases, these creatures glow only when they are mating or feel threatened, so there are biological on-off switches. There are other microorganisms that can sense the presence of arsenic. And there are countless types of bacteria that are harmless to humans and easy to work with in the lab.

To combine these elements in your lab, you need to install an appropriate software program on your laptop and search the databases of relevant companies to locate and purchase the proper DNA units that code for luminescence, on-off switches, and arsenic sensing. Then, you need to purchase a supply of some sort of harmless bacteria. At that point, you just have to put the DNA components in a sensible sequence, insert the resulting DNA code into the bacterial DNA, and test to see if the bacteria are healthy and capable of replicating themselves. To test the results, all you have to do is drop some arsenic in a bottle of water, add some of your man-made bacteria, and shake: if the water starts to glow, bingo. (This slightly oversimplified scenario is based on one that was actually carried out by a team from the University of Edinburgh in the International Genetically Engineered Machine contest in 2006.)

The most difficult part of the process now is putting the DNA components in a sensible sequence, but that is unlikely to be true for long. The world of biosynthesis is hooking up with 3-D printing, so scientists can now load nucleotides into a 3-D "bioprinter" that generates genomes. And they can collaborate across the globe, with scientists in one city designing a genetic sequence on a computer and sending the code to a printer somewhere else—anywhere else connected to the Internet. The code might be for the creation of a life-saving medicine or vaccine. Or it might be information that turns the tiny phi X174 virus that Venter worked on a decade ago into something that kills human cells, or makes nasty bacteria resistant to antibiotics, or creates some entirely new viral strain.

INFORMATION, PLEASE

What stymies the very few national security and law enforcement experts closely following this biological revolution is the realization that the key component is simply information. While virtually all current laws in this field, both local and global, restrict and track organisms of concern (such as, say, the Ebola virus), tracking information is all but impossible. Code can be buried anywhere—al Qaeda operatives have hidden attack instructions inside porn videos, and a seemingly innocent tweet could direct readers to an obscure Internet location containing genomic code ready to be downloaded to a 3-D printer. Suddenly, what started as a biology problem has become a matter of information security.

When the WHO convened its second dual-use summit, therefore, in February 2013, about a third of the scientists and government officials in attendance were from the United States, representing at least 15 different agencies as diverse as the FBI, the Centers for Disease Control and Prevention, the Department of Defense, and the Office of the U.S. Trade Representative. Although other countries brought strong contingents, the message from the Obama administration was clear: we are worried.

Each country party to the Biological Weapons Convention is required to designate one agency to be responsible for guaranteeing compliance with the treaty's provisions. For the United States, that agency is the FBI. So now, a tiny office of the FBI, made even smaller through recent congressional budget cuts and sequestration, engages the scientific community and tries to spot DURC. But the FBI has nothing like the scientific expertise that the biologists themselves have, and so in practice, it must rely on the researchers to police themselves—an obviously problematic situation.

Other countries have tried to grapple with the dual-use problem in other ways. Denmark, for example, has a licensing procedure for both public- and private-sector research. It requires researchers to register their intentions before executing experiments. The labs and personnel are screened for possible security concerns and issued licenses that state the terms of their allowable work. Some of the applications and licenses are classified, guaranteeing the private sector trade secrecy. Such an effort is possible there, however, only because the scale of biological research in the country is so small: fewer than 100 licenses are currently being monitored.

The Dutch government sought to control Fouchier's publication of how he modified the H5N1 virus through the implementation of its export-control laws, with the information in question being the commodity deemed too sensitive to export. Although the government lifted the ban after the first WHO summit, a district court later ruled that Fouchier's publication violated EU law. Fouchier is appealing the decision, which could have profound implications across Europe for the exchange of similar research. Among the lessons of the recent U.S. intelligence leaks, however, is that it may well be impossible to have airtight controls over the transmission of digital information if the parties involved are sufficiently determined and creative.

In line with their emerging engineering perspective, many biologists now refer to their genomics work as "bar-coding." Just as manufacturers put bar codes on products in the supermarket to reveal the product's identity and price when scanned, so biologists are racing to genetically sequence plants, animals, fish, birds, and microorganisms all over the world and taxonomically tag them with a DNA sequence that is unique to the species—its "bar code." It is possible to insert bar-code identifiers into synthesized or GOF-modified organisms, allowing law enforcement and public health officials to track and trace any use or accidental release of man-made or altered life forms. Such an approach has been used for genetically modified seeds and agricultural products, and there is no good reason not to mandate such labeling for potentially worrisome dual-use work. But bar-coding has to be incorporated by the original researchers, and it is not going to be implemented by those with malicious intentions. So there are no quick or easy technological fixes for the problem.

FROM WHO TO HAJ

The 2013 WHO summit failed to reach meaningful solutions to dual-use research problems. The financially strapped WHO couldn't find the resources to follow up on any of the recommendations produced by the summit. Worse, the attendees could not even manage to come up with a common framework for discussion of the issue. Poor nations felt it was an extremely low priority, with African representatives complaining that their countries didn't have the resources to implement biosafety guidelines. As one representative put it, speaking on the condition of anonymity, "We are the ones that actually suffer from all of these diseases. We are the ones that need this research. But we cannot do it. We do not have the facilities. We do not have the resources. And now, with all these DURC worries, our people cannot get into your laboratories to work by your side [in the United States or Europe] for security reasons. This whole DURC issue is simply holding us back, whether that is the intention or not."

Noticeably quiet at the three-day conference were the representatives from large developing countries such as Brazil, China, India, and South Africa. And when any of them did speak up, it was to emphasize their concerns about who would hold the patents on products made with dual-use research, to insist on the need for technology transfer, or to mouth platitudes about how their countries' researchers already operated under strict scrutiny. The Chinese delegates, in particular, were adamant: all necessary provisions to ensure biological safety, they assured the gathering, are in place in their country. Two months after the meeting, a team of scientists at China's National Avian Influenza Reference Laboratory at the Harbin Veterinary Research Institute used GOF techniques to manufacture 127 forms of the influenza virus, all based on H5N1, combined with genetic attributes found in dozens of other types of flu. The Chinese team had taken the work of Fouchier and Kawaoka and built on it many times over, adding some synthetic biological spins to the work. And five of their man-made superflu strains proved capable of spreading through the air between guinea pigs, killing them.

Less than a decade ago, the international virology community went into an uproar when U.S. scientists contemplated inserting a gene into stockpiled smallpox viruses that would have made solutions containing the virus turn green, for rapid identification purposes. What the U.S. researchers thought would be a smart way to track the deadly virus was deemed a "crime against humanity."

Earlier this year, in contrast, when a new type of bird flu called H7N9 emerged in China, virologists called for GOF research as a matter of public health urgency. When the virus was subjected to genetic scrutiny, both Fouchier and Kawaoka declared it dangerous, noting that the very genetic changes they had made to H5N1 were already present in the H7N9 strain. In August, Fouchier's group published the results of experiments that showed that the H7N9 virus could infect ferrets and spread through the air from one animal to another. And Fouchier, Kawaoka, and 20 other virologists called for an extensive series of GOF experiments on the H7N9 virus, allowing genetic modifications sufficient to turn the bird flu into a clear human-to-human transmissible pathogen so as to better prepare for countering it.

As health research authorities in the relevant countries mull the scientists' request to manipulate the H7N9 virus, other microbes offer up mysteries that might be resolved using GOF techniques. The Middle East respiratory syndrome, or MERS, appeared seemingly out of nowhere in June 2012 in Saudi Arabia, and by September 2013, it had infected 132 people, killing almost half of them. Although the virus is similar to SARS, much about the disease and its origins is unknown. There were numerous cases of apparent human-to-human transmission of MERS, especially within hospitals, and Saudi health officials worried about the possible spread of MERS throughout the Islamic world. There is no vaccine or cure for MERS. If work to determine the transmissibility of H7N9 is to be permitted, shouldn't researchers do something similar to see what it would take to transform MERS into a casually transmitted form, likely to spread, for example, among haj pilgrims?

When HIV emerged in the early 1980s, nobody was sure just how the virus was transmitted, and many health-care workers feared that they could contract the then 99 percent lethal disease through contact with their patients. Schools all over the United States banned HIV-positive children, and most sports leagues forbade infected athletes from playing (until the NBA star Magic Johnson bravely revealed that he was infected, turning the tide against such bans). Had it been technically possible to do so, would it have been wise to deliberately alter the virus then, giving it the capacity to spread through the air or through casual contact?

WHAT NOW?

Scientists and security experts will never come to a consensus about the risks of dual-use research in synthetic biology. After all, almost 35 years after smallpox was eradicated, debates still rage over whether to destroy the last remaining samples of the virus. The benefits of synthetic biological research are difficult to assess. Its proponents believe it will transform the world as much as the ongoing revolution in information technology has, but some others are skeptical. Moving aggressively to contain the possible downsides of dual-use research could hamper scientific development. If it were to get truly seized by the issue, the U.S. government, for example, could start to weave a vast bureaucratic web of regulation and surveillance far exceeding that established elsewhere, succeeding only in setting its own national scientific efforts back while driving cutting-edge research to move abroad. Unilateral action by any government is destined to fail.

What this means is that political leaders should not wait for clarity and perfect information, nor rush to develop restrictive controls, nor rely on scientific self-regulation. Instead, they should accept that the synthetic biology revolution is here to stay, monitor it closely, and try to take appropriate actions to contain some of its most obvious risks, such as the accidental leaking or deliberate release of dangerous organisms.

The first step in this regard should be to strengthen national and global capacities for epidemiological surveillance. In the United States, such surveillance has been weakened by budget cuts and bureaucratic overstretch at the federal, state, and local levels. The Centers for Disease Control and the U.S. Department of Agriculture represent the United States' first line of defense against microbial threats to human health, plants, and livestock, but both agencies have been cut to the bone. The Centers for Disease Control's budget has been cut by 25 percent since 2010, and it recently dropped by a further five percent thanks to sequestration, with the cuts including funding that supported 50,000 state, territorial, city, and county public health officers. It should be a no-brainer for Congress to restore that funding and other support for the nation's public health army.

At the same time, the Centers for Disease Control and the Department of Agriculture must become better at what they do. In the coming age of novel microbes, focusing attention on a small list of special pathogens and toxins, such as the Ebola virus, anthrax, and botulinum, offers a false sense of security. Even the recent suggestion that H5N1 be added to the National Select Agent Registry, which keeps track of potentially dangerous biological agents and toxins, seems beside the point: a simple, ubiquitous microbe such as *E. coli*, a bacterium that resides in the guts of every human being, can now be transformed into a killer germ capable of wreaking far more havoc than anything on that registry.

Solving the puzzle of just what to watch for now and how to spot it will require cooperative thinking across national and professional boundaries. Within the United States, leaders of organizations such as the Centers for Disease Control, the FBI, the Department of Health and Human Services, the Department of Defense, and the intelligence agencies will need to collaborate and pool their information and expertise. And internationally, multilateral groups such as the WHO and its food and agriculture counterparts will need to work with agencies and institutions such as Interpol, the Association of Southeast Asian Nations, the Pan American Health Organization, and the African Union.

The Biological Weapons Convention process can serve as a multilateral basis for DURC-related dialogue. It offers a neutral platform accessible to nearly every government in the world. But that process is weak at present, unable to provide verification akin to that ensured by its nuclear and chemical weapons counterparts.

Given their own problems, in fact, international institutions are currently ill equipped to handle the dual-use research issue. Grappling with severe budget constraints for the third year in a row, the WHO, for example, has shrunk in size and influence, and its epidemiological identification-and-response capacity has been particularly devastated.

It is in the United States' own interests, as well as those of other countries, to have a thriving global epidemiological response capability housed within the WHO, acting under the provisions of the International Health Regulations. U.S. disease sleuths may not be welcome everywhere in the world, but WHO representatives, at least in principle, are allowed inside nearly every country. Congress should therefore appropriate $100 million a year for five years for direct support of the WHO's epidemiological surveillance-and-response system. To make sure U.S. underwriting doesn't become a meaningless crutch, Washington could make it clear to the WHO's World Health Assembly that some of that American support should be directed toward building indigenous epidemiological surveillance capabilities in developing countries, in order to bring them into compliance with the International Health Regulations. If U.S. legislators feared that such support for the WHO would morph into a multiyear entitlement program, they could have Washington's financing commitment start in 2014 and gradually decrease to zero by 2019, as other donor countries added their own assistance and recipient countries reached sustainable self-reliance. Congress should also continue the U.S. Agency for International Development's PREDICT Project, which is tasked with identifying new disease threats and to date has trained 1,500 people worldwide and discovered 200 previously unknown viruses.

Any global surveillance effort will require harmonized standards. At present, however, there are no agreed-on biosafety laboratory standards or definitions of various aspects of biosecurity, GOF research, or even DURC. So key U.S. agencies need to work closely with their foreign counterparts to hash out such standards and definitions and promulgate them. A model for emulation here might be the Codex Alimentarius, established by the UN Food and Agriculture Organization and the WHO in 1963 to standardize all food-safety guidelines worldwide.

In an era when e-mailed gene sequences have rendered test-tube transport obsolete, the proper boundaries of export and its control are increasingly difficult to define. At the core of the dual-use research problem is information, rather than microbes, and overregulating the flow of information risks stifling science and crippling international collaborative research. To deal with this problem, the U.S. Department of Commerce, the U.S. Department of Agriculture's Animal and Plant Health Inspection Service, and the Office of the U.S. Trade Representative must create a regulatory framework appropriate to dual-use research. Here, a model for regulation might draw from the experiences of the International Plant Protection Convention and the Animal and Plant Health Inspection Service's engagement through the U.S. Trade Representative's Office of Services and Investment. For Internet traffic in genomes, many nucleotide distribution centers already monitor "sequences of concern," demanding special information on individuals seeking pathogen-related genetic details. This approach should be embraced by governments.

So what should governments and institutions be on the lookout for? Evidence of the covert deliberate alteration of a life form that turns a creature into a more dangerous entity. If governments permitted or supported such research, they would be accused of violating the Biological Weapons Convention. The United States is by far the largest funder of basic science and the world's powerhouse of biological research, and so it would be at the greatest risk of being the target of such accusations. But sunlight is a good disinfectant, and it is legitimate to ask for any such research to be explained and defended openly. The State Department, in concert with the Department of Health and Human Services' Office of Global Affairs, should develop briefing materials for diplomatic personnel, explaining synthetic biology, GOF work, and DURC and thus balancing the United States' image as the foremost center of biomedical research against concerns about the creation of man-made pathogens. The State Department should promote cooperation on detecting and controlling DURC and on managing the shared global risk of the inappropriate release of synthetic pathogens; it should also support assistance programs aimed at hardening the safety of labs and monitoring them worldwide.

The tracking of novel DNA and life forms should be implemented on a voluntary or mandatory basis immediately. Private biotechnology companies and distributors of DNA components should assign biosecurity tags to all their man-made products. The trade in genomic sequences should be transparent and traceable, featuring nucleotide tags that can be monitored. The genomic industry should self-finance the necessary monitoring and enforcement of standards of practice and permit unrestricted government inspections in the event of breakdowns in biosafety or lab security.

Last year, Friends of the Earth, the International Center for Technology Assessment, and the ETC Group jointly issued a report called *The Principles for the Oversight of Synthetic Biology*, which called for the insertion of suicide genes in man-made and GOF-altered organisms—sequences that can be activated through simple changes in the organisms' environs, terminating their function. Although such suicide signals may be technically difficult to implement at this time, dual-use research should strive to include this feature. The three organizations have also called on industry to carry damage and liability insurance covering all synthetic biological research and products, a seemingly obvious and wise precaution. The BioBricks Foundation, meanwhile, is the loudest proponent of synthetic biology today, proclaiming its mission as being "to ensure that the engineering of biology is conducted in an open and ethical manner to benefit all people and the planet. . . . We envision synthetic biology as a force for good in the world." Such ethics-based scientific organizations can drive awareness of the field and its problems and increase sensitivity among researchers to legitimate public concerns, and so their activities should be encouraged and expanded.

The controversies and concerns surrounding dual-use research in synthetic biology have arisen in less than four years, starting from the moment in 2010 when Venter announced his team's creation of a new life form described as "the first self-replicating species on the planet whose parent is a computer." Before Venter's group raced down such a godlike path, it went to the Obama White House, briefing officials on a range of policy and ethical issues the project raised. For a while, the administration considered classifying the effort, worrying that it might spawn grave dangers. Instead, much to Venter's delight, the White House opted for full transparency and publication. "Perhaps it's a giant philosophical change in how we view life," Venter said with a shrug at a Washington press conference. He wasn't sure. But he did feel confident that what he called "a very powerful set of tools" would lead to flu vaccines manufactured overnight, possibly a vaccine for the AIDS virus, and maybe microbes that consume carbon dioxide and emit a safe energy alternative to fossil fuels. Now that synthetic biology is here to stay, the challenge is how to ensure that future generations see its emergence as more boon than bane.🌐

Google's Original X-Man

A Conversation With Sebastian Thrun

S ebastian Thrun is one of the world's leading experts on robotics and artificial intelligence. Born in Solingen, Germany, in 1967, he received his undergraduate education at the University of Hildesheim and his graduate education at the University of Bonn. He joined the computer science department at Carnegie Mellon University in 1995 and moved to Stanford University in 2003. Thrun led the team that won the 2005 DARPA Grand Challenge, a driverless car competition sponsored by the U.S. Defense Department, and in 2007, he joined the staff of Google, eventually becoming the first head of Google X, the company's secretive big-think research lab. He co-founded the online-education start-up Udacity in 2012. In late August, he spoke to *Foreign Affairs* editor Gideon Rose in the Udacity offices.

How and why did you first get into science and technology?
As a child, I spent a lot of time with things like Lego, building trains, cars, complex structures, and I really liked that. When I was about 11, I got a TI-57 programmable calculator. This let you write programs of up to 50 steps, which would be erased when you switched it off. I got very enthusiastic about seeing just what you could do with that. Could you program a game, could you program complex geometry, could you solve financial equations? (The answer for all of those is yes.) I had a little booklet in which I kept my 50-step programs, of which I was very proud. A few years later, I

got a NorthStar Horizon computer, which I used to program my own video games, which was extremely fun.

As a college student, what really interested me was the human brain and human intelligence. I dabbled in philosophy and medicine and psychology and eventually found that the most constructive way to approach those problems was through computer science and artificial intelligence: you could actually build something from the ground up that would then manifest intelligence, even if only a little bit of it, and that fascinated me.

Why robotics?

I ultimately got into robotics because for me, it was the best way to study intelligence. When you program a robot to be intelligent, you learn a number of things. You become very humble and develop enormous respect for natural intelligence, because even if you work day and night for several years, your robot isn't that smart after all. But since every element of its behavior is something that you created, you can actually understand it.

I started out in 1994 programming a robot called RHINO that we shipped to the United States to a big robotic competition. The goal was to build a robot that could clean up a kitchen. It wasn't a real kitchen; it was sort of a researchers' version, where all the objects that had to be picked up were clearly marked. But it represented the state of the art at the time. We came home with second prize, which was wonderful because we were the only non-U.S. team in that competition.

Then, we came up with this idea of building robotic tour guides for museums. In 1997, we got a chance to install one in the Deutsches Museum in Bonn, and the following year, we got our big chance at the Smithsonian's National Museum of American History, where we had a two-week exhibition at which you would be greeted by a robotic tour guide. We built the tour guide, a robot we named Minvera, from scratch. It was completely autonomous; it made all its own decisions. It was programmed to find visitors and interact with them, directing them to and explaining specific exhibits that we had pre-chosen. It had a face, it could smile, it could frown, and it was great fun.

One of my favorite moments was actually when the robot was switched off in the middle of the night, and we were sitting in a corner programming. A human tour guide came by, and not realizing I was watching, she looked the robot up and down and said to it, "You are not going to replace me."

My next big project, after I had moved to Carnegie Mellon University, was Nursebot. I started a number of interdisciplinary courses with the University of Pittsburgh and became an adjunct professor of nursing there, and we built robots for elderly care. Then, we built a robotic system for mapping abandoned mines. Around Pittsburgh, there are an enormous number of abandoned coal mines. There are mine fires that have been going for decades. And many of these mines lack active maps—where the mines were done illegally or where the maps got lost over the decades. So we decided to look into what it would take to make robots that could explore abandoned mines. In this period, I also did a lot on autonomous helicopters and helicopter mapping. But eventually, I decided to move from Carnegie Mellon to Stanford.

How did you get involved with driverless cars?
In 2004, my CMU colleague Red Whittaker engaged in an epic race called the DARPA Grand Challenge. The U.S. government had put up a million bucks as prize money for whoever could build a car that could drive itself. The original mission was to go from Los Angeles to Las Vegas, but that was quickly found not to be safe, so the race moved to going from Barstow, California, to Primm, Nevada, along a 140-mile premarked desert route. In the first race, which I did not participate in, Red had the best-performing team, but his robot went less than eight miles. DARPA scheduled a second race for the following year, and having come freshly to Stanford and having nothing to do because it was a new job, I decided, why not give it a try?

So we put together a team to build a robot car, Stanley, that could drive by itself in desert terrain. We started with a class of about 20 students. Some of them stayed on, some of them went as far away as they could when they realized what a consuming experience it is to build a robot of that proportion. And over the next several months, I spent most of my time in the Mojave Desert, behind the steering wheel, writing computer code on my laptop together with my graduate students.

What was the result?

Well, we were lucky. Five teams finished that year, and in my book, they all won equally. But we happened to be the fastest by 11 minutes, so we got the $2 million check. [DARPA had doubled the prize for the second race.]

Had you expected to actually complete the race?

I always love to be careful with my expectations, so that life has pleasant surprises for me. But I was very proud—not just proud of myself but proud of the community. There were about a thousand people from various countries and various grad schools and companies that jointly tried to solve this problem, and I think we achieved something big that day together.

Why did your project end up working so well?

Many of the people who participated in the race had a strong hardware focus, so a lot of teams ended up building their own robots. Our calculus was that this was not about the strength of the robot or the design of the chassis. Humans could drive those trails perfectly; it was not complicated off-road terrain. It was really just desert trails. So we decided it was purely a matter of artificial intelligence. All we had to do was put a computer inside the car, give it the appropriate eyes and ears, and make it smart.

In trying to make it smart, we found that driving is really governed not by two or three rules but by tens of thousands of rules. There are so many different contingencies. We had a day when birds were sitting on the road and flew up as our vehicle approached.

And we learned that to a robot eye, a bird looks exactly the same as a rock. So we had to make the machine smart enough to distinguish birds from rocks.

In the end, we started relying on what we call machine learning, or big data. That is, instead of trying to program all these rules by hand, we taught our robot the same way we would teach a human driver. We would go into the desert, and I would drive, and the robot would watch me and try to emulate the behaviors involved. Or we would let the robot drive, and it would make a mistake, and we would go back to the data and explain to the robot why this was a mistake and give the robot a chance to adjust.

So you developed a robot that could learn?

Yes. Our robot was learning. It was learning before the race, and it was learning in the race.

Was this connected to the probabilistic learning that you had worked on?

Yes. That's the core of what was this was all about.

How would you describe that to a layman?

When you raise a child, you don't sit down and take all the rules of life, write them into a big catalog, and start reading the child all these individual rules from A to Z. When we raise a child, a lot of what we do is let the child experiment and guide the experimentation. The child basically has to process his own data and learn from experience.

We did exactly the same thing with the robot. We said, "Look, we could write down all the rules, but there are so many of them, it would take us so long. It'll be much better if we just let the robot grow up like a child." And when the robot made a mistake, we sat there as the parents, observed the mistake, and said, "This was a mistake; don't do it again." And the robot would then reason about what things to do differently to avoid making the same mistake in the future.

It was at that event that you met Larry Page?

Yes. Larry had a long-standing interest in many things and chose to come to the DARPA Grand Challenges. He came unnoticed, wearing sunglasses, but we hooked up during the morning. In most races that I've participated in, during the race you sweat a lot. In this race, there was nothing to do. We were just sitting on the sidelines and letting our creations compete on our behalf. So we started talking about robotics.

In the middle of the race, there was a point where I was absolutely certain that our car had failed. I'd been watching the progress of the little dot on the map very carefully, and our robot hadn't moved in six minutes. I knew the robot was never programmed to stop, so the fact that it had stopped had to mean that it was broken. It turned out, in hindsight, that the car had been paused by the organizers to give more space to another car that was ahead of us. The time didn't count against us, and the robot was perfectly fine. But for a moment, I was conceding defeat and trying to explain [to Larry] why we lost.

Did this lead to a connection with Google?

The connection with Google came a little later. Larry and I remained friends. There was another race two years later called the DARPA Urban Challenge, in which we came in second, after a team from Carnegie Mellon. Then, I got involved in Google Street View. I had a brilliant master's student who effectively built a small version of Street View. And when I showed it to Larry, it became clear that the scope of photographing the world was beyond what a single master's student at Stanford could accomplish, so we decided to join forces. The decision entailed my taking a sabbatical and joining Google as a full-time manager, and four of my students switched over, too.

Why driverless cars?

It's a no-brainer. If you look at the twentieth century, the car has transformed society more than pretty much any other invention. But cars today are vastly unsafe. It's estimated that more than a million people die every year because of traffic accidents. And driving cars consumes immense amounts of time. For the average American worker, it's about 52 minutes a day. And they tie up resources. Most cars are parked at any point in time; my estimate is that I use my car about three percent of the time.

But if the car could drive itself, you could be much safer, and you could achieve something during your commute. You can also envision a futuristic society in which we share cars much better. Cars could come to you when you need them; you wouldn't have to have private car ownership, which means no need for a garage, no need for a driveway, no need for your workplace to have as many parking spots.

Like Zipcars on a grand scale?

Yes, think car sharing on a grand scale. One of the difficulties in car sharing today is that you have to pick up the car being shared. If the car came to you, it'd be much, much easier.

Is this personal for you?

Absolutely. When I was 18, my best friend lost his life when his friend made a split-second poor decision to speed on ice and lost control of the vehicle and crashed into a truck. And one morning, when I myself was working on driverless cars, when we were expecting a government delegation to be briefed on my progress, my head administrator at Stanford went out to get breakfast for us and never came back. She was hit by a speeding car at a traffic light, and she went into a coma, never to wake up. This is extremely personal for me.

These moments make clear to me that while the car is a beautiful invention of society, there's so much space for improvement. It's really hard to find meaning in the loss of a life in a traffic accident, but I carry this with me every day. I feel that any single life saved in traffic is worth my work.

We are now at a point where the car drives about 50,000 miles between what I would call critical incidents, moments when a human driver has to take over, otherwise something bad might happen. At this point, most of us believe the car drives better than the best human drivers. It keeps the lane better, it keeps the systems better, it drives more smoothly, it drives more defensively. My wife tells me, "When you are in the self-driving car, can you please let the car take over?"

Another big project at Google X, where you were working on the driverless car, was Google Glass. How did that come about, and how does it relate to the lab's other projects?
One of the things that has excited me in working at Google and with Google leadership is thinking about big, audacious problems. We often call them "moonshot" problems.

The self-driving car was a first instance of this, where we set ourselves a target that we believed could not be met. When the project started, we decided to carve out a thousand miles of specific streets in California that were really hard for humans to drive, including Lombard Street in San Francisco and Highway 1, the coastal route from San Francisco to Los Angeles. Even I believed this was hard to do.

So we set this audacious goal, and it took less than two years to achieve it. And what it took to get there was a committed team of the world's best people basically left alone to do whatever it took to reach the goal.

I wanted to test that recipe in other areas. So Google entrusted me with the founding of a new group called Google X. (The "X" was originally a placeholder until a correct name could be found.) We looked at a number of other audacious projects, and one of them was, can we bring computation closer to our own perception?

We hired an ingenious professor from the University of Washington, Babak Parviz, who became the project leader. And under his leadership, we developed early prototypes of Google Glass and shaped up the concept into something that people know today— that is, a very lightweight computer that is equipped with a camera, display, trackpad, speaker, Bluetooth, WiFi, a head-tracking unit.

It's a full computer, not dissimilar to the PCs I was playing with when I was a teenager, but it weighs only 45 grams.

How did you get from there into online education?

I went into education because I learned from my friends at Google how important it is to aim high. Ever since I started working at Google, I have felt I should spend my time on things that really matter when they are successful. I believe online education can make a difference in the world, more so than almost anything else I've done in my life.

Access to high-quality education is way too limited. The United States has the world's most admirable higher education system, and yet it is very restrictive. It's so hard to get into. I never got into it as a student. There are also fascinating opportunities that exist today that did not exist even 20 years ago.

The conventional paradigm in education is based on synchronicity. We know for a fact that students learn best if they're paired one-on-one with a mentor, a tutor. Unfortunately, we can't afford a tutor for every student. Therefore, we put students into groups. And in these groups, we force students, by and large, to progress at the same speed. Progression at the same speed can cause some students—like me, when I was young—to feel a bit underwhelmed. But it can also cause a lot of students to drop out.

A lot of students, when they aren't quite up to the speed that's been given to them, get a grade like a C. But instead of giving them more time to get to the mastery it would take to get an A, they get put into the next cohort, where they start with a disadvantage, with low self-esteem. And they often end up at that level for the rest of their student career.

Salman Khan, whom I admire, has made this point very clearly by showing that he can bring C-level math students to an A+ level if he lets them go at their own pace. So what digital media allow us to do is to invent a medium where students can learn at their own pace, and that is a very powerful idea. When you go at your own pace, we can move instruction toward exploration and play-based learning.

When I enter a video game, I learn something about a fictitious world. And in that video game, I'm allowed to go at my own pace. I'm constantly assessed—assessment becomes my friend. I feel good when I master the next level. If you could only take that experience of a video game back into student learning, we could make learning addictive. My deep, deep desire is to find a magic formula for learning in the online age that would make it as addictive as playing video games.

So the "gamification" of education is a good thing?

I'm hesitant to say that gamification is a good thing, because it comes with many superficial things. And I don't wish to replace a master's degree in physics with mastery in Angry Birds. That's obviously not good enough. But on the other hand, when you play Angry Birds, there is no lecture, there are no office hours, there is no final exam. You get in, and many of us get addicted. So you could take the addiction and excitement and personalization of Angry Birds back into mainstream learning and marry the best of both worlds—go after very deep academic topics but do it with playfulness, with student choice, with student empowerment, and with active exploration. Then, I think we can change everything.

I've read that you feel the high points of your life are when you feel stupid, because you're confronted with something that you don't understand and you have an opportunity to learn. Is that true?

Yes. It's true that for me the biggest moments are when I have a new insight. And one of the reasons why I love to venture into new territories is because I don't know what the solution is, so it affords me a chance to explore and to learn something new. With the desire to learn comes the acknowledgement that I don't know, otherwise no learning would take place. And in the presence of ignorance, it follows logically that I will make poor choices, make mistakes that in hindsight could have been easily avoided. Those are called failures. So failures are an essential component of the process of innovation. If there are no failures, I'm not really innovating.

Therefore, failures make me very proud. I'm actually happy to fail, because it gives me a chance to learn and iterate and avoid the same mistake in the future. I honestly believe that if we were to embrace failure as much as success, and celebrate failure as much as success, then we could shed the fear of failure. And if you shed the fear of failure, then you'd be much more able to make the right choices.

Is what you're doing with your educational transformation, trying to create a system that will inculcate that kind of attitude?

I would hope so. We have a very strong emphasis on experiential learning, in which the student is asked to solve a problem. We don't give them the solution in advance; we only give them the solution after the student has had a chance to solve it first. The reason we do this is that we believe the mind grows much faster by trying to find a solution itself. And the mind is open for input after having tried it.

Now, I have to admit that we have students that don't like this. They say, "I'm used to the teacher telling me the solution, and then I just learn that solution and practice it." And a number of students have left Udacity for that reason, because it feels kind of stressful to be asked a question without knowing the answer.

But the students that are actively engaged have all shown enormous growth in their ability to solve problems. And the growth doesn't come from listening to a famous professor. It comes almost exclusively from working on actual problems. The role of the professor then becomes to curate those challenges and make them gradually more difficult, so you can unfold the student's full potential.

Your wife is a professor of comparative literature. Does this kind of approach work as well for the humanities as it does for the sciences?

I would argue that the humanities people have been a step ahead of most of the engineering professors in that they already employ what's called the "flipped classroom" model, in which the students read the literature at home and come to class to discuss it. That's different from what most engineering classes look like, where the professor tends to lecture. In both cases, I would argue, the students are forced to learn at the same pace at the same time. The magic of the online world will be that we can give people their own paths and their own pace and thereby really change everything.

Are you using the concepts and tools of artificial intelligence to develop this kind of personalized tutorial approach?

More and more so. One of the great advantages of teaching online is that we have enormous amounts of data about student behavior. And just as we were able to teach Stanley to maximize its chances to navigate a desert floor, we are using data to maximize the chances of educating a student. That might sound a little uninspirational, but to me, it's an amazing way to turn education into a truly data-driven science.

Your projects are extraordinarily radical. Is that what attracts you to them?

I aspire to work on subjects where a number of things have to be the case. One is they have to really change the world if they succeed. I need to be able to tell myself a story that, no matter how slim the chances of success, if it succeeds, it is going to massively change society for the better. I think that's the case for safety in driving and transportation. It's the case for bringing the Internet to everybody. And it's the case for education.

I love to work on problems that are hard, because I love to learn. And all these problems have their own dimension of hardness. Some of them are more technological, some are more societal. When these things come together, I get very excited.

What drives or generates innovation? What creates a Sebastian Thrun?

I feel like I'm overrated. Most of what I do is just listen carefully to people. But truly great innovators, like Larry Page and Sergey Brin, or Elon Musk, or Mir Imran, bring to bear really great visions of where society should be, often fearless visions. And then just a good chunk of logical thinking—as Elon Musk puts it, "thinking by first principles." Not thinking by analogy, whereby we end up confining our thought to what's the case today, but thinking about what should be the case, and how we should get there, and whether it is feasible to do it.

Once you have the vision and the clear thought together, what's missing is just really good execution. And execution to me is all about the way you would climb a mountain you've never climbed before. If you waver along the way, if you debate, if you become uncertain about the objective, then you're not going to make it. It's important that you keep climbing. And it's important that you acknowledge that you don't have all the answers. So you will make mistakes, and you will have to back up, learn, and improve. That is a normal component of the innovative process. But you should not change your goal.

Are there drivers of innovation at the societal and national level? You've said that you moved from Germany to the United States because the more open, less hierarchical system here was one in which you felt more able to thrive.

Yes. I think there's a genuine innovative element in America that you find in almost no other culture. And I believe it goes back to the founding of this wonderful country, where the people who came over had to be innovative to make their own rules and clear the land and build society up from scratch. And I think that gene, that genuinely American gene that is behind the American dream, remains here today, more than in any other place I know of. And it's a wonderful thing, it makes me very happy to be part of such an amazing group of smart and driven entrepreneurs in Silicon Valley.

Does the government have a role to play in fostering innovation?

I'm hesitant to give governments a strong role. And the reason is the pace at which innovation happens in Silicon Valley is so much faster than the pace at which government intervention can keep track. And there's always a danger in all our legislative and regulatory efforts of overspecifying a status quo when the world has moved on.

What about funding for basic public goods of innovation? Aside from Google, isn't private-sector R & D diminishing rather than expanding?

I would love to see more companies push basic innovation. For one thing, it's their responsibility, but even more so, any company that wishes to survive over the next 30 years needs to focus on basic innovation. Google has been criticized for investing in issues such as self-driving cars or mobile technologies such as Android. But I believe it's a big gamble that will pay out in the long term as the needs of society change. So if there's any point in the history of this country when basic research and basic innovation should really be funded, it's today, when societies are moving at a faster pace than ever before.

As robots get more autonomous, are we going to get to a point where we enter Isaac Asimov territory, where we need his "three laws of robotics" or something similar?

We have already created life forms that can't be extinct and that will be with us for a long time to come—they're called viruses and computer worms. But I am a strong believer that at the end of the day, the technologies that we build, we also tame. In many dimensions of human skills, technology has long taken over. Your pocket calculator can calculate numbers better than most people. Computers can play chess better. Soon, computers will be able to drive better. Does this mean that robotic cars or self-driving cars are taking over the world? No. We will use them to make our lives better and make ourselves more effective.

Are we going to see emerging consciousness in robots or computers in the next generation or two?

There's emerging consciousness in my spell checker, which tells me what word is spelled wrong. There's emerging consciousness in my fuel-injection car. My elevator is conscious because it knows what floor to go to. These are not consciousness on the level of human consciousness. But I believe we have reached a level where the line between human intelligence and machine intelligence is clearly blurred. In some cases, the intelligence or ability of machines is superior. Wikipedia knows more about the world than I do. I don't see a danger of machines becoming hostile in that context. People can be hostile and can use technology against other people. But I think machines will continue to be subordinate to humans, and that makes me happy.

There are people who feel that the prospects of life are diminishing and that the next generation is not going to have a better life than the previous one. Do you think your child's life will be more interesting and exciting and filled with larger prospects than yours?

If you look at history, the fear that the next generation would be worse off than the previous one has been around for many centuries. It's not a new fear. And it's often due to the lack of imagination of people in understanding how innovation is moving forward. But if you graph progress and quality of life over time, and you zoom out a little and look at the centuries, it's gotten better and better and better and better.

Our ability to be at peace with each other has grown. Our ability to have cultural interchanges has improved. We have more global languages, we have faster travel, we have better communication, we have better health. I think these trends will be sustained going forward, absolutely no question. If you look at the type of things that are happening right now in leading research labs, I see so many great new technologies coming out in the next ten to 20 years. It ought to be great.

So you disagree with the notion that innovation is dead, or that we're in a great stagnation, or a period of decline?
I think anybody who believes that we are in a period of decline or stagnation probably hasn't been paying attention. If you look at the way society has transformed itself in the last 20 years, it's more fundamental than the 50 years before and maybe even bigger than the 200 years before.

I'll give an example. With the advent of digital information, the recording, storage, and dissemination of information has become practically free. The previous time there was such a significant change in the cost structure for the dissemination of information was when the book became popular. Printing was invented in the fifteenth century, became popular a few centuries later, and had a huge impact in that we were able to move cultural knowledge from the human brain into a printed form. We have the same sort of revolution happening right now, on steroids, and it is affecting every dimension of human life.

A century or two ago, you had innovations such as steam, electricity, railroads, the internal combustion engine, the telegraph and telephone and radio. Those things had ramifications that fundamentally changed the structure of society, the structure of political organization. Is the information technology revolution going to have that kind of impact?
I think the impact will be greater. I don't want to belittle any innovation. I think the steam engine, the car, television, all the examples you mentioned are landmarks of history. But if you zoom out a little bit, most of these inventions come from the last 150 to 200 years. Very few are a thousand years old or older, and given that humanity is much older than that, you could say that almost all

inventions are recent. I believe the full potential of the Internet has not been realized yet, and we're not very used to it. But a hundred years from now, we will conclude this was one of the biggest revolutions ever.

I believe we live in an age where most interesting inventions have not been made, where there are enormous opportunities to move society forward. I'm excited to live right now. But I would rather live 20 years from now or 50 years from now than live today. It's going to be better and better. ✪

Making Sense of Mali

The Real Stakes of the War Rocking West Africa

Susanna Wing

T he last few months have shaken Mali to its core. In March 2012, the country's 20-year relationship with democracy ended abruptly after a group of low-ranking military officers overthrew the government. Within weeks of the coup, the National Movement for the Liberation of Azawad (MNLA), a Tuareg separatist group, seized several cities in northern Mali. Adding to the chaos, just weeks after that, fundamentalist Islamist groups, such as Ansar Dine, al Qaeda in the Islamic Maghreb (AQIM), and the Movement for Unity and Jihad in West Africa (MUJAO), overran those same cities.

Regional mediators attempted to help resolve the conflict, but their efforts yielded no tangible results. By late 2012, West African leaders had agreed to send 3,000 soldiers to halt the insurgents' advance, but the soldiers' arrival lagged. Earlier this month, the jihadist groups marched into the town of Konna. They seemed primed to make the short hop to Sevaré, which is home to a Malian military base and airstrip, and then onward to Bamako, Mali's capital.

But on January 11, France, impatient for the African-led intervention, responded to Bamako's pleas for help with air strikes and, soon after, with ground troops. The war, which already involves local, regional, and international troops, is not likely to end soon.

SUSANNA WING is an associate professor of political science at Haverford College and the author of *Constructing Democracy in Africa: Mali in Transition*.

As Bamako struggles to regain control of the northern part of the country and maintain stability in the south, observers have explained the conflict and the intervention with crude simplifications that do not reflect the reality on the ground and which point to incorrect solutions to the country's problems.

For starters, the conflict in the North is often reduced to two actors: Tuareg separatists and radical Islamists. For example, in an op-ed in *The New York Times* called "Nationalists or Islamists?," the Wesleyan Professor Peter Rutland argued that the core of the conflict is the "nationalist secession movement of the Tuareg people," as opposed to the actions of militant Islamists that have caught the world's attention. He refers in passing to the other ethnic groups as "the Africans who inhabit southern Mali."

In fact, the Tuareg are a minority population in northern Mali; Fulani, Songhai, Bambara, and other groups have also historically occupied much of the area. Some individuals from these groups have fled the region in the wake of the fighting, and others have joined insurgent forces. In addition, the Tuareg are not a unified bloc. Some of them have also fled the region, others have joined Ansar Dine, others the MNLA, and still others have stayed but joined neither. Finally, although over 90 percent of Malians and a vast majority of Tuareg practice Islam, most Malians agree with celebrated Malian religious leaders such as Chérif Ousmane Madani Haidara, the moderate Sufi preacher and Vice President of the High Islamic Council of Mali, and refuse to be governed by sharia law. Wahhabism has been on the rise, but the population has long practiced a more moderate form of Islam.

Simplifications of the ethnic, religious, and political dynamics of this crisis will not help to resolve the complex issues that are at its root. Thanks to 20 years of (admittedly shaky) democracy, most Malians treasure political participation as a key component of citizenship. What they want now is not less democracy—precisely what, to their minds, the Islamists and separatists would bring— but broader participation and greater freedom. In an op-ed in *The New York Times*, Oumou Sall Seck, mayor of Goundam in northern

Mali, shared a common view among Malians when she wrote that "Lawless and godless men—who hide behind Shariah and demands for Tuareg independence—are now beating and raping women and conscripting children to fight their 'holy' war." It is no surprise that a majority want to live in a secular Mali with its current borders intact and, preferably, a legitimately elected president.

Similarly, reports have erroneously implied that France's intervention is nothing more than neocolonial adventurism. May Ying Welsh, a correspondent for Al Jazeera English, argued on *Democracy Now* that France's campaign was driven by its resource interests in the region. Meanwhile, the archbishop of Accra wondered if the intervention was not another "colonisation attempt."

To be sure, the weakness of the Malian state is tied, in part, to the legacy of French colonialism. And critics are not wrong to point out that France has important strategic and economic interests in the region. (France's nuclear power plants feed off the uranium mines in nearby Niger.) But the idea that these factors drove France's intervention is incorrect.

In reality, the Malian army could not withstand the advances of Tuareg separatists last March and had no chance of holding off an offensive by the jihadists. Particularly after the fall of Konna, the Malian government was in real need of help. The troops that ECOWAS (the Economic Community of West African States) promised to send were simply too slow to materialize, so France stepped in.

On the street, Malians are generally supportive of international assistance. According to accounts from the field, the majority of Malians support France's intervention. For now at least, people are waving the French flag in the streets of Bamako (merchants claim that the flags are in short supply) and some Malian mothers are even naming their newborns "Hollande."

Of course, France's welcome will wear thin as the conflict drags on. And not everyone is happy with the French presence: the crisis in Algeria, in which an offshoot of AQIM took dozens of workers at a gas facility hostage, is one indication of that. But, as Bamako and Paris have stated, the uproar in Algeria is only further evidence that the insurgency in Mali reflects a problem that reaches far beyond Mali's borders and must therefore be addressed at the international level.

So what is next? Since Mali is landlocked and not a single neighboring country supports AQIM's or MUJAO's presence in the region, it is feasible that Mali's borders could be sealed to halt or significantly reduce the flow of supplies to the rebels. The outpouring of Malian support for France and the desire to rebuild a democratic, secular state across the country are also positive indications.

But this conflict will not be resolved quickly—Tuareg grievances are long-standing, and jihadists will not easily give up their fight. Even when fighting subsides, moreover, it will be a tall order for Mali to establish a stable and legitimate government. The government needs to follow through on its promise of decentralization—and the entire country including the north, is starved for economic development. The last year has destroyed many of the advances that NGOs and the government had managed to achieve in northern Mali, such as the construction of new schools and health and community centers. Unless Malian officials uphold their promises and support local governance and development, it is unlikely that peace and democracy will return.⊛

Saving the Euro, Dividing the Union

Could Europe's Deeper Integration Push the United Kingdom Out?

R. Daniel Kelemen

In an article I wrote last May, I argued that Europe's future would be defined by a "new normal." The road to economic recovery would be long and painful, but thanks to aggressive intervention by the European Central Bank and the new continent-wide governance structures being put in place, the eurozone's collapse was no longer a serious risk. The credit ratings agencies now seem to agree. The year 2012 ended with Standard & Poor's upgrading its assessment of Greek sovereign debt. Last week, Fitch declared that the odds of a eurozone breakup are now "very unlikely." Although record unemployment persists in the periphery of the common currency area and growth prospects have dimmed for Germany and other core countries, there is a growing consensus that the worst may be over.

Instead of unraveling, as so many skeptics had predicted, European countries responded to the economic crisis by taking significant steps toward deepening their integration. The continent's leaders granted EU institutions greater control over the fiscal

R. DANIEL KELEMEN is Professor of Political Science and Director of the Center for European Studies at Rutgers University. He is the author of *Eurolegalism: The Transformation of Law and Regulation in the European Union.*

policy of member states, ratified a fiscal compact, and reached an agreement on the outlines of a banking union. European Central Bank President Mario Draghi emphasized the bank's commitment to do "whatever it takes" to save the common currency.

But this incremental deepening of European integration may come at a cost: Not all 27 member states want to be part of a closer union—least of all the United Kingdom. Talk of a "Grexit" from the euro has been replaced by talk of "Brexit"—a British exit—from the European Union itself. Euro-skepticism in the United Kingdom has reached historic heights. The U.K. Independence Party, which is committed to London's leaving the EU, has overtaken the Liberal Democrats as the third most popular party. Recent polls suggest that a majority of British residents favor an exit. British Prime Minister David Cameron, facing enormous pressure from Euro-skeptic backbenchers in his own party, will soon deliver a major speech on the United Kingdom's relationship with the EU. He is likely to call for the repatriation of powers from the EU in areas such as social policy, employment, and justice, and promise a national referendum on a "new deal" with Europe. Meanwhile, many leaders on the continent are tiring of Cameron's anti-European rhetoric and his demands for special treatment and opt-outs.

As the EU takes steps to strengthen its economic and political union, it is likely to drive a deeper wedge between core eurozone states and member states outside of the common currency that are unwilling to go along. Officials in Brussels have suggested that tensions caused by tighter coordination in the common currency area can be addressed by developing new forms of what is known as two-speed or multi-speed integration, whereby core groups of countries move ahead with deeper union on certain policies, while others opt out. Although this flexible approach has worked in the past, including for the establishment of the eurozone itself, there are reasons to believe it may be less tenable today as the EU moves toward an unprecedentedly close economic, fiscal, and political union. Flexible, à la carte approaches will not by themselves resolve the tensions between the countries committed to deepening their union and those refusing to take part.

ORIGINAL ARTICLE: MAY 16, 2012

The eurozone's troubles no longer qualify as a crisis, an unstable situation that could either quickly improve or take a dramatic turn for the worse. They are, instead, a new normal—a painful situation, to be sure, but one that will last for years to come. Citizens, investors, and policymakers should let go of the idea that there is some magic bullet that could quickly kill off Europe's ailments. By the same token, despite the real possibility of Greek exit, the eurozone is not on the brink of collapse. The European Union and its common currency will hold together, but the road to recovery will be long.

It has been nearly two and a half years since the incoming socialist government in Greece revealed the extent to which its predecessor had accumulated debt, precipitating an economic storm that has left slashed budgets, collapsed governments, and record unemployment in its wake. With each dramatic turn, observers have anticipated the story's denouement. But again and again, a definitive resolution—either a policy fix or a total collapse—has failed to emerge.

The truth is that there are no quick escapes from the eurozone's predicament. Divorce is no solution. Although some economists suggest that struggling countries on the periphery could leave the euro and return to a national currency in order to regain competitiveness and restore growth, no country would willingly leave the eurozone; doing so would amount to economic suicide. Its financial system would collapse, and ensuing bank runs and riots would make today's social unrest seem quaint by comparison. What is more, even after a partial default, the country's government and financial firms would still be burdened by debt denominated largely in euros. As the value of the new national currency plummeted, the debt would become unbearable, and the government, now outside the club, would not be able to turn to the eurozone for help.

Some economists go further and argue that countries on Europe's periphery could thrive outside the euro straitjacket. This is equally unconvincing. Southern European countries' economies suffer from deep structural problems that predate the euro. Spanish unemployment rates fluctuated between 15 and 22 percent throughout most of the 1990s; Greece has been in default for nearly half of its history as an independent state. These countries are far more likely to tackle their underlying problems and thrive inside the eurozone than outside it.

Others have suggested that Germany and other core countries—weary of funding endless bailouts—might abandon the euro. That is even less plausible. Germany has been the greatest beneficiary of European integration and the common currency. Forty percent of German exports go to eurozone countries, and the common currency has reduced transaction costs and boosted German growth. An unraveling of the eurozone would devastate German banks, and any new German currency would appreciate rapidly, damaging the country's export-led economic model.

A number of policy reforms may improve economic conditions in the eurozone, but none offers a panacea. Eurobonds, increased investment in struggling economies through the European Investment Bank and other funds, stricter regulations of banks, a common deposit insurance system, a shift from budget cuts to structural reforms that enhance productivity and encourage private-sector job creation—all of these could improve Europe's economic situation and should be implemented.

But none of these measures would quickly restore growth or bring employment back to pre-crisis levels. That is because they do not address Europe's central economic problem: the massive debt accumulated by the periphery countries during last decade's credit boom. The 2000s saw a tremendous amount of capital flow from the northern European countries to private- and public-sector borrowers in Greece, Ireland, Portugal, and Spain. Germany and other countries with current account surpluses flooded the periphery with easy credit, and the periphery gobbled it up. This boosted domestic demand and generated growth in the periphery but also encouraged wage inflation that undermined competitiveness and left massive debt behind. As the economists Carmen Reinhart and Kenneth Rogoff have pointed out, when countries suffer a recession caused by a financial crisis and debt overhang, they take many years to recover.

With both breakup and immediate solutions off the table, then, the eurozone is settling into a new normal. As the union slowly digs itself out of the economic pit, it is important to recognize that its system of economic governance has already been fundamentally transformed over the past two years.

First, the eurozone has, at least in practice, done away with its founding documents. In any monetary union in which states retain the autonomy to tax, spend, and borrow, there is a risk that some countries' excessive borrowing could threaten the value of the common currency. Recognizing this, the euro's creators drafted the Stability and Growth Pact and the "no bailout" clause in the Maastricht Treaty. The SGP placed legal restrictions on member-state deficit and debt levels, and the no-bailout clause forbade the European Union or individual member states from bailing out over-indebted states to avoid moral hazard.

The Maastricht governance regime is dead. The SGP was never strictly enforced, and when the crisis hit, the European Union tossed aside the no-bailout clause. Fearing contagion, it extended emergency loans to Greece, Ireland, and Portugal and set up a permanent bailout fund—the European Stability Mechanism (ESM)—which will be up and running this summer.

Having broken the taboo on bailouts, Europe had to find a way to limit the moral hazard of states turning again and again to the European Union for aid. EU lawmakers introduced the so-called six-pack legislation, which strengthened the European Commission's ability to monitor member states' fiscal policies and enforce debt limits. Twenty-five EU member states signed a fiscal compact treaty, which committed them to enshrining deficit limits into national law. Only those states that eventually ratify the treaty will be eligible for loans from the ESM.

Such legal provisions alone will not overcome the moral hazard, but they have been accompanied by evolution in bond markets, which now distinguish between the debt of healthy governments in the core and weak ones on the periphery. For the first decade of the euro's young life, bond markets priced the risk associated with the peripheral economies' bonds nearly the same as that associated with German ones. Today, the yield spreads are substantial and increase at the first sign of heightened risk. And by forcing private investors to take a nearly 75 percent loss on Greek bonds in conjunction with the second Greek bailout in February 2012, European leaders made clear that private bondholders should not expect bailouts to cover their losses, too. Now, more vigilant bond markets will police governments that run up unsustainable deficits or whose banking sectors grow fragile.

The second major structural change is that the European Central Bank—legally prohibited from purchasing any member state's debt—has thrown its rules aside and directly purchased billions in Greek, Irish, Italian, Portuguese, and Spanish bonds. Moreover, the ECB has indirectly financed billions more loans through its long-term refinancing operation, which extended over a trillion euros in low-interest loans to commercial banks.

ECB President Mario Draghi has repeatedly insisted that the bank is not engaging in "monetary financing" of member-state debts. If I were an Italian president of a central bank located in Frankfurt with a mandate designed by German inflation hawks, I would say that, too. But in practice, the ECB has shown itself to be far more flexible than many had anticipated. It has revealed, quite simply, that it will not oversee the demise of the currency that justifies its existence.

This new system of eurozone governance is more sustainable than the pre-crisis regime set in place by the Maastricht Treaty. It will withstand a Greek exit, for example. If Greece refuses to adhere to the terms of its bailout package and is forced out of the eurozone in the coming weeks, the ECB will likely scramble to stop contagion, but it will not be faced with the entire system's collapse. Meanwhile, by standing firm on Greece, the European Union will have further demonstrated that the conditions attached to its bailouts are serious, motivating other states to stick to their reform programs.

Greece's exit from the eurozone would be a catastrophe for Greece and a trauma for Europe, but it would not change the fundamentals of the post-2008 eurozone governance regime, which will still be based on stronger fiscal surveillance, more robust enforcement procedures, more vigilant bond markets, and a more activist central bank. With such a system in place, and with their commitment to fiscal discipline established, EU leaders will now face the slow, difficult tasks of adjustment and structural reform. And those burdens must be shared by all. It is understandable that Germany and the ECB initially demanded austerity as the condition for bailouts, but this one-sided approach has driven peripheral economies deeper into recession. Moving forward, austerity, wage reductions, and structural reform on the periphery must be coupled with public spending and wage increases in Germany, which will boost demand. There will be no quick fix, but the eurozone will recover, slowly but surely.✪

The Real Reason Putin Supports Assad

Mistaking Syria for Chechnya

Fiona Hill

Few issues better illustrate the limits of the Obama administration's "reset" with Russia than the crisis in Syria. For more than a year, the United States has tried, and failed, to work with Russia to find a solution to end the violence. Moscow has firmly opposed international intervention to remove Syrian President Bashar al-Assad from power, arguing that the conflict must be resolved through negotiations and that Assad must be included in any transitional arrangement leading to a new government. Although the Russian foreign minister, Sergey Lavrov, reached out recently to the leaders of the Syrian opposition, these talks produced no indication that the Kremlin is seriously recalibrating its positions on Syria. And that's hardly surprising: the main obstacle to any shift in Russia's calculations is President Vladimir Putin himself, whose aversion to forcible regime change is intense and unwavering.

Why has Putin offered such steadfast support to Assad? On the surface, Moscow seems to profit from exporting arms to Syria, and it depends on the regime's good will to maintain Russian access to a naval facility at the Mediterranean port of Tartus. But these are marginal and symbolic interests. Putin is really motivated to

FIONA HILL is the Stephen and Barbara Friedman Senior Fellow in Foreign Policy at the Brookings Institution and the co-author, with Clifford Gaddy, of *Mr. Putin: Operative in the Kremlin*.

support the Assad regime by his fear of state collapse—a fear he confronted most directly during the secession of Russia's North Caucasus republic of Chechnya, which he brutally suppressed in a bloody civil war and counterinsurgency operation fought between 1999 and 2009. (In Russia, the republics are semi-autonomous federal units comprising the historic territories of the country's non-ethnic Russian groups.) In a series of interviews he gave in 2000 for an authorized biography, Putin declared that "the essence of the . . . situation in the North Caucasus and in Chechnya . . . is the continuation of the collapse of the USSR. . . . If we did not quickly do something to stop it, Russia as a state in its current form would cease to exist. . . . I was convinced that if we did not immediately stop the extremists [in Chechnya], then in no time at all we would be facing a second Yugoslavia across the entire territory of the Russian Federation—the Yugoslavization of Russia." And we know how Putin feels about the demise of the Soviet Union; in 2005 he called it "the greatest geopolitical catastrophe of the [twentieth] century," a comment that was meant to bemoan the collapse of the Soviet state rather than the demise of communism.

For Putin, Syria is all too reminiscent of Chechnya. Both conflicts pitted the state against disparate and leaderless opposition forces, which over time came to include extremist Sunni Islamist groups. In Putin's view—one that he stresses repeatedly in meetings with his U.S. and European counterparts—Syria is the latest battleground in a global, multi-decade struggle between secular states and Sunni Islamism, which first began in Afghanistan with the Taliban, then moved to Chechnya, and has torn a number of Arab countries apart. Ever since he took office (first as prime minister in 1999 and then as president in 2000) and was confronted by the Chechen war, Putin has expressed his fear of Sunni Islamist extremism and of the risks that "jihadist" groups pose to Russia, with its large, indigenous, Sunni Muslim population, concentrated in the North Caucasus, the Volga region, and in major cities such as Moscow. A desire to contain extremism is a major reason why Putin offered help to the United States in battling the Taliban in Afghanistan after 9/11. It is also why Russia maintains close relations with Shia Iran, which acts as a counterweight to Sunni powers.

In the case of Chechnya, Putin made it clear that retaking the republic from its "extremist opposition forces" was worth every sacrifice. In a speech in September 1999, he promised to pursue Chechen rebels and terrorists even into "the outhouse." He did just that, and some opposition leaders were killed by missile attacks at their most vulnerable moments. The Chechen capital city of Grozny was reduced to rubble. Tens of thousands of civilians were killed, along with jihadist fighters who came into Chechnya with the encouragement of extremist groups from the Arab world, including from Syria. Moscow and other Russian cities endured devastating terrorist attacks. Putin's treatment of Chechnya became a cautionary tale of what would happen to rebels and terrorists—and indeed to entire groups of people—if they threatened the Russian state. They would either be eliminated or brought to their knees—exactly the fate Putin wishes for today's Syrian rebels.

After two decades of secessionist strife, Putin has contained Chechnya's uprising. Ramzan Kadyrov, a former rebel who switched his allegiance to Moscow, now leads the republic. Putin granted Kadyrov and his supporters amnesty and gave them a mandate to go after other militants and political opponents. Kadyrov has rebuilt Grozny (with ample funds from Moscow) and created his own version of an Islamist and Chechen republic that is condemned by human rights organizations for its brutal suppression of dissent.

For the past two years, Putin has hoped that Assad would be able to do what he did in Chechnya and beat back the opposition. Based on the brutal record of Hafez al-Assad, Bashar's father, in suppressing uprisings, Putin anticipated that the regime would have no problem keeping the state together. But now Assad seems to have failed, and Putin is not one to back a losing horse. He and the rest of the Russian leadership are well aware that their staunch support for Assad has damaged Russia's standing in the Arab world, but they have no alternative plan to get out of the stalemate. Putin is still not ready to sanction an intervention that could lead to the dismantling of the Syrian state and to risk creating a situation akin to that in Afghanistan in the 1990s, when warring groups of extremists fought each other and created a breeding ground for global jihadism. In Putin's view, lawless post-Qaddafi Libya, which has become an exporter of guns, fighters, and refugees to its neighbors, only further underscores the dangers of international intervention.

Before abandoning Assad, Putin will need to have answers to some pressing questions: Who will be responsible for the fallout from the regime's collapse? Who will keep Sunni extremists in check? Who will keep extremists away from the North Caucasus and other Russian regions with large Sunni Muslim populations? And finally, who will ensure the security of Syria's chemical weapons? Putin certainly does not trust the United States to play this stabilizing role: as he sees it, when the United States pulled out of Iraq, it left behind a Shia strongman, Nouri al-Maliki, to suppress the Sunnis; the U.S. withdrawal from Afghanistan is leaving only uncertainty in its wake. In short, Putin doubts that the United States and the international community can deliver stability to Syria, so he continues to stand by the flailing regime as the only means of avoiding the collapse of the state altogether.

Although Putin looks at Syria and sees Chechnya, the situations are quite different. All of Syria is in the throes of civil war, and Assad does not have the same resources that Putin had in dealing with Chechnya. He cannot eliminate key representatives and supporters of the opposition abroad as Putin did with the Chechens, including by assassinating the former acting Chechen President Zelimkhan Yandarbiyev in Qatar in 2004 to stop his fundraising and recruiting activities. Unable to crush or co-opt the opposition, Assad has taken Syria over the precipice. Syria is also bristling with conventional weaponry along with an arsenal of weapons of mass destruction that pose a significant threat to neighboring states. Those neighbors—Lebanon, Jordan, Turkey, Iraq, Israel, and Iran farther afield—have been engulfed in the conflict. In contrast, in spite of the flows of money and men into Chechnya and the spill-over of refugees and terrorist acts into the rest of Russia (and sometimes into Azerbaijan, Georgia, and Turkey), there was no similar proliferation threat in the Chechen war, and no outside powers ever became heavily involved. Chechnya is in a bad neighborhood, but Syria is in a terrible neighborhood, and the effects of the Syrian conflict cannot be contained in the way that Chechnya's were.

Neither these differences nor the scale of the humanitarian tragedy will convince Putin to change his mind on Syria. The Russian president will continue to hold out against intervention and insist that negotiations with Assad must be part of the way forward, until some strongman can be found to restore a semblance of order to Syria's chaos. If, by some miracle, Syria does not turn into a full-scale regional disaster, Putin will pat himself on the back and say it was thanks to him because he prevented an intervention. If the more likely scenario plays out, Putin will blame Washington. He will hold the United States responsible for destroying Syria and empowering Sunni Islamist extremists by championing democracy and the Arab revolutions. Meanwhile, Putin's obstinacy is already turning his worst nightmare—the fracturing of a geopolitically important state—into a reality.

How Iran Won the War on Drugs

Lessons for Fighting the Afghan Narcotics Trade

Amir A. Afkhami

"Selling poppies is easier than selling diamonds and gold in Afghanistan, and just as valuable," an official in the Afghan Ministry of Public Health told me in 2011. "The [police] is corrupt, the farmer is poor, and the addict always buys."

He was right. The failure of international forces in Afghanistan to curb the narcotics trade presents one of the gravest threats to the country's long-term stability and security. Even though the U.S.-led coalition has spent more than $6 billion on stopping drug shipments, creating incentives for farmers to exchange poppies for other crops, and disrupting illicit financial networks over the past decade, Afghanistan remains the world's largest supplier of heroin and other illegal opiates.

In NATO countries alone, Afghan narcotics cause more than 10,000 heroin-overdose deaths per year—making them far deadlier than the munitions that have claimed the lives of approximately 3,200 coalition personnel since the start of the war. Meanwhile, needle-sharing among intravenous drug users has led to an

AMIR A. AFKHAMI is Assistant Professor of Psychiatry and Behavioral Sciences, and of Global Health, at George Washington University. Follow him on Twitter @Psych_Doc.

explosion of HIV infections from the Russian heartland to communities in the Baltics and Eastern Europe. The Afghan drug trade presents a unique threat to international security, since it has created unlikely bedfellows out of ideologically divergent terrorist organizations, such as Hezbollah, which has its hands in narcotics transport and financing from Lebanon to South America, and the Taliban, which controls production.

Within Afghanistan, the drug trade provides the funding for the ongoing insurgency and perpetuates a culture of impunity and corruption—major impediments to the establishment of good governance and a healthy civil society. Furthermore, from a public health standpoint, the skyrocketing rate of drug addiction there has created a potentially insurmountable challenge for the central government. A 2010 study by the United Nations Office on Drugs and Crime reported that roughly one million Afghans between the ages of 15 and 64 are addicted to narcotics, up from 860,000 in 2005. Afghanistan's eight percent addiction rate among adults is twice as high as the global average.

Most troubling, Afghans are turning to intravenous drug use in large numbers—heroin use increased by 140 percent between 2005 and 2010 alone. This raises the risk of lethal blood-borne diseases, including HIV/AIDS and hepatitis, which can be transmitted through shared needles. Left unchecked, Afghanistan's growing HIV outbreak has the potential to upend the gains made since the Taliban era in limiting the death caused by infectious diseases.

Since the U.S.-led antinarcotics efforts have made scant progress, it is time for Afghanistan to look to other models. As it turns out, neighboring Iran's failures and successes in reducing both the demand for drugs and the harm they cause offer a good example.

HOW TO STOP A PLAGUE

For much of the twentieth century, Iran's strategy for curbing drug addiction looked a lot like Afghanistan's current one: stopping the flow of narcotics and destroying crops. When, in the early 1970s, it became clear that this method wasn't working, Iranian authorities adopted policies that focused more on prevention and treatment, with promising results.

But the 1979 revolution changed all that, and the Islamic government it brought to power implemented strict zero-tolerance narcotics laws. The regime, which saw drug use not as a medical or public health issue but as a moral shortcoming, believed that addiction and abuse could be beaten out of the public through punitive measures. Penalties for addicts included fining, imprisonment, and physical punishment; drug dealers and smugglers were often considered to be "at war with God" and executed. By the late 1980s, the government was sending thousands of addicts to prison camps, where they were supposed to detoxify and atone for their sins through forced labor.

These draconian social measures against drug users and dealers were matched with similarly aggressive operations to prevent the flow of opiates across the border from Afghanistan. By the late 1980s, an estimated 50 percent of Afghan opiate production was passing through Iranian territory, and the Iranian markets were flooded with Afghan opium, heroin, and morphine. Starting in the early 1990s, Tehran constructed more than 260 kilometers of static defenses—including concrete dams that blocked mountain passes, anti-vehicle berms, trenches, minefields, forts, and mountain towers—at a cost of over $80 million. By the late 1990s, more than 100,000 police officers, army troops, and Revolutionary Guardsmen were committed to antinarcotic operations.

Yet both the social policies and the border fortifications were fruitless. Although the Iranian authorities seized nearly eight times the amount of narcotics in 1999 than they had in 1990, they could not keep up with the expansion of Afghan opium production, which rose in those years from approximately 1,500 metric tons to roughly 4,500. Iran also found that the number of intravenous drug users was growing. Ironically, the prisons and camps where addicts were expected to kick their habits became epicenters of drug use, in which people learned how to inject heroin and shared primitive infection-prone needles.

The rise in malignant drug use brought with it more deaths, more cases of addiction, and, most embarrassingly for Iran's leaders, a full-blown HIV/AIDS epidemic. After years of blaming the West's moral turpitude and decadence for the virus, Iran's leadership had to face an outbreak at home, fueled by its own failed antinarcotic policy. By the late 1990s, in some provinces, double-digit percentages of heroin users were falling prey to the disease. In 2005, biological surveillance data from the Kermanshah province showed a 13.5 percent HIV prevalence rate among the adult prison population.

These setbacks prompted a complete turnaround in Iran's approach to fighting narcotics. Instead of focusing on punishing addicts and trying to stop the drug supply, Iran decided to try to reduce the harm of narcotics and the demand for them. By 2002, over 50 percent of the country's drug-control budget was dedicated to preventive public health campaigns, such as advertisement and education. Iran's conservative and previously intransigent leadership opened narcotics outpatient treatment centers and abstinence-based residential centers in Tehran and the provinces.

The Islamic Republic also began to allow nongovernmental organizations to launch their own prevention and treatment efforts. The government began to implicitly support needle-exchange programs, going so far as to encourage the distribution of clean needles in the Iranian prison system. Gradually, the road was paved for methadone maintenance treatment centers and clinics that dispensed locally produced opium pills, in a bid to turn injection drug users into medicated patients.

In making this shift, Iran sought not only to halt the growing HIV/AIDS epidemic but also to reduce the demand for illicit narcotics and to reintegrate drug users back into the economy. These new measures began to show results: the number of new HIV cases among intravenous drug users dropped from a high of 3,111 in 2004 to 1,585 in 2010. This trend was particularly notable among Iran's prison population, which witnessed a drop in HIV prevalence from a high of 7.92 percent in 1998 to a low of 1.51 percent in 2007.

Additionally, in areas where the country set up harm-reduction programs, improvements were observed in addicts' life expectancies and psychological well-being, coupled with an overall reduction in the illicit consumption of opiates.

INTERVENING IN AFGHANISTAN

Iran's experience is particularly instructive for Afghanistan; both are Islamic republics that are inclined to see drug addiction through a religious prism. Yet the Iranians demonstrated that it is possible to overcome this inclination and to view drug use primarily as a public health issue. Going forward, the United States and other donor countries need to encourage Kabul to take a page out of the Iranian playbook and adopt a broader, medically oriented approach to its drug problem.

In the past several years, several European organizations have begun to train Afghans in harm reduction strategies. Médecins du Monde, a French nongovernmental organization, has established a handful of methadone treatment centers to treat HIV-positive patients with antiretrovirals in addition to caring for intravenous drug users. These efforts, however, have run up against inadequate funding and significant ideological barriers within Afghanistan's strictly conservative government. Moreover, powerful members of President Hamid Karzai's ruling clique still have financial stakes in the poppy trade, and are therefore unenthusiastic about such efforts.

But as Iran's experience shows, the only way to actually drive down drug use and contain its negative effects is to focus on prevention and treatment. To make this shift, Afghanistan should start by creating a drug-oriented policymaking body that could operate outside the corrupting confines of the Afghan government. For this measure to succeed, the international forces in the country would need to move beyond their counterproductive focus on crop exchanges and interdiction. Western investments in Afghan counternarcotic efforts should emphasize education, treatment, and reducing the overall demand for the drugs. If these efforts fail, much of the international efforts to stabilize Afghanistan will have been for naught: the country will remain a dangerous narco-state, home to a devastating public health epidemic, and an exporter of addiction and death to the rest of the world.●

The Egyptian State Unravels

Meet the Gangs and Vigilantes Who Thrive under Morsi

Mara Revkin

"Everybody needs a weapon," said Mahmoud, a 23-year-old Egyptian arms dealer, as he displayed his inventory of pistols, machetes, and switchblades on the living room floor of his family's apartment in the crime-ridden Cairo neighborhood of Ain Shams.

With Egyptian government statistics indicating a 300 percent increase in homicides and a 12-fold increase in armed robberies since the 2011 revolution, Mahmoud and other black-market entrepreneurs are capitalizing on a growing obsession with self-defense and civilian vigilantism among Egyptians who have lost patience with their government's inability to restore security. Frustration with lawlessness is among the numerous grievances that will drive antigovernment protesters to the streets on June 30, the one-year anniversary of President Mohamed Morsi's inauguration.

Mahmoud is one of many post-revolutionary lawbreakers who were victims of crime before they became perpetrators. When I asked him how he made the decision to start selling black-market weapons, he replied sarcastically, "What decision? I had no choice." Over lukewarm Pepsi served by his mother, Mahmoud explained

MARA REVKIN is a student at Yale Law School currently based in Cairo and the former Assistant Director of the Atlantic Council's Rafik Hariri Center for the Middle East. Follow her on Twitter @MaraRevkin.

that he used to earn a living as a taxi driver. But shortly after the revolution, his car was hijacked at gunpoint by a local gang. Like many of the amateur black marketeers responsible for Egypt's current crime wave, Mahmoud is a far cry from the hardened criminal I had been expecting; he is just a young man hoping to earn enough money to move out of his parents' house, marry his fiancée, and replace his stolen taxi.

Mahmoud's neighborhood is home to one of Cairo's most active black markets in unlicensed weapons, where vendors hawk a variety of small arms—stolen police pistols, locally made shotguns, knives, switchblades and Tasers—at below-market prices. Although Egyptian law prohibits the sale of unlicensed weapons, these informal markets have thrived since the early days of the revolution. They operate openly and often in plain view of the police, who until recently showed little interest in regulating the illicit trade, despite soaring crime rates. Even in downtown Cairo, unlicensed weapons dealers have been known to set up shop just steps away from prominent symbols of judicial authority, the Lawyers' Syndicate building (Egypt's version of the Bar Association) and the headquarters of the Supreme Judicial Council.

In the days leading up to the June 30 protests, police have attempted to crack down on the illegal weapons trade. But dealers like Mahmoud are adept at evading the authorities. When police approach, they simply move their wares elsewhere, selling weapons from the safety of private homes or parked vehicles.

Black-market weapons range in price from cheap to high-end: a switchblade goes for about L.E. 75 ($10.75), a Taser costs around L.E. 350 ($50), and for L.E. 700 ($100), you can purchase a locally manufactured birdshot gun. Stolen police pistols, at the upper end of the market, sell for upwards of L.E. 2000 ($285). Small knives have become a popular choice for women, who have been plagued by an increase in sexual assault and harassment since the revolution.

Like good entrepreneurs, weapons dealers have been quick to exploit fears of violent crime. Just down the street from the crowded

Naguib Metro station, in broad daylight, one cardboard sign urged, "Protect yourself for L.E. 10." That $1.40 would buy you a dull but nonetheless menacing blade that looks guaranteed to inflict at least tetanus, if not more serious harm.

Many of the guns for sale come from the thousands of firearms that were ransacked from police departments during the revolution. Others are smuggled across Egypt's borders with Libya and Sudan. The cheapest firearms are the birdshot guns, known as "fards," which are handmade by underemployed craftsmen who cobble together the frighteningly inaccurate weapons from machine parts and scrap metal.

ANYTHING GOES

The proliferation of small arms in Cairo and across Egypt is just one symptom of the security vacuum that persists two years after the uprising that shattered Hosni Mubarak's seemingly unbreakable police state. Distrustful of a police force known for being simultaneously abusive and incompetent, and wary of an increasingly politicized judicial system that rarely delivers justice, many Egyptians are administering law and order on their own terms.

In one particularly extreme case in March, two young men accused of stealing a rickshaw in a Nile Delta town were stripped naked, hung upside down from the roof of a bus station, and beaten to death by a mob of 3,000 people. Not all of the vigilantism is violent, however. Take Namaa, a civil society organization that works on sustainable development. The group is funding a crowd-sourcing initiative that solicits reports about neighborhood hazards—damaged electrical wires, for example—and dispatches volunteers to respond to problems that might otherwise be ignored by local authorities.

Meanwhile, facing intermittent strikes by judicial workers and police officers, Egypt's overextended government is all too willing to outsource some of its law enforcement functions to nonstate actors and informal institutions. In the notoriously lawless Sinai Peninsula, official state courts have long preferred to delegate the adjudication of tribal disputes to customary courts. Since the revolution, local authorities there have tolerated the expansion of informal Sharia committees that administer Islamic law, creating what is beginning to resemble a state within a state. Informal justice is not limited to Egypt's most remote regions, and unofficial customary courts in the greater Cairo area have seen demand for their services, ranging from dispute resolution to marriage licenses, increase notably since 2011.

Instead of working to reform the country's dysfunctional institutions, some political leaders have embraced the devolution of core security functions to community-based policing initiatives or private contractors. Earlier this year, the Building and Development Party, the political wing of the formerly militant Islamist group al-Gamaa al-Islamiya, proposed draft legislation that would legalize unarmed "popular committees" to supplement the uniformed police force. In another instance of state-sponsored community policing, the Ministry of Supply recently announced the formation of unarmed, civilian-staffed popular committees to curb the smuggling of flour.

The outsourcing of traditional law enforcement functions to civilian and nonstate actors is a common pathology of weak states and transitioning democracies, in which security and judicial institutions are viewed as either illegitimate or ineffective. And indeed, Egyptians complain that the police never fully redeployed after they withdrew from the streets during the revolution. Those few who are present in the streets are doing nothing to combat crime.

Ahmed al-Shenawi, an Egyptian criminologist, told me about a neighbor in Alexandria who owns an empty lot and recently discovered that a stranger was unlawfully constructing an apartment building on his property. When the owner asked the local police to intervene on his behalf, he was told that there was nothing the authorities could do. The police did advise him, however, to hire some *baltagiyya* (Egyptian slang for "thugs") to forcibly expel the interloper. Another common complaint, by victims of car theft, is that police refuse to assist them and instead recommend that they seek out the thieves and offer to buy back their stolen vehicles.

In yet another account of the state's indifference to disorder, Shahinaz Nabeeh, a British-Egyptian journalist, once called the police after she saw a group of thugs beating a man in the Cairo neighborhood of Agouza. When she asked if the police could please be sent quickly, the dispatcher who answered the phone replied nonchalantly, *"Inshallah"* (God willing), and promptly hung up on her. The police never arrived, and the fight continued for two hours until the victim finally died.

In these cases, the refusal of police to do their job has more to do with apathy and incompetence than it does with corruption. But other reports suggest that a much more malignant phenomenon is at work: direct police complicity in organized crime. Criminal gangs are among the biggest beneficiaries of post-revolutionary lawlessness. They function as a substitute for state security personnel in the most dangerous slums of Cairo, allegedly with the tacit permission and even encouragement of police. According to Haitham Tabei, an Egyptian journalist who reports on urban crime, the police have willingly abdicated control over entire neighborhoods of the city to criminal gangs. These predatory groups operate illicit fiefdoms of racketeering, trafficking, and prostitution with total impunity, hiring thugs (and sometimes even children) to staff their private militias.

In Mahmoud's neighborhood, gangs have been known to extort payments from shopkeepers in exchange for protection from break-ins. Some of them base their operations out of nearby Pharaonic tombs that were unearthed in the middle of a densely populated neighborhood over a decade ago and have been neglected by Egypt's dysfunctional Antiquities Ministry ever since. Among the deteriorating ruins, local gangs are illegally constructing slum dwellings and extracting rent from hapless tenants who would otherwise be homeless.

Outside of Cairo, the problem is even more severe. Gangs control entire sections of major highways in Upper Egypt and Sinai, where they terrorize truck drivers with semiautomatic weapons and use the threat of carjacking to extort royalties from companies that rely on ground transport to ship their goods. As one truck driver told *al-Masry al-Youm*, a daily newspaper, "No road is safe after the revolution."

"THE POLICE HAVE BEEN DEFANGED"

Although the primary function of the Mubarak regime's security apparatus was to protect the state from its political opponents, one of its few positive side effects was an overall chilling effect on crime. Before the revolution, Cairo had one of the lowest homicide rates in the world, with significantly fewer murders per capita than Oslo, Helsinki, Toronto, Brussels, and New York, according to 2009 UN statistics.

Crime waves are to be expected in post-authoritarian transitions, and the tradeoff between democratic reform and insecurity has been widely studied in the context of the Soviet Union's demise. So it is perhaps unsurprising that violent crime rates have soared since the collapse of the Mubarak regime. In particular, Egyptian criminologists attribute the uptick both to the presence of a significant number of escaped criminals who broke out of jails during the revolution and to first-time offenders who have resorted to crime for lack of legitimate job prospects. (Unemployment in Egypt now stands at a record 13.2 percent.)

During the 18-day uprising in 2011, more than 23,000 prisoners escaped, and some 5,000 escapees remain at large. But when I contacted Cairo police stations to ask whether the government has a strategy for recapturing the wanted fugitives—or even has a list of their names—I was repeatedly told that no such information exists. Ahmad Bastamy, a criminologist, explained that much of the paperwork documenting the names and charges against the at-large escapees was destroyed during the revolution, making their recapture all but impossible.

Crime has never been more of a problem, yet the government's capacity to enforce law and order is at an all-time low. Egypt's government has made a number of symbolic—and almost entirely superficial—gestures at security sector reform. A dizzying succession of cabinet reshuffles over the last two years has ushered in five new interior ministers. Mubarak's hated domestic security agency, the State Security Investigations Service (SSIS), was rebranded with a new name, the National Security Agency, in an effort to signal its supposed commitment to protecting the people from the state, rather than the other way around. But despite the new signage and a handful of personnel changes, the core of Mubarak's security apparatus has been largely preserved.

Meaningful security sector reform, a central demand of the revolution and one of Morsi's forgotten campaign promises, has all but fallen off the political agenda. Egypt's partially dissolved parliament and recently reshuffled government are preoccupied instead with mass protests, the deteriorating economic situation, and a legal battle over the design of the electoral system that has postponed elections indefinitely. A former police official, Mohamed Mahfouz, is leading a campaign to reform the national police force and rehabilitate its public image. But when I asked him how much progress has been made on the issue, he replied bluntly, "Absolutely none."

In March, a senior official in the Building and Development Party estimated that 80 percent of the state security employees formerly employed by the Mubarak regime are still working for the supposedly reconstituted National Security Agency. Of those few officers who were prosecuted for crimes and rights violations during the revolution, the vast majority have been acquitted and reinstated. This has only reinforced an institutional culture of impunity that may prove to be Mubarak's most intractable legacy.

Meanwhile, human rights activists are concerned that an expanding private security industry—one of the few sectors creating jobs in Egypt today—operates with alarmingly little oversight or legal accountability. Private contractors are increasingly being used to prop up the dysfunctional state security apparatus. The Brotherhood was forced to hire private security companies to protect its headquarters on June 30, after the Interior Ministry announced that the police would only be responsible for "state institutions." The growth of a largely unregulated industry of private security guards, some of whom are licensed to carry weapons, presents another obstacle to comprehensive security sector reform.

Ironically, the non-Islamist opposition, which campaigned so vocally for state security reform during the revolution, is now itself preventing institutional change. Liberal parties that were calling for a purge of state institutions a year ago are now deeply suspicious of any new appointments or legislative reforms initiated by the Muslim Brotherhood-led government, which they fear is maneuvering to repopulate the state security apparatus with Islamists. Accusations of "Brotherhoodization" have put Morsi's government on the defensive, and any attempts at reform will likely be resisted by an opposition whose primary agenda seems to consist of obstructing that of the Brotherhood.

Mahfouz fears that the entrenched culture of state security institutions is deeply resistant to change. "For decades," he told me, "the police were taught that the people were their enemy and the state was their friend. Now, they need to be retrained to see the people as their friend." But a new report documenting 359 cases of torture by security personnel since Morsi's inauguration is a reminder that old habits are hard to break.

Despite the persistence of police brutality since the revolution, Egyptians are more likely to describe law enforcement officers as incompetent than dangerous. As one American diplomat who wished to remain anonymous put it, "The police have been defanged." Convincing the police to protect people who hate them— and no longer fear them—is no easy task.

The police themselves complain that they are increasingly the victims of preemptive attacks by criminals and unruly protesters. In recent months, reports of stolen police vehicles and deadly attacks on officers—sometimes in broad daylight—have become commonplace. The government has responded by adopting new legislation that imposes harsher penalties for assaulting security personnel—an admission of the growing vulnerability and ineptitude of a police force that once inspired terror.

Nabeel Zakaria, a retired army general, told me that Egyptians have given up on the police. "Everyone is responsible for his own protection now," said Zakaria, who lives with his family in an affluent suburb north of Cairo. He says the two-hour-long commute into the city and back is well worth the peace of mind that comes with living in a gated community insulated from urban crime.

Zakaria's assessment of the police is consistent with recent polling data, which found a stark disparity between levels of public support for the military and police. Whereas the military is by far the most popular institution in Egypt today (73 percent believe it has a positive influence on the country), only 35 percent of Egyptians expressed positive views about the police, and 63 percent believe that the police are doing more harm than good

BROKEN LAW

The courts have not fared much better. The Islamist-controlled executive and legislative branches have been engaged in a protracted power struggle with the judicial system, seeing it as an obstacle to their agenda. In recent months, Morsi and Islamist lawmakers have repeatedly called into question the neutrality of Mubarak-appointed judges and accused them of protecting the interests of the former regime. They are still reeling from decisions that the courts made last June, when judges dissolved the lower house of parliament and issued controversially lenient sentences in the trials of the former president and other regime officials. The entanglement of the judiciary in politics through repeated confrontations with the executive and legislative branches has eroded the institution's legitimacy in the eyes of the public. As Shenawi described the situation, "If the president doesn't even respect the courts, how can we expect the people to respect them?"

The conflict between the judiciary and the legislature escalated again in May, when Egypt's Supreme Constitutional Court issued a provocative ruling invalidating the new electoral law and postponing parliamentary elections indefinitely. Meanwhile, Egypt's judges have threatened to take to the streets over a draft law regulating judicial authority that they say would undermine the independence of the courts. These maneuvers have led the public to conclude that Egypt's purportedly neutral judiciary is now functioning as a political interest group that may be tempted to prioritize its own self-serving agenda over the rule of law.

Without a serious effort to rebuild confidence in Egypt's security apparatus and judicial institutions, there are few incentives to abide by laws that are neither enforced nor respected. Egyptians once lived in fear of the state. Now they fear its absence. Against the backdrop of antigovernment protests, the black-market weapons boom in a context of unchecked lawlessness is an alarming reminder that Egypt's government, which so recently oversaw a vast police state, has now lost its monopoly on violence.

During a widely ridiculed speech on June 26 that was intended to placate the opposition, Morsi tried to deflect blame for the unrest onto former regime loyalists known as *feloul*, whom he accused of hiring gangs to instigate trouble. These paranoid allegations of organized thuggery, whether true or not, were the words of a leader who knows he is not fully in control. The diffusion of lethal weapons among civilians who no longer fear or respect their government has created a highly combustible atmosphere in which violence is viewed as a legitimate and even necessary response to insecurity.

On both ends of an intensely polarized political spectrum, Morsi's supporters and his opponents insist that they are committed to diffusing violence. But the two camps are behaving in ways that make armed confrontation inevitable. Islamists organized a rally under the slogan "No to Violence" on June 21, yet a Brotherhood-affiliated televangelist, Safwat Hegazy, took to the stage to proclaim, "If anyone so much as sprays Morsi with water, we will spray him with blood." Two days later, anti-Morsi protesters violently attacked the Brotherhood's headquarters in the Nile Delta town of Damanhour, killing one person and injuring sixty more. Neither the opposition nor the Brotherhood is doing much to reduce the probability of a bloodbath on June 30, other than to engage in a mutually discrediting display of blame-shifting.

Meanwhile, the looming specter of violence has inspired nostalgia for the days of military rule. Earlier this month, protesters gathered outside of the Ministry of Defense to demand that Morsi transfer power to the head of the armed forces. But the restoration of martial law would be a superficial and ultimately unsustainable solution to a security vacuum that requires much deeper institutional reforms. Egypt's precarious democratic experiment hinges on whether the country can build an accountable state that can be trusted to maintain a monopoly on violence and wield it lawfully and humanely. Until then, Egyptians will continue to take security into their own hands.⊛

Even Good Coups Are Bad

Lessons for Egypt from the Philippines, Venezuela, and Beyond

Omar Encarnación

To understand the swift and dramatic demise of Egypt's first democratically elected leader and what it might portend for the country's future, it helps to take a broad comparative perspective. The manner in which the country's military deposed President Mohamed Morsi, of the Muslim Brotherhood–affiliated Freedom and Justice Party, is by no means an isolated case. In fact, it fits rather perfectly within the model of a civil society coup, a concept I first described in a 2002 *World Policy Journal* essay that explained the brief removal from power of Venezuela's Hugo Chávez by a coalition of business, labor, and civic groups. Other scholars have subsequently applied the idea to other coups, such as those in the Philippines in 2001, in Ecuador in 2002, in Thailand in 2006, and in Honduras in 2009. All of these cases show that civil society coups are not the fix for democracy that they purport to be, which looks to be true in Egypt as well.

Endemic to new democracies, civil society coups entail the removal from power of an elected leader through sustained protest, usually with the aid of the military. Indeed, it is the partnership between civil society and the military—not usually known for acting in concert—that distinguishes a civil society coup from an

---

OMAR ENCARNACIÓN is Professor of Political Studies at Bard College.

ordinary one. More often than not, those behind the coup justify it by claiming that they intend to rescue democracy, which is paradoxical since they are, in fact, uprooting it. This is Tocqueville's civil society gone rogue; rather than working patiently and discreetly toward improving the quality of democracy, it turns angry and restless and plots for sudden and radical political change.

In my original essay on Chávez's removal from office, I identified three preconditions for a civil society coup. The first is the rise to power of a leader whose commitment to democracy is at best suspect. The second is a political apparatus that fails to meet public expectations about economic growth and stability, usually because of its corruption, incompetence, and neglect of the country's basic needs. The third is the emergence of civil society actors—trade unions, religious associations, and civic groups—rather than formally organized political forces, which have either disintegrated or which never fully developed in the first place, as the main opposition to the government. The combined result of these conditions is the emergence of an adversarial relationship between an invigorated civil society and a delegitimized political system against a background of widespread societal discontent and the collapse of the rule of law. Under such conditions, disputes and political crises are solved on the streets rather than in the legislature.

All of these conditions materialized in Egypt. Once in office, Morsi wasted very little time showing his ambivalence toward democracy. Last November, he attempted to give himself extrajudicial powers that would have essentially put him above the law. He claimed that he needed these powers to get around a hostile judiciary that remains staffed primarily by holdovers from the previous regime. But Egyptians saw it as nothing more than a power grab. The following month, when Morsi pushed through a new constitution that dialed back women's rights and enhanced the military's power, among other things, many Egyptians felt betrayed.

Morsi's brief time in office was also marred by economic turmoil. Living conditions in Egypt are worse now than they were under Mubarak. According to the IMF, before the revolution, 40 percent of the country lived in poverty. Now, 50 percent do. And in the weeks leading up to the coup, acute shortages of food, fuel, and other basic necessities followed one on top of the other. To be sure, Morsi inherited a very troubled economy. As Ibrahim Saif, an economist at the Carnegie Endowment, put it, the revolution left "a hostile environment for private-sector investment," fueled by "a perceived risk of expropriation," as well as damaging "taxation, stringent regulations, export and production subsidies, and high transaction costs associated with red tape." At the same time, however, Morsi's policies aggravated political instability and uncertainty. That, in turn, made it nearly impossible to restore the once vibrant tourist sector, shore up investor confidence, or convince international donors, such as the IMF and the World Bank, that the new democracy was on firm footing.

Finally, for the past year and a half, it has been difficult to discern who, exactly, comprises the opposition. That is a common characteristic of democratic transitions engineered from below, which tend not to generate a unified political opposition but, rather, a constellation of opposition groups whose divisions are bigger than whatever difference they may have with the government. That makes it hard to forge compromises between the government and its discontents, and even harder to construct a loyal opposition that counterbalances the party in power but channels people's grievances through the political system. The emergence of a loyal opposition is just as important to democratic consolidation as an effective democratic leader. The disorganized nature of the Egyptian opposition was on full display during the protests that led to the military's intervention, as a motley crew of pro-democracy groups came together with no more common purpose than driving the Muslim Brotherhood out of power.

There is an inherent tendency to view civil society coups as good coups (as opposed to bad ones masterminded by the military without the support of the masses). After all, civil society coups hold the alluring promise of resetting the democratization process by flushing out an experiment with elections gone awry and creating a tabula rasa upon which to create a new democracy. That is the view adopted by Egyptian liberals, who have been at pains to even avoid using the word "coup." Mohamed El Baradei, the Nobel-laureate diplomat, former Director of the International Atomic Energy Agency, and Egypt's most prominent liberal, told *The New York Times* that "Morsi had bungled the country's transition to a inclusive democracy." He added, "As Yogi Berra said, it's déjà vu all over again, but hopefully this time we will get it right."

But the notion that a civil society coup can restart democracy is wildly optimistic. Venezuela and the Philippines suggest two likelier scenarios. In Venezuela, waves of strikes followed the proposed nationalization of Venezuela's national oil company (PDVSA). The military took Chávez hostage for some 48 hours before withdrawing plans to install an interim president and to call new elections, and accepting Chávez's restoration. Forcing the military's reversal was its realization that it could not contain Chavismo, the best-organized political force in the country, which had fierce loyalty to its founding leader—a point driven home by violent counter-coup demonstrations that left some 20 people dead. Chávez ruled Venezuela for another decade, until his death, earlier this year, becoming more vengeful and authoritarian as he went. He also turned increasingly anti-American, since he blamed the United States for his ouster. Although the evidence of American participation in the Venezuelan coup is contested, the Bush administration did cheer Chávez's ousting as "a victory for democracy" before correcting course after most Latin American governments had denounced developments in Venezuela as a coup.

The parallels with Egypt are worth noting. As in Venezuela, the coup in Egypt pushed from power the best-organized political force in the country, the Muslim Brotherhood. Unlike Chávez, of course, Morsi is not seen by the Brotherhood rank and file as the very embodiment of the movement. But so far the movement's leadership is resolute in its insistence that Morsi be returned to power, suggesting that his restoration cannot be ruled out. "There is no plan B," a spokesman for the Brotherhood said to ABC News, adding, "We either return the president back to his rightful place or they are going to have to shoot us in the street."

In the Philippines in 2001, the military ousted President Joseph Estrada after four days of intense popular protests during the Second People Power Revolution, a name that paid homage to the People Power revolution, which ousted strongman Ferdinand Marcos in 1986. After giving Estrada the boot, the military installed Vice President Gloria Arroyo as the country's new leader. Arroyo, who served as president until 2010, had a rocky tenure. In no small part, that was because she was tainted by the illegitimate manner in which her predecessor had been deposed. She managed to survive several violent counterprotests by supporters of Estrada (who himself became a shadow figure that haunted Arroyo's entire presidency), including a massive storming of the presidential palace by some three million protesters in 2001 who claimed to represent the Third People Power Revolution. In Egypt, finding an acceptable replacement to Morsi is already proving a challenge, as can be seen in the quick rise and fall of El Baradei as a potential interim prime minister.

Civil society coups are seldom, if ever, a good thing for democracy. Indeed, Egyptians might have been better off letting Morsi serve his full term in office rather than aborting his clumsy but democratic tenure. For now, Egypt might be lucky to wind up like Venezuela or the Philippines, since it could certainly chart a more tragic course—a civil war—a prospect that only looks likelier as violence against Morsi supporters continues. If the last few decades have taught observers anything, it is that democracy depends, in no small measure, on people waiting to defeat the incumbent government at the ballot box rather than in the streets.🌀

How Yemen Chewed Itself Dry

Farming Qat, Wasting Water

Adam Heffez

I n a little over a decade, Sana'a, Yemen, may become the world's first capital to run out of water. Failed governance and environmental mismanagement share some of the blame for drying up the city. But there is also a more surprising culprit: a national addiction to qat, a narcotic that is incredibly water-intensive to cultivate.

If current trends continue, by 2025 the city's projected 4.2 million inhabitants will become water refugees, forced to flee their barren home for wetter lands. In preparation, some officials have already considered relocating the capital to the coast. Others have proposed focusing on desalination and conservation to buy time.

As policymakers butt heads over the best course for Yemen, the dwindling water supply is already leading to instability: according to *Al-Thawra*, one of the country's leading newspapers, 70 to 80 percent of conflicts in Yemen's rural regions are water-related. And across the country, Yemen's Interior Ministry estimates, water- and land-related disputes result in about 4,000 deaths each year—35 times the number of casualties in the deadliest al Qaeda attack in the country's history.

ADAM HEFFEZ is a research assistant in the Program on Arab Politics at the Washington Institute for Near East Policy.

THE QAT CAME BACK

The cultivation of qat, a mild narcotic plant that releases a stimulant when chewed, accounts for up to 40 percent of the water drawn from the Sana'a Basin each year, and that figure is rising. That is both because qat takes a lot of water to farm (much more than coffee, another plant that does well in Yemen's fertile soil) and because cultivation of it increases by around 12 percent each year, according to Yemen's Ministry of Agriculture and Water Resources. Not only is the crop drying the Sana'a Basin, it has displaced over tens of thousands of hectares of vital crops—fruits, vegetables, and coffee—which has sent food prices soaring. According to the World Bank, rising food prices, in turn, pushed an additional six percent of the country into poverty in 2008 alone.

Why the increasing reliance on qat production? Farmers are willing to put up with the plant's high demand for water because it has a more regular yield than other crops and because the market for it is virtually guaranteed. Every cubic meter of water used for qat cultivation returns a profit five times as great as that for the next most lucrative crop, grapes. No wonder: according to the World Health Organization, up to 90 percent of adult men in Yemen chew qat for three to four hours daily, and women literally sing its praises. (A popular song goes: "Long live qat, which . . . makes us stay peacefully at home with our friends.") At weddings and special events, a family's social standing is gauged by the value of qat served to guests. One might think that such a popular drug would have deep roots in a culture, but its widespread use is actually relatively new: in the 1970s, when Yemen had few paved roads, qat, which has a shelf life of only 24 to 48 hours, often could not reach its markets in time, so fewer people had access to it.

Yemen cannot continue using water this way. In 2011, the rate of water consumption from the Sana'a Basin exceeded the rate of natural recharge by a factor of five. And, even understanding this, Yemenis have placed little value on conservation: much of the country's 68 billion cubic meters of annual rainwater is wasted due to mismanagement and inadequate dams.

Part of the problem is that farmers, for whom the physical labor exerted in agriculture is a source of pride, are attached to wasteful practices, such as flood irrigation (the uncontrolled distribution of water over soil). Drip irrigation—a practice that is about 35 percent more efficient and widely available at low cost—could easily increase returns on water. But when asked about drip irrigation, one farmer told me that "flood irrigation is more honorable . . . all [drip irrigation] requires is pumping water up into the tank."

Making things worse, the country's decaying dams seep water that could otherwise be used productively. May 2010 saw flooding—the worst to hit Sana'a in decades—but very little of the water was captured for later use. Moreover, the country's well system is a disaster. By law, only the government is allowed to dig and maintain wells. But according to some interpretations of sharia, which Yemen's constitution specifies as the sole legal framework, a well drilled on privately owned land is the property of the landlord, not of the state. So drilling continues. Today, Yemen's National Water and Sanitation Authority, which is tasked with urban water administration, supplies water to only 36 percent of Sana'a's households. The other two-thirds get their supplies from groundwater wells.

The wells are a public health nightmare—the country's groundwater is increasingly contaminated by sewage effluent. Beyond that, the wells prevent the National Water and Resource Authority, which is responsible for managing the country's water resources in a sustainable way, from enforcing conservation measures, such as improving irrigation efficiency.

DON'T GO CHASING WATERFALLS

Of course, those officials know that Sana'a is facing an arid future. Moving the capital city, as some have proposed, would cost over $40 billion, according to some estimates. Securing the funds would be nearly impossible: approximately 75 percent of the government's revenue is derived from rapidly depleting oil reserves, and the World Bank predicts that oil will stop generating income for the Yemeni government by 2017. Foreign aid is similarly scant.

Even if it were possible to raise the funds, moving an entire city of over two million people would surely lead to internal strife. The tribal concept of *juwarah* (rights of neighbors) often inhibits the sale of land to members of other tribes. The transfer of land to Sana'a's two million displaced residents could thus lead to chaos.

Another idea, which the Ministry of Agriculture and Water Resources (MAWR) has discussed, is to transfer water to Sana'a from other sources. Unfortunately for Yemen, all the rest of the country's fresh water is currently in use. Therefore, transferring water to Sana'a would essentially involve siphoning it away from others, also inviting conflict.

Policymakers have also toyed with the idea of alleviating the strain on the Sana'a Basin by decreasing agriculture in the region. But that would only kick the can down the road, because, even without agriculture, and given all of Yemen's other poor water practices, the growing population would eventually dry out the basin anyway. In addition, decreasing agriculture would push up food prices even further.

LIQUID ASSET

Instead, the government should do three things to secure its water future: push farmers and the public away from qat, shore up Yemen's existing water infrastructure, and manufacture new potable water through desalinization.

First, the government should encourage farmers to switch to less water-intensive crops, such as cactus fruits. For now, the government subsidizes diesel—the main fuel used to extract groundwater—which accounts for 80 percent of the cost of qat cultivation. The low cost of extraction gives farmers little reason to switch to other crops or use sustainable farming practices. Attempts to lift a portion of the subsidy several times between 1995 and the present raised the price of diesel and dragged water up closer to its true economic price. Those changes were not enough to discourage qat production altogether, but at least obliged farmers to start thinking about more efficient irrigation techniques.

Should the government opt to decrease the subsidy again, the farmers could be pushed even further.

On the supply side of the equation, the government should also launch a public campaign against qat use. Although qat is not deadly, the health risks associated with it are many—they include hyperactivity, increased blood pressure, liver complications, ulcers, and impotence—and the societal costs are nothing to sneeze at. Across the country, around 30 percent of household income, on average, is used for buying qat, despite the fact that 45 percent of Yemenis live below the poverty line. Qat has also been linked to diminished productivity at work.

In its campaign against qat use, the Yemeni government has a good model to follow: its own water conservation campaign from 2007, for which it developed a character named Rowyan (meaning "to have quenched one's thirst"). Rowyan's face appeared on wheel covers and in storefronts throughout Sana'a, and the campaign managed to at least convince some Yemenis that water scarcity was a problem A similar campaign against qat could help gradually wean some chewers away from the habit.

Second, the government needs to encourage improved irrigation techniques in all agricultural areas—ones that grow the narcotic as well as other crops. It should obligate more farmers to opt for rain irrigation instead of groundwater use, which wouldn't run counter to their desire to do things by hand. More than one million acres of arable land that used to be irrigated by rainfall (as of the 1970s) are now doused with water drawn from nonrenewable sources. There is no reason that those acres can't be reclaimed.

The National Water and Resource Authority also needs to cooperate with Yemen's local leadership, which, because it makes money off private wells and other water sources, has a vested interest in inefficient use. The NWRA can do so by taking advantage of the political transition in Yemen that accompanied the Arab Spring. For one, the ongoing national dialogue conference, which brings together 565 Yemenis from all segments of society to collaborate on forming a new government, might ease distrust of state institutions. A relationship of cooperation, rather than antagonism, will help the NWRA gain legitimacy in the eyes of local leadership, which will aid with the implementation of conservation measures in places that are outside of the government's reach.

The government should also take care of Yemen's leaky water pipes, which waste up to 60 percent of the water they contain. Money for that, too, will be hard to find. But it could court more investment from countries such as Saudi Arabia, whose security interests are inseparable from its southern neighbor's. Finally, the government must limit the drilling of wells for domestic purposes.

Conserving the water that Yemen has now will only go so far. The depletion of nonrenewable groundwater might leave Yemen with no real option other than to manufacture new water through desalinization. Pumping desalinated water from plants near the sea to Sana'a would be costly, but the fixed startup costs would be distributed across time and would be far less than moving the capital. In the beginning, the government will have to temporarily subsidize desalinated water so that it would be within reach for most consumers. The government would likely need foreign aid to implement this subsidy and to develop the desalination infrastructure.

In ancient times, Yemen was a world leader in agricultural production and water efficiency practices. Between 750 and 700 BC, in what is today northern Yemen, the Kingdom of Saba'a (Sheba) built the Marib Dam, which captured irrigation from rainfall for roughly a millennium. If it improves management of existing water resources and builds up infrastructure for conservation and desalination, Yemen, once a model of water conservation, may yet have hope for reviving its capital. ☻

The Arab Sunset

The Coming Collapse of the Gulf Monarchies

Christopher Davidson

S ince their modern formation in the mid-twentieth century, Saudi Arabia and the five smaller Gulf monarchies—Bahrain, Kuwait, Oman, Qatar, and the United Arab Emirates (UAE)—have been governed by highly autocratic and seemingly anachronistic regimes. Nevertheless, their rulers have demonstrated remarkable resilience in the face of bloody conflicts on their doorsteps, fast-growing populations at home, and modernizing forces from abroad.

One of the monarchies' most visible survival strategies has been to strengthen security ties with Western powers, in part by allowing the United States, France, and Britain to build massive bases on their soil and by spending lavishly on Western arms. In turn, this expensive militarization has aided a new generation of rulers that appears more prone than ever to antagonizing Iran and even other Gulf states. In some cases, grievances among them have grown strong enough to cause diplomatic crises, incite violence, or prompt one monarchy to interfere in the domestic politics of another.

It would thus be a mistake to think that the Gulf monarchies are somehow invincible. Notwithstanding existing internal threats, these regimes are also facing mounting external ones—from

CHRISTOPHER DAVIDSON is a reader in Middle East politics at Durham University and the author of *After the Sheikhs: The Coming Collapse of the Gulf Monarchies,* from which this article is adapted.

Western governments, from Iran, and each other. And these are only exacerbating their longstanding conflicts and inherent contradictions.

HOME BASES

The existence of substantial Western military bases on the Arabian Peninsula has always been problematic for the Gulf monarchies. To their critics, the hosting of non-Arab, non-Muslim armies is an affront to Islam and to national sovereignty. Their proliferation will likely draw further criticism, and perhaps serve as yet another flashpoint for the region's opposition movements.

Among the largest Western installations in the Gulf is al-Udeid Air Base in Qatar, which owes its existence to the country's former ruler, Sheikh Hamad bin Khalifa al-Thani. In 1999, al-Thani told the United States that he would like to see 10,000 American servicemen permanently based in the emirate, and over the next few years, the United States duly began shifting personnel there from Saudi Arabia. Today, al-Udeid houses several thousand U.S. servicemen at a time and has also served as a forward headquarters of U.S. Central Command (CENTCOM), a U.S. Air Force expeditionary air wing, a CIA base, and an array of U.S. Special Forces teams. Nearby Bahrain hosts the U.S. Naval Forces Central Command and the entire U.S. Fifth Fleet, which includes some 6,000 U.S. personnel. The United States recently downsized its force in Kuwait, but four U.S. infantry bases remain, including Camp Patriot, which is believed to house about 3,000 U.S. soldiers and two air bases.

The United States plans to further expand its regional military presence in the near future. As CENTCOM recently announced, the country will be sending the latest U.S. antimissile systems to at least four Gulf states. These are new versions of the Patriot antimissile batteries that the United States already sent to the region and are meant to assuage the Gulf rulers' fears of Iranian missile attacks. Tellingly, the announcement did not reveal exactly which states had agreed to take the U.S. weapons. Yet analysts widely assume that the unnamed states are Bahrain, Kuwait, Qatar, and the UAE.

Equally, if not more, problematic than hosting so many foreign military bases has been the Gulf monarchies' ever-rising spending on Western arms. Although much of the equipment is inappropriate for bolstering defensive capabilities or is superfluous to peacekeeping operations—the kinds of missions Gulf soldiers are likely to find themselves undertaking—Gulf leaders regarded the trade as necessary for their protection.

By most measures, such spending has gotten out of hand. As a proportion of GDP, the Gulf monarchies' purchases make them the biggest arms buyers in the world. Even the poorer Gulf states, which are grappling with declining resources and serious socioeconomic pressures, spend far beyond their means.

Of all of the monarchies' purchases, Saudi and UAE procurements have attracted the most attention. In 2009 alone, the UAE purchased nearly $8 billion in U.S. military equipment, making it the United States' biggest arms customer that year. Saudi Arabia, for its part, purchased about $3.3 billion in hardware. In December 2011, the United States announced that it had finalized a $30 billion sale of Boeing-manufactured F-15 fighter jets to the Saudi Royal Air Force. And a UAE firm has reportedly partnered with a U.S. company, General Atomics Aeronautical Systems, to bring predator drones to the UAE. This venture makes the UAE the first foreign buyer to acquire U.S. drone technology.

In the West, the sales have not been without criticism. The pro-Israel lobby, for example, has repeatedly argued that the sale of such high-grade equipment to the Gulf monarchies will erode Israel's "qualitative edge" in the region. The programs will also prove troublesome inside the Arab kingdoms, as the region's ruling families will find it increasingly difficult to justify such massive transactions to their beleaguered national populations. Given existing regional tensions, they are likely to continue increasing spending anyway—be it on tanks, warplanes, or naval vessels.

COMMON CAUSE

The monarchies are also under pressure to deal with Iran, and some of them see posturing against Tehran as a convenient mechanism for containing domestic opposition, distracting from growing socio-economic pressures, and manipulating sectarian tensions. Since the beginning of the Arab Spring, the Gulf monarchs have gone to great lengths to highlight Shia membership in opposition movements, a tactic that has allowed them to delegitimize critics—falsely—as Iranian agents.

Thus far, the strategy has enjoyed some limited success; members of the Gulf's Sunni populations have been quick to accuse Shia activists of being traitors. Many Western authorities continue to lend support to the monarchies on the grounds that the alternative would be Iran-style theocratic, revolutionary, and anti-Western governments.

Still, the risks of such rabid anti-Iran sentiments are serious and possibly existential. By acting on such attitudes, Gulf monarchs have undermined their longstanding position as neutral peace brokers and distributors of regional development aid, and made themselves into legitimate targets in any conflict in the Persian Gulf. It is unlikely that the fathers of today's Gulf rulers would have allowed that to happen, no matter how deeply they distrusted their neighbor across the Gulf. This previous generation sidelined most confrontations with Iran—including even the 1971 seizure of three UAE islands by the Shah—in recognition of shared economic interests and the substantial Iranian expatriate populations that reside in many of the monarchies.

All that is now ancient history in states like Bahrain, Saudi Arabia, and the UAE. Saudi officials have taken a particularly aggressive stance. According to a leaked U.S. diplomatic cable from 2008, the Saudi king has "repeatedly exhorted the United States to cut off the head of the snake"—Iran's nuclear weapons program. Another cable from the same year quoted a veteran Saudi minister for foreign affairs suggesting a U.S. or NATO offensive in southern Lebanon to end Iran-backed Hezbollah's grip on power there. And a former Saudi intelligence chief has said publicly that Saudi Arabia should "consider acquiring nuclear weapons to counter Iran."

In early 2011, Bahrain's rulers took full advantage of anti-Iranian sentiments to act against domestic opponents, announcing that they would deport all Shia residents who had "links to Hezbollah and Iran's Revolutionary Guard." In practice, that meant expelling hundreds of Bahrain's Lebanese residents, suspending all flights between the capital Manama and Beirut, and warning Bahraini nationals not to travel to Lebanon due to "threats and interference by terrorists."

Abu Dhabi's attitude toward Iran originally appeared to have been more hesitant, perhaps because of its previous ruler's more moderate policies. According to a 2006 cable from the U.S. Embassy in Abu Dhabi, the UAE government told U.S. officials that "the threat from al-Qaeda would be minor compared to if Iran had nukes . . . but that it was reluctant to take any action that might provoke its neighbor." Nevertheless, as Abu Dhabi's forceful Crown Prince Muhammad bin Zayed al-Nahyan and his five full brothers gained control over most of the country's foreign policy, the emirate's views have fallen in line with those of Saudi Arabia and Bahrain. Since 2007, the crown prince's circle has pushed Western officials to put more troops in the region to counter Iranian hegemony. In 2009, the crown prince forcefully warned the United States of appeasing Iran, reportedly saying that "Ahmadinejad is Hitler."

Qatar, which has sought a role as regional peace broker, has been more careful with its public statements on Iran. Even so, in a private meeting in 2009, Qatar's then prime minister Sheikh Hamad bin Jassim bin Jaber al-Thani, characterized Qatar's relationship with Iran as one in which "they lie to us and we lie to them." Qatar's calculated diplomacy perhaps owes to its precarious balancing act: the country hosts major U.S. military facilities while sharing its largest gas resource—the offshore North Field—with Iran.

THE ENEMY OF MY ENEMY

Perhaps even riskier than their hawkishness toward Iran is the Gulf monarchies' dovishness toward Israel. Since independence, the

Gulf monarchies have upheld laws requiring government personnel, businesses, and even individual residents to boycott Israel. In the UAE, the federal government has always housed an Israel boycott office. One federal law, passed in 1971, stipulates that "any natural or legal person shall be prohibited from directly or indirectly concluding an agreement with organizations or persons either resident in Israel, connected therewith by virtue of their nationality of working on its behalf."

For many years, however, the boycott extended well beyond such restrictions. The state-owned telecommunications company has barred telephone calls to Israel and blocked Web sites with an Israeli suffix. The government has not permitted Israeli nationals to enter the UAE, nor—in theory—any visitors that possess Israeli visa stamps in their passports. Yet trade opportunities have occasionally prompted the UAE to ignore its own boycott. After joining the World Trade Organization in 1996, UAE authorities were clearly under pressure to drop or at least relax their stance. When Dubai agreed to host the WTO's annual meeting in 2003, delegations from all of the organization's member states had to be invited; there was no way to prevent the arrival of an Israeli delegation or the flying of an Israeli flag on top of the Dubai World Trade Centre tower.

Concerns over Iran have further thawed relations between some of the Gulf monarchies and Israel. An open channel of communication now exists between Qatar and the Israeli security services. In late 2010, Qatar hosted a large delegation of senior Israeli policemen, among them the head of the Israeli police's investigations and intelligence branch, ostensibly as part of an Interpol meeting. Thus far, there is little firm evidence of growing security ties between Saudi Arabia and Israel, or at least there have been no blatant admissions of them (as has been the case with Bahrain and Qatar). Nevertheless, rumors of significant Saudi-Israeli cooperation, prompted by the existence of a mutual enemy, have circulated in diplomatic circles for years.

The monarchies' new policies toward Israel are particularly dangerous given domestic political realities. The Gulf's national populations are, for the most part, anti-Israeli and pro-Palestinian. Gulf nationals grew up watching the Palestinian intifada on television, and the liberation of Palestine remains a shared ideal among the region's youth. There are also substantial communities of Palestinians in every monarchy; naturalized Gulf nationals who were born in Palestinian refugee camps are even known to hold powerful official posts in some rulers' courts.

SUCCESSION STRUGGLES

The pressures facing the Gulf states make for a very tense region, one in which disagreements over the United States, Iran, and Israel threaten to boil over. Quarrels between the kingdoms have at times grown so bitter that one monarchy has tried to alter the course of dynastic succession in another. Following the death of a ruler or a petty internal dispute in one monarchy, it is now commonplace for neighboring monarchs to interfere, either by discreetly backing a preferred candidate, or, in the more extreme cases, by sponsoring a coup d'état. The resulting power vacuums have often allowed foreign powers to interfere as well.

The best example of a modern-day coup and subsequent foreign interference took place in the UAE's northernmost emirate of Ras al-Khaimah. In 2003, after allegedly burning an American flag at an anti-Iraq war demonstration, Prince Sheikh Khalid bin Saqr al-Qasimi, the emirate's long-serving crown prince, was replaced in the order of succession by a younger half-brother, Sheikh Saud bin Saqr al-Qasimi. Their very elderly father, Sheikh Saqr bin Mohammed al-Qasimi, later signed a decree in support of this change, but many analysts questioned the ruler's decision-making abilities, given his advanced age and poor health. The new crown prince had the apparent backing of Abu Dhabi, which sent military tanks to take positions on the streets of Ras al-Khaimah. The ousted crown prince's supporters still took the streets to show their support; security forces with water cannons disbursed them. The crown prince was then duly exiled, crossing the border to Oman before leaving for the United States.

As the emirate's Dubai-like development program began to flounder in 2008, the new crown prince Saud became increasingly vulnerable to criticism, including widespread allegations that he accepted kickbacks from the construction industry. The deposed prince, who was still in exile, enlisted a U.S. public relations firm and a British lawyer to conduct an international media campaign to persuade Abu Dhabi and the international community that the incumbent crown prince was a liability.

The campaign focused on Saud's apparent connections to Tehran, claiming that his effective deputy—a Shia Lebanese businessman— had major commercial interests, including factories, in the Islamic Republic. In 2009, the campaign even claimed that Iranian customs officers had been visiting Ras al-Khaimah's port and that the emirate was serving as a conduit for nuclear materials destined for Iran. Local media alleged that recent terror plots there, including a 2009 attempt to blow up Dubai's incomplete Burj Khalifa skyscraper, had originated in Ras al-Khaimah. The exiled crown prince even courted Israeli support, reportedly meeting with Israel's ambassador to the United Kingdom, who said that he was "working with certain people from his side" and "promised that the matter will be solved in his [the former crown prince's] favor."

In late 2010, the campaign appeared to be gaining traction. Abu Dhabi's ruling family allowed Khalid to return from exile to visit his father Sheikh Saqr, who still held the throne but was undergoing treatment in an Abu Dhabi hospital. When Saqr died in October, Khalid quickly returned to Ras al-Khaimah and installed himself in his former palace with some 150 heavily armed guards and even more loyal tribesmen. He seemed confident that, having received Abu Dhabi's blessing to attend his father's funeral, he would be officially installed as ruler of Ras Khaimah later that day. But in the early evening, the UAE Ministry for Presidential Affairs in Abu Dhabi announced that his younger brother Saud had been named the new ruler of Ras al-Khaimah.

Abu Dhabi, which holds the presidency of the Emirates, deployed UAE tanks on the outskirts of the emirate and all of the deposed crown prince's retainers—including two of his cousins, several Omani citizens, and a Canadian military adviser—were arrested and detained for questioning. Two months later, the emirate's new ruler was invited to a banquet in Abu Dhabi held in his honor, where the ruler of Abu Dhabi congratulated him on his success.

The Gulf's immediate future is likely to be marked by many more such coup and countercoup attempts. Several current monarchs are very old, and powerful factions in growing royal families have coalesced around rival successors. In each of these cases, internecine contests will develop and, given the high stakes involved, the involvement of foreign powers is all but inevitable.

In the end, however, the monarchies may all suffer from such meddling, for these regimes are only as strong as the weakest links in their chain. An especially brittle monarchy succumbing to pressure over Western involvement, Iran, or Israel could easily be the first domino to fall, undoing the illusion of invincibility that the Gulf monarchies have so painstakingly built to distinguish themselves from the floundering Arab republics next door.

Reprinted from After the Sheikhs: The Coming Collapse of the Gulf Monarchies, *by Christopher M. Davidson, with the permission of Oxford University Press. © Oxford University Press 2013.*

Where Have All the Workers Gone?

China's Labor Shortage and the End of the Panda Boom

Damien Ma and William Adams

I t became fashionable after the Soviet Union's collapse to say that breakneck economic growth was the only thing postponing the Chinese Communist Party's (CCP) day of reckoning. Communist ideology was discredited, went the argument, but as long as the economic pie kept growing, citizens would set aside broader concerns and take their piece. But what if growth were interrupted by, say, a global financial crisis, collapse of world trade, and mass layoffs on the Chinese factory floor? The music would stop, the masquerade party would end, and Jennifer Connelly would smash her way through David Bowie's bubble prison, so to speak.

Except that it didn't. The Chinese economy faced exactly this cataclysmic scenario in the final months of 2008. Collapsing confidence and worldwide financial dysfunction forced businesses to cancel orders en masse. It was a huge blow to the Chinese manufacturing industry, compounding the weaknesses of a domestic economy already fragile after months of government efforts to cool a real estate bubble and overheating inflation. Tens of millions of Chinese migrant workers were laid off in the lead up to the Lunar

DAMIEN MA is a Fellow at The Paulson Institute. **WILLIAM ADAMS** is a Center Associate of the University of Pittsburgh Asian Studies Center. They are authors of *In Line Behind a Billion People*, from which this essay is adapted.

New Year holiday in late January 2009. They returned to the countryside, passed the holiday with relatives, and waited for the crisis to abate.

Meanwhile, Zhongnanhai's poobahs began to sweat. The global economy was plunging into the worst recession since the 1930s. China responded hastily with an outsized stimulus package that boosted confidence, but was insufficient to create jobs for both the laid-off workers and the millions of college graduates and young migrant workers who had flocked to urban job markets every year for decades. Early in 2009, Chinese officials were openly worrying about maintaining social stability in the Chinese countryside.

The economy in 2009 was indeed shaky by Chinese standards, if not in comparison to the rest of the world. China's real GDP growth slowed to single digits—the lowest it had been in nearly a decade. Accordingly, the China bears rose from hibernation to swarm op-ed pages and talk show panels, predicting the collapse of the Chinese labor market, an economic crisis, and a political crisis.

Instead, the labor market overheated.

Over the next two years, China's economic policymakers flooded the economy with bank credit, funding countless new housing projects, amazing feats of infrastructure modernization, and some fantastical white elephants along the way. Migrant workers gravitated toward the millions of jobs created on construction sites, or back to the factories whose order books were filled by investment-led demand. By early 2010, job postings began to outnumber job-seekers for the first time since the start of China's resource-intensive economic boom at the beginning of the twenty-first century, a period we call the Panda Boom (after that cuddly creature's voracious habit of eating 10–15 percent of its body weight in bamboo each day). Suddenly, in 2010, it was a lack of workers rather than a lack of orders keeping factories from running at full tilt.

In the heat of the moment, it was unclear exactly what had saved the country from disaster. Did the massive stimulus program pull the economy from the brink of recession? Or did the crisis fundamentally transform the labor market in some unanticipated way?

With the benefit of several years' hindsight, it seems clear that the labor market had been transforming even before the crisis hit.

SOCIALIST EMPLOYERS PARADISE LOST

The structure of the Chinese labor force changed—and is still changing—much faster than Beijing had anticipated.

During the Panda Boom, all the major factors guiding Chinese labor relations had swung in employers' favor, the foremost being supply and demand. First came demographics: the country was enjoying a mini–baby boom that boosted the number of annual workforce entrants around the end of the twentieth century, an echo of the baby boom amid the relative peace and social stability of the decade following China's 1949 reunification. Second came urbanization: a massive movement of workers gravitated toward factory work on the coasts in the 1990s and 2000s after the earliest market-oriented reforms of the 1980s, which freed up farm laborers by dramatically increasing agricultural productivity per worker. And third came tens of millions of layoffs in state-owned enterprises in the late 1990s, which helped keep true unemployment in urban China (as opposed to what meaningless official unemployment statistics said) elevated for most of the 2000s. Add to this the millions of teenagers aging into the workforce each year, and you have an employer's paradise: workers needed jobs much more urgently than employers needed labor.

During China's demographic explosion, maintaining job growth was the government's paramount priority. Occupational safety, collective bargaining rights, and other costly labor protections were vastly less important, and summarily ignored. That started to change a little with the Chinese Labor Contract Law of 2008, the centerpiece of a stronger labor regulatory package that increased worker protections against layoffs, obliged employers to negotiate with the party-controlled unions over pay rates and benefits, and provided workers with new avenues to defend their rights against employers in courts. Fully enforced, the regulation's provisions were estimated to increase the cost of employing Chinese workers by some 10–20 percent. But at the time the law was enacted, no one gave that much thought. After all, there were still nearly 200 million migrants in the cities and millions more waiting to move off farms. As long as the supply remained abundant, the employer's paradise would endure.

By 2010, however, cracks were starting to show. They became most visible in a string of highly publicized wildcat strikes at foreign-owned factories that year. Multinational and Chinese manufacturers had cut wages during the downturn of 2008–2009 and had been slow to raise them as production began normalizing over the following year—even as inflation had taken off in a hurry.

It was a double shock for foreign employers. First, they were flummoxed that workers were emboldened to shut down production so soon after many manufacturers had been driven to the brink of bankruptcy. Managers were still twitching at the memories of 2008, when the economy was so bad that many owners in Shenzhen had snuck over the factory wall in the cover of night, leaving their unpaid workers behind. Second, that the strikes happened at all turned preconceived notions on their heads: China was not supposed to have strikes.

Double-digit wage increases eventually ended the strikes, but they didn't bring back the old labor market. Factory employers who were slow to keep wage increases in line with market rates quickly saw their workers walking away. Annual workforce turnover of half or more were not uncommon at some factories. After lagging behind GDP growth for the previous decade, average Chinese wages grew faster than GDP in 2011 and 2012, right alongside a major slowdown of the economy as a whole.

MIGRANTS CAME, SAW, AND LEFT

The recent labor drought revealed that the usual explanation of how the Chinese blue-collar labor market works is insufficient. It significantly overestimated the amount of excess labor. In particular, it misunderstood the dynamics of a large rural labor force that could have potentially entered the workforce as migrant workers. It was widely believed that Chinese would leave the farms, come to the cities where they would be vastly more productive, GDP would boom, and the countless underemployed laborers still idling on the farm would keep wages from rising.

But that story ignores an ugly truth of how the Chinese workforce functions, or at least how it functioned historically.

Many westerners have failed to recognize, for example, that the size of the Chinese labor market is significantly limited by Chinese prejudices. By Western standards, China would be considered a racist, ageist place. Nondiscrimination is a foreign legal concept to Chinese employers. During the previous decade of unrelenting growth, many factories would only hire female Han Chinese workers under the age of 25, because they were believed to be more easily managed than men and more energetic than older workers. For migrant workers over the age of 40, finding work was exponentially more difficult than it was for younger migrants (and sometimes impossible). Based on employers' preferences, if one wanted to understand the real supply of potential laborers for Chinese factories, it would have been unrealistic to include many potential workers in their 40s and 50s.

Analysts overestimated the blue-collar labor force in another important way, as well. It is true that, in the last decade, high schools graduated millions of students who might have gone straight to work. But many of them opted to go to college rather than to factories and construction sites. From 2000 to 2010, the number of young people enrolling in higher education programs rather than entering the workforce after high school tripled, growing from 2.2 million to 6.6 million. With so many young people hitting the books, the usual squeeze through the factory gates became less tight.

Chinese factory managers have more or less adapted, willingly or otherwise, to the new reality. Employers are, of course, increasing wages as necessary to keep their workers from walking off the line. Manufacturers are also shifting factories further inland, away from the largest Chinese cities where costs of doing business (and wages) are highest, and where they might find more willing migrants—those who would rather work six hours from their home village instead of 26 hours away in Guangdong.

A job close to home appeals not only to older migrant workers as a practical way to balance work and family obligations, but also to migrants of the post-1980s and 1990s generations, though for different reasons. The younger migrants tend to weigh lifestyle considerations heavily and approach the workforce with radically different expectations and attitudes than previous generations.

Early on in the post-1978 reform and opening period, migrant workers often left their parents and siblings (the one-child policy was not as strictly enforced in the countryside as in cities) for life in the factory town or the city. To be sure, the work they found in Chinese factories was tough and mind numbing, but still compared favorably to the exhausting rigors of farm life.

The new generation of migrant workers, by contrast, hardly worked on the farm, if ever at all, and often never saw their parents doing field labor either. Recent studies from Chinese think tanks have shown that these new migrants are less motivated by simple financial opportunities than by their own career advancement and individual interests. Moreover, they tend to put a premium on social justice and fair treatment. These lifestyle considerations make living closer to home, family, friends, and a familiar dialect and culture (which range as much in China as do the modern-day variations of Latin spoken in different corners of Europe) as important as their salary, if not more so in some cases.

SCHOOL OF HARD KNOCKS

The flip side of the dearth of blue-collar labor has been the glut of recent college graduates that scarcely qualify for work in China's competitive job market. During the beginning of the market economy era in the 1980s, less than three percent of Chinese young people received a four-year university education. This exclusive cabal of credentialed elites was placed into high flying careers and lived lifestyles befitting their social status.

That was then. College graduates now face a life that would be totally unrecognizable to those a generation earlier, who had the fortune of first-mover advantage. Tripling the size of the higher education system in only a decade has meant a rapid proliferation of new institutions, most of which provide educations—and professional prospects—that can't compare with those of the graduates of the top tier institutions. A massive riot in 2006 illustrated how different the prospects are for graduates of elite universities and those of newer ones: Some graduates of the satellite campus of a university in central China apparently went berserk when they discovered that their diplomas designated them graduates of the satellite, not of the parent university as they were originally promised.

In a situation that would sound familiar to Americans, graduates of new and lower-ranked universities have struggled to find good entry-level jobs. They live in small, crowded, shared apartments at the edge of major cities, scraping by to make rent. The plum jobs for university graduates at state-owned enterprises, in government, or at glitzy multinationals are no more attainable for these young people than for migrant laborers of the same age. And the college graduates won't take the manufacturing jobs, perhaps to their detriment: average starting wages for college graduates were actually lower than average migrant worker salaries in 2011. Without a good employer to secure their place in urban China, these young people do not simply struggle economically; in many ways, they can be as marginalized from the economic and social fabric of their urban life as are migrant workers.

WHAT NOW?

The consequences of China's transforming labor market are by no means all bad; in fact, they will make the task of managing the Chinese economy easier in several crucial ways. A simultaneous influx of college graduates and lack of blue collar workforce entrants will narrow the wage gap between more and less educated Chinese, and also between rural and urban households. It must be a relief for the government that a secular demographic change is narrowing inequality in a way that its own policies have not. However, the strains of a rapidly changing population also bring new and unfamiliar complexities. Growth is slowing as China's economy runs short of underemployed laborers to power its export juggernaut and anchor the "China price" for which the country is so famously known.

These changes are quite visible in China's recent economic statistics. In nominal terms, GDP rose 9.8 percent from 2011 to 2012, but in a change for China, more of the gains from growth accrued to workers, thanks to a tight labor market, than to the owners of capital. Median urban disposable incomes rose by 15 percent. The corporate profits of industrial firms, by contrast, rose by only five percent. Rapidly rising wages accelerated the country's shift from an export-oriented to domestically focused economy. Economic underperformance in the United States, Europe, and Japan also did China no favors.

Yes, to a certain extent, China's demographic hangover and the country's transition to a consumption-based economy are actually good news. Overreliance on investment and exports is not exactly sustainable. But the process of transition will have winners and losers. Rebalancing means households living on their salaries get more of the economic pie. Entrepreneurs, "red capitalists," multinationals, and tax collectors, commensurately, will likely be left with less.

Meanwhile, governing and encouraging economic development will become considerably more challenging. Economic management is much easier with an enormous demographic gust blowing at a government's back, propelling its economy forward even if policies are less than optimal. As the wind dies, individual policies and economic decisions are starting to matter much more. Now, China will need to be a whole lot smarter and more creative in designing policy incentives.

Productivity growth (that is, growth in output per worker) is likely to slow markedly. This is partly because of a less productivity-friendly mix of economic activity. Expanding demand for services means that a larger share of Chinese GDP will be generated by the service sector. It is much harder to double GDP per person employed in these parts of the economy than it is in the manufacturing sector. Slower growth, in turn, will blunt some of the government's most effective tools at managing its hybrid market economy. Beijing has been incredibly successful at growing out of economic problems. The bad loans crippling the banking sector at the dawn of the hyper-growth era, which began in the early 2000s, weren't fully repaid, for example—they just shrank relative to the rest of the financial industry and gradually stopped being a systemic risk to the economy. China still has to deal with the fallout from the credit boom of 2009–2010, which will inevitably generate hefty bad loans; its old strategy of growing out of the problem may not be as effective in a post double-digit growth era.

There are also several challenges to companies, foreign and domestic. They are already moving factories inland and raising wages to adapt to the new balance of power between migrant workers and employers. Inevitably, many companies will also start incorporating business practices for managing a mature workforce, analogous to those adopted in the United States or Europe.

More broadly, corporate strategy has to adapt to the end of cheap Chinese labor. The shift matters most for multinationals, which allocate investment, R & D, and managerial resources between China and other markets. Some U.S. companies have contemplated bringing operations back to the United States, Mexico, or Vietnam. But a lower growth and more expensive China won't drive all the multinationals away. There is still value to being in proximity to the world's largest high-growth market, which contributes the most to global aggregate demand each year. Those that do stay, though, will likely opt for increased mechanization. As labor becomes more expensive, machines become relatively cheaper and a more attractive option for maximizing efficiency.

Finally, China's demographic hangover could coincide with a rightsizing of expectations about what China can do for a multinational business. Managers might become less willing to accommodate "Chinese characteristics"—the combination of regulatory uncertainty, intellectual property violations, and the risk of becoming embroiled in corruption scandals that seem much harder to avoid there than in a developed market. In other words, these dynamics might serve as a catalyst for the government to renew economic and institutional reforms as new enticements to attract foreign investment.

China's demographic hangover is here, and it is as unexpected and unpleasant as the morning after a 30th birthday. Given the facility with which the government has managed difficult economic transitions in the past 20 years—forcing the military out of the market economy in the 1990s and initiating the Panda Boom later that decade—the purely economic dimensions seem daunting, but no more so than the other feats the CCP has pulled off. Instead, it's the social and political dimensions of the demographic hangover that seem most perplexing.

Most obviously, the prospect of an independent labor movement, albeit a small one, holds the potential to trigger revolutionary changes. Much more so than a decade ago, Chinese workers, historically poorly represented in the country's politics, seem aware of their own interests and more vocal about their demands. If China's leaders want to keep the music playing, the emergence of labor as an interest group could well require them to rethink the grand bargain—growth in exchange for stability—they strike with the public they govern. ❷

Love in the Time
of Bollywood

India's Strained Romance Revolution

Ira Trivedi

At nine every morning, Sana dons her burqa and rides pillion on her father's scooter. He drops her off at the all-women's college in Bhopal where she is completing a Master's degree in English literature. On most days, though, Sana does not attend classes. Once inside the college gates, she throws off her burqa, changes into her "Westerns" (typically low-rise jeans and a fitted t-shirt), and leaves. Her boyfriend of two years, Aftab, picks her up on his motorbike, and they zoom off to spend the day together.

Sana's hometown is the sleepy capital of the central Indian state of Madhya Pradesh. Situated on the banks of a glorious lake, Bhopal is beautiful. But it is known around the world for something else: an industrial disaster in 1984 that killed 2,259 people. Today however, Bhopal seems much like any other bustling Indian city. Next to sepia Mughal-era ruins are the familiar signs of urban development: glitzy new shopping malls, McDonald's, and bright new coffee shops, such as Bake-n-Shake and Cafe Coffee Day. These are the kinds of places that one can take a boyfriend when cutting class, and they are filled with young couples in love.

Despite the new additions to Bhopal's landscape, though, it still is not easy to carry on an illicit romance. "I can never let my family find out," Sana says. "If they do, they will drag me out of college

IRA TRIVEDI is an author, most recently, of *India in Love* (forthcoming from Aleph).

and marry me off." In fact, she has been betrothed to her cousin, a customary practice in her Muslim family, since she was 16. At the time of her engagement, Sana says, she was too young to understand what was happening. She was still in school and had, until then, led a rather sheltered life. She only realized the implications of her engagement after she began college. But by then, she had "adjusted" to the idea of marrying her cousin. In all these years, she has met him only twice. She is still expected to marry him when she graduates. Of her boyfriend, Aftab, she says, "I would love to marry him, but my family does not agree. He is Shia; I am Sunni. Also, he is unemployed."

A baby-faced 23-year-old, Aftab graduated college with a degree in mass communications three years ago. He has been looking for a job since then, but he has been unable to find anything that suits. His parents, who work for the local government, want him to try the public sector. Aftab admits that he finds the prospect of a stable but unglamorous government job boring. His passion is music; he has a band, which performs a fusion of rock and Sufi music. Gigs in Bhopal are few and far between, though, so to pass his time, he takes computer classes and hangs out with Sana.

WHAT'S LOVE GOT TO DO WITH IT

Sana and Aftab's story is a familiar one. All over India, men and women like them are living through a romantic revolution, much like the one that rocked the United States. In the United States, the revolution came in two stages. First, the development of a market-driven and individualistic economy led to the erosion of traditional social systems. By the late 1800s, young people began embracing the radical idea that love should be the primary reason for marriage. And, as such, it no longer made sense for their families or religious groups to choose their partners. The love revolution, of course, did not upend sexual politics: men and women were still seen as fundamentally different beings, sexually and otherwise. That did not begin to change until the mid-1960s, which was marked by the breakdown of traditional gender roles, rising female independence, the advent of birth control, and more liberated sex lives: the sexual revolution.

In India, as is often the case, everything seems to be happening at once. Thanks to years of urbanization and economic growth, there is more opportunity, more entertainment, and more freedom. Social barriers are weakening, the mingling of sexes is more permissible, and birth control is more widely available. Gender biases are waning, and women are suddenly less dependent on men. Today, almost a third of India's 480 million jobs are held by women and, over the past decade, urban women's incomes have doubled. These days, according to IMRB, a market research firm, about 60 percent of urban women say that they are responsible for their own lives.

But it might all be too much, too quick. The legacy of the gradual, two-step love and sexual revolution, according to Stephanie Coontz, the author of *Marriage, a History*, is that, by the time the West got to the more radical second stage, parents' ability to control their children had already been diminished. But in India, "even though you are getting this very rapid trend of young people wanting relationships," Coontz told me, "you're also getting much more pushback than Western young women and men have got." And that is why India's love and sexual revolution is a much more tense affair.

In hundreds of interviews for my upcoming book, *India in Love*, I found that, across India's towns, notions of love and longing—of dating and romance—are quickly changing. In the biggest cities, such as Mumbai and New Delhi, more young people are starting to expect independence, especially when it comes to their personal lives. Their counterparts in smaller ones, such as Bhopal, are fast following suit. A recent study of over 50,000 young people across India conducted by the International Institute for Population Sciences and Population Control found that fully 77 percent of unmarried women and 59 percent of unmarried men said that women should be able to choose their own husbands. At the same time, however, the age-old forces of caste, community, religion, and family expectations are pushing back. Many young people are thus squeezed between tradition and modernity.

Economic woes only compound the problem. The World Bank's latest World Development Report found that youth unemployment in India was about 50 percent higher than overall unemployment. Many unemployed young people delay their entry into the workforce by extending their years of education. And as a result, the Reserve Bank of India reports, outstanding personal educational loans have more than doubled over the past four years. These days, then, most young people simply cannot afford to take financial control of their own lives—which means frustration, disappointment, and sometimes, suicide. According to Vikram Patel, the lead author of a *Lancet* study on suicide in India, "young educated Indians from the richer states are killing themselves in numbers that are almost the highest in the world." And many of those deaths are for love: the state of Tamil Nadu has the highest number of what the police term "love failure suicides," with over 500 cases reported each year.

One bright and cool New Year's Eve, I met with Sana and some of her friends at Bhopal's lakeside. The friends, emblematic of modern young India, wear the latest western fashions and watch MTV and American sitcoms. Most of them are pursuing university degrees, but all of them live with their families. They have dreams, but no concrete plans for the future. As we stand around one friend's cherry-red motorbike (a gift from his parents), he raps a song by Yo Yo Honey Singh, a popular musician who combines English and Punjabi lyrics. "Your waist sways. Your high heels are to be blamed for it," he chants. "Your heart slips. Your high heels are to be blamed for it."

The all-at-once revolution and increasingly bleak economic situation has unmoored many young Indians. Women can wear high heels, go to malls and, like everyone else, dream about the future. But many cannot realize those dreams because they are unable to take responsibility for their own lives. Sana's older sister had an arranged marriage to a man in Hyderabad. She divorced him after a year when she found out that he was having a longtime affair with another woman. Sana fears that she will end up like her sister, finding herself in a marriage that does not work with a man that she does love. Still, she tells me, she has no option but to listen to her parents. She has two years left before she finishes college. If she and Aftab—both jobless—marry against their families' wishes, they will have no way of surviving.

Beside the lake, the day slips by. At long last, Sana returns to college and throws on her burqa as we wait for her father to pick her up. "My future is not in my hands," she says to me with a shrug. "So at least I should enjoy the present."

HONOR THY MOTHER AND THY FATHER

If Sana seems resigned to her fate, other young Indian women have taken their future into their own hands. In a country with entrenched traditions of patriarchy, caste, and family honor, that can be life threatening—usually because the lovers' own families take matters into their own hands. Reports of "honor-killings" of young lovers, especially those who cross caste or religious lines, have become routine. The risk of honor killings is so dire, especially in more conservative, patriarchic states in northern India, that the government has opened guarded shelters for runaway couples. According to lawyers, the High Court for Punjab and Haryana receives as many as 50 applications per day from couples seeking protection. That is a staggering tenfold rise from the five or six per day applications they got five years ago.

I meet Neha and Mukul at the New Delhi shelter of the Love Commandos, an organization that, according to its popular Facebook page, is dedicated to "helping India's love birds who want to marry for love." The group has received national and international attention for its work, and, although its facilities are basic—it can only offer couples access to a crowded rooftop shed—it is flooded with men and women on the run.

Neha and Mukul are from Mahendragarh, a bucolic city in Haryana, where buffaloes wade in ponds next to a new four-lane highway. It is home to one million people, along with several sparkling schools and engineering colleges, which were built recently to turn the city into the state's education hub. Neha and Mukul fell in love at the co-ed college they attended. They are from different castes: she is a high-caste Rajput, and he is a Dalit (referred to in British times as an Untouchable). Neha and Mukul mostly kept in touch via cell phone; there were few places they could meet without word getting back to their families. Eventually, it was the cell phone that gave them away. After six months, Neha's mother found the incriminatory text-messages. Neha's family told her she must get married to a man of their liking, and threatened to kill her and Mukul if she refused. To save their love and their lives, Mukul and Neha got married in a hasty ceremony and then made their way to the Love Commandos' shelter in New Delhi.

In a sense, their story shows how little has changed in India. It is still dangerous for love to cross social (or parental) redlines. According to some reports, 94 percent of honor killings are carried out by the woman's family—usually with the support of a local village council, or *khap panchayat*. Run mostly by elderly men, *khap panchayat* once dominated political life across northern India, regulating everything from marriage to property disputes. Even today, and despite the fact that India's supreme court has condemned them as illegal, *khap panchayat* continue to wield vast influence in many villages across north India. Some have endorsed child marriage and have argued that, in order to reduce rapes of young women, girls should be married by age 16. The head of the council in Baliyan, Mahendra Singh Tikait, has even gone on record saying that "Love marriages are dirty...and only whores can choose their partners." *Khap panchayat* might be a vestigial organ—more suited to the country's rural past—but they persist because some still support their views.

In another sense, though, Neha and Mukul's story shows that India has changed—at least a little. The country sees more love marriages there than ever. A decade ago, around five percent of marriages were not arranged. Today, estimates range from ten percent (UNICEF) to 30 percent (Shaifali Sandhya, a psychology professor at the Adler School). Mixed marriage, too, is increasingly common. Annually, around 984 Dalits who marry non-Dalits get protection orders in runaway marriages. And about ten establishments in Chandigarh, the capital city of both Haryana and Punjab, conduct mixed-marriage ceremonies. In one temple, an officiant claimed that his facility had solemnized 1,500 mixed marriages over the last five years.

Neha and Mukul will stay in the rooftop shelter in New Delhi until they figure out what to do next—a dismal honeymoon if there ever was one. Their dream is to scrape together some money to go to Mumbai, which is a popular destination for runaways. Increasingly, young people chose to live in such big cities, where they believe they will be free from family regulations and pressure. Better infrastructure—new road projects, extensive railways, half a dozen new airlines, including several low-cost ones—has made it easier for Neha, Mukul, and those like them to move. They reflect broader national trends: Over the next four decades, 31 villagers will show up in an Indian city every minute—700 million people in all. A 2010 McKinsey Global Institute study predicts that 590 million people, about 40 percent of the country's population, will live in cities by 2030, and 70 percent of net new employment will occur in cities, up from 30 percent in 2008.

As I speak with Neha and Mukul, I realize that that they don't talk about the past or the families, relatives, and friends they have left behind. All they want to do is talk of tomorrow—of new cities, new lives, and new plans. They are excited to make a fresh start in the India they have seen on television. They brush away my warnings about city living, including the grim job scenario. "We have run away in support of each other," Neha says, clutching Mukul's hand. "Our parents just want to kill me, kill him, kill everyone. But we love each other, and we won't let anything stop us."

LOVE CONQUERS

In 2013, India is still at the beginning of a major social revolution. New ideas about love and gender are born every day, but old ones are slow to die. In law and in practice, love marriage is creeping across urban India. So, too, is an increasingly liberal attitude towards sexuality. And social structures are changing as young people begin to prize independence. Liberation (sexual and otherwise) is exhilarating. But it also creates new tensions that a society might not be prepared for or equipped to face. As Indian sexual behavior changes, there is bound to be turbulence and conflict—and Sana and Aftab, Neha and Mukul, and couples like them will bear the brunt. Still, despite the strains and broken hearts it may induce in the near term, the revolution could bring more equality between the genders and increased personal freedom in the long run.